HOW TO READ THIS BOOK:

Although I color-coded the different documents gone over, it is very unlikely the testing will be so memory-based as to ask where the content is found. Testing centers are more concerned that you understand the concepts within rather than code numbers. I have color-coded them so you know which document you are reading from (30-40 or title 174) while reading the book.

I like to group things mentally and visually as it makes the document more readable when I understand why things are where they are. What things can or might change, and how can they end up in the more permanent law. Title 174 is more easily added to and retracted, whereas Article 30-40 is not. I go onto explain more of this later in the book. As for now hopefully you see why I organized it like I did.

COLORS

Yellow signifies that you are reading the law code from West Virginia Real Estate License Act, W. Va. Code § 30-40.

Blue means you are reading law code from W. Va. Code R. § 174 Title 174 of the West Virginia Code of State Rules.

COLUMNS

The left-hand column presents the original law code verbatim and has no color associated with it.

The right-hand column interprets the code in a more understandable, familiar way and is either yellow or blue. The goal is to provide the reader with both views, side by side, to better understand the documents as a whole.

CONTENTS

WV Real Estate License Act
Chapter 30- Article 40

30-40

Taking some national course is NOT going to accomplish the needed details of the WV Law Code required to pass the state portion of the licensing exam. All too often course providers try to generically produce national content and blanket sell courses everywhere without going into the fine details of state law.

IF THERE WAS ONE SUBJECT MOST EVERY COURSE SKIMPS ON, THIS IS IT.

This is why we so often brag that Spruce School of Real Estate is local to West Virginia! We specialize in West Virginia.

Remaining small benefits you. We have the ability to know our states guidelines at a masterful level.

It's easier for the larger corporate schools to make money, but this comes at the cost of you failing the licensing exam portion specific to your state if you haven't figured out how to get that info.

This textbook provides the law code information for the state of West Virginia. Congratulations, you found it. You will walk away after reading this book, understanding the law code regarding West Virginia Real Estate at an expert level and being capable of passing any exam on the matter.

You will understand the real estate law code in WV at the master level needed to pass the state portion.

The West Virginia Real Estate Law Code Bible

1st Edition

By Billy Zwiener

Published by Spruce School of Real Estate
Books are available for educational, business, or sales promotional use. 1-800-864-7318
https://SpruceSchool.com
Online edition is available for download

credits:

Throughout this textbook, references are made to the following legal code:

West Virginia Real Estate License Act, W. Va. Code § 30-40 et seq. (2024).

W. Va. Code R. § 174
Title 174 of the West Virginia Code of State Rules.

Back Cover Image:
"Girl Reading Book with Glasses Bold Silhouette in Pastel Shadows" © Ni / Adobe Stock

Interior Images:
"Hand drawn illustration graphic of a money icons" © Robert Wicher / Adobe Stock
"Detective investigation corkboard with crime evidence cartoon icon" © ssstocker / Adobe Stock
"Hand Holding Black Empty Wallet, Financial Concept Cut Out PNG." © Pixel Corner / Adobe Stock
"A young beautiful woman in anticipation of a surprise" © BillionPhotos.com / Adobe Stock
"Confused woman gesturing with open hand, neutral expression, isolated on white background. PNG transparent." © Asier / Adobe Stock
"American thin blue line flag on map of West Virginia" © Karen Roach / Adobe Stock
"Credit Card Icon with Dollar Sign Representing Online Payment and Financial Transactions" © Cherrita07 / Adobe Stock
"cartoon man with complaint with speech bubble" © lineartestpilot / Adobe Stock
"Hot deal tag with colorful rays and rustic design, perfect for promotions" © NongKirana / Adobe Stock
"Smiling business woman in white shirt and glasses holding and showing blank empty card" © Prasanth / Adobe Stock
"Business woman best employee of month holds large medal." © Valery / Adobe Stock
"Confused Man" © xadartstudio/ Adobe Stock
"West Virginia pin map location" © Patsiri / Adobe Stock
"3D chubby piggy bank" © YGStocks / Adobe Stock
"Fingerprint" © Graphics / Adobe Stock
"Illustration of a lawyer with arms crossed in front of a stack of books" © Teppi / Adobe Stock
"Risky Business" © Lisa F. Young / Adobe Stock

All other images and graphics created by author of this texbook.

CONTENTS

WV Real Estate License Act
Chapter 30- Article 40

30-40

CONTENTS Title 174

CONTENTS Title 174

CONTENTS Title 174

§30-40-1 LEGISLATIVE FINDINGS

Legislative findings. The Legislature hereby finds and declares that the practice of real estate brokerage is a privilege, and any person engaged in the professional practice of real estate brokerage should possess the requisite experience and training and be subject to adequate regulation and control.

Imagine you want to buy or sell a house. It's a big deal, right? Well, the government thinks so too!

They want to make sure that the people who help you buy or sell houses (we call them real estate brokers) know what they're doing. The government says:

1. Being a real estate broker is a special job.
2. People who do this job need to learn a lot and practice a lot.
3. We need to make sure these people follow rules to keep everyone safe.
4. It's important to protect people from someone who doesn't know how to do this job properly.
5. We made these rules to help everyone and keep things fair.

It's kind of like how you need to learn and practice before you can ride a bike without training wheels. The government wants to make sure real estate brokers have their "training wheels" off before they help people with houses!

§30-40-2 SHORT TITLE

Short title. This article shall be known and may be cited as the "West Virginia Real Estate License Act".

Imagine you're writing a book about rules for people who help buy and sell houses in West Virginia. You need to give your book a name. The governing body who makes rules for West Virginia decided to call their set of rules about this "The West Virginia Real Estate License Act". It's like giving a title to your favorite storybook, but for important rules instead. When people want to talk about these rules, they can use this name to make sure everyone knows which rules they're talking about. So, if someone says, "The West Virginia Real Estate License Act", they mean all the rules about helping people buy and sell houses in West Virginia. The yellow sections of this textbook are Spruce School of Real Estate's down to earth interpretation of the WV Real Estate License Act. The left hand column that is the unedited precise wording of the WV Real Estate License Act so that you can read the original code and then read it broken down in easier to understand concepts using the right hand column.

§30-40-3 LICENSE REQUIRED

License required. It is unlawful for any person to engage in directly or indirectly, or to advertise or hold himself or herself out as engaging in or carrying on the business or act in the capacity of a real estate broker, associate broker, or salesperson within this state without first obtaining a license as provided for in this article. Prior to practicing real estate brokerage in this state, a license shall be obtained from the commission even if the person or entity is licensed in another state and is affiliated or otherwise associated with a licensed real estate broker in this state.

If you want to help people buy or sell houses, you need a special permission slip called a license. It's against the rules to do this job or tell people you can do it without this permission slip. Even if you have a permission slip from another place, you still need to get one from the people in charge here before you can help with houses. It's important to follow these rules so everything is fair and safe for everyone.

§30-40-4 DEFINITIONS

(a) "Applicant" means any person who is making application to the commission for a license.

(a) **"Applicant"** is just a fancy word for someone who's trying to get permission to do something official. In this case, it means a person who's filling out paperwork and asking a group of people (called a commission) if they can have a special document called a license. Think of it like this:

1. You want to do something that needs official approval
2. You fill out forms and answer some questions
3. The people in charge look at your information
4. While you're waiting to hear back, you're called an "applicant"

It's kind of like when you apply for a job or to get into college. During that time when you're waiting to hear back, you're an applicant. In this situation, instead of a job or school, you're applying for a license from a commission.

(b) "Associate broker" means any person who qualifies for a broker's license, but who is employed or engaged by a licensed broker to engage in any activity regulated by this article, in the name of and under the direct supervision of the licensed broker.

(b) An **"associate broker"** is like a highly skilled real estate professional who has leveled up in their career. Here's what you need to know:

1. Qualifications: They've studied hard and passed the tests to become a full-fledged real estate broker. This means they have more knowledge and experience than a regular real estate agent.
2. Working arrangement: Even though they're qualified to be a broker, they choose to work for another licensed broker instead of running their own brokerage.
3. Job duties: They do all sorts of real estate tasks, like helping people buy and sell homes, just like other real estate professionals.
4. Supervision: They work under the guidance of the main broker who owns or runs the real estate company. This broker is responsible for overseeing their work.
5. Using the company name: When they do their job, they represent the real estate company they work for, not themselves as an independent broker.

Think of it like this: An associate broker is like a highly skilled chef who could run their own restaurant but chooses to work in someone else's kitchen instead. They have the skills to be in charge but prefer to be part of a team under someone else's leadership.

(c) "Broker" means any person who for compensation or with the intention or expectation of receiving or collecting compensation: (1) Lists, sells, purchases, exchanges, options, rents, manages, leases, or auctions any interest in real estate; or (2) Directs or assists in the procuring of a prospect calculated or intended to result in a real estate transaction; or (3) Advertises or holds himself or herself out as engaged in, negotiates, or attempts to negotiate, or offers to engage in any activity enumerated in subdivision (1) of this subsection.

(c) **"Broker"** A broker is someone who helps people buy, sell, or rent properties. They do this as a job and get paid for their work. Here's what a broker might do:

1. Help people list their homes for sale or rent
2. Assist buyers in finding properties to purchase
3. Manage rental properties for landlords
4. Organize auctions for real estate
5. Help people exchange one property for another

Brokers also:

6. Look for potential buyers or sellers (we call these "prospects")
7. Advertise properties or their services
8. Negotiate deals between buyers and sellers

Basically, if someone is involved in any part of a real estate transaction and gets paid for it, they're probably working as a broker. This includes advertising themselves as someone who can help with these kinds of deals. The main point is that a broker is a professional who helps make real estate deals happen and earns money for doing so.

(d) "Cancelled" means a license that was not renewed by December 31 of the year in which license expired.

(d) **"Cancelled"** in this context means:

You had a license.

This license had an expiration date which was July 1st.

You were supposed to renew the license before July 1st. You were also given multiple opportunities to renew it after July 1st, with a late fee, up until December 31st of that same year. You didn't renew it by December 31st. So now, your license is considered "cancelled" because you missed the deadline to renew it.

Think of it like a subscription to a streaming service. If you don't pay to renew it by the due date, your access gets cut off. In this case, if you don't renew your license by the end of the year it expired in, it gets cancelled, and you can't use it anymore.

(e) "Commission" means the West Virginia real estate commission as established in section six of this article.

(e) **"Commission"** in this case refers to a specific group of people, not the money you might earn from a sale. It's talking about the West Virginia Real Estate Commission. Think of this commission like a team of experts who oversee real estate activities in West Virginia. Their job is to make sure that people buying, selling, or working with property in the state are following the rules and doing things properly. This group was created by law, specifically in section six of the article being discussed. It's an official organization that helps regulate the real estate industry in West Virginia. So when you see "Commission" mentioned in this context, just remember it's shorthand for this official group of people who manage real estate matters in West Virginia.

(f) "Compensation" means fee, commission, salary, or other valuable consideration, in the form of money or otherwise.

(f)**"Compensation"** is basically a fancy word for payment or reward that someone gets for doing work or providing a service. It covers different ways people can be paid, such as:
Money: This is the most common form of compensation. It includes:

1. Salary: A fixed amount of money you get regularly, like every month.
2. Commission: Extra money you earn based on how much you sell or accomplish.
3. Fee: A set amount paid for a specific job or service.
4. Other valuable things: Sometimes, compensation isn't just money.

   It can be:
5. Benefits: Things like health insurance or vacation days.
6. Stock options: A chance to buy company shares at a special price.
7. Perks: Special advantages like a company car or free meals.

In simple terms, compensation is anything of value that you receive in exchange for your work or efforts. It's not always just cash in your pocket – it can come in different forms, but it's all meant to reward you for what you do.

(g) "Designated broker" means a person holding a broker's license who has been appointed by a partnership, association, corporation, or other form of business organization engaged in the real estate brokerage business, to be responsible for the acts of the business and to whom the partners, members, or board of directors have delegated full authority to conduct the real estate brokerage activities of the business organization.

(g) A **"designated broker"** is like the captain of a real estate team. This person:

1. Has a special license to work in real estate (called a broker's license)
2. Is chosen by a real estate company to be in charge
3. Is responsible for making sure everyone in the company follows the rules
4. Has permission from the company's leaders to make important decisions

Imagine a real estate company as a ship. The designated broker is the captain who:

1. Makes sure the ship (company) sails smoothly
2. Keeps an eye on all the crew members (other real estate agents)
3. Takes responsibility if something goes wrong
4. Has the power to steer the ship in the right direction

The company trusts this person to lead their real estate business and make sure everything is done correctly and legally. It's a big job with a lot of responsibility!

(h) "Distance education" means courses of asynchronous instruction in which instruction takes place through media where the teacher and student are separated by time.

(h) **Distance education** is a way of learning where you don't have to be in the same place or even learning at the same time as your teacher. It's like this:

1. You get your lessons and assignments through things like the internet, email, or even old-school mail.
2. You can do your work whenever it fits your schedule. There's no set class time where everyone has to show up together.
3. Your teacher creates the lessons ahead of time, and you access them when you're ready.
4. You might watch pre-recorded videos, read online materials, or complete assignments on your own time.
5. You and your teacher are "separated by time" because you're not interacting live or in real-time.
6. Think of it like this: Instead of going to a classroom at a specific time, you're getting your education delivered to you, and you can tackle it when it works best for you. It's flexible and allows you to learn at your own pace.

(i) "Entity" means a business, company, corporation, limited liability company, association, or partnership.

(i) An **"entity"** is basically any group that's set up to do business. It's like a team that's formed to make money or provide services. Here are some examples:

- Business: This could be anything from a small shop to a big store.
- Company: Think of companies like Apple, Nike, or Netflix.
- Corporation: These are usually larger businesses that are officially registered with the government.
- Limited liability company (LLC): This is a special type of business where the owners have some protection if the business gets into trouble.
- Association: This could be a group of people or businesses that come together for a common goal, like a trade association.
- Partnership: This is when two or more people team up to run a business together.

So, when you hear the word "entity" in a business context, it's just a fancy way of saying "any type of official business group." It's used as a catch-all term to cover all these different ways people can organize themselves to do business.

(j) "Expired" means a license that was not renewed by July

(j) **"Expired"** for a license means it's no longer valid because the person didn't renew it in time. It's like this:Imagine your license is a subscription to a streaming service. Every year, you need to pay to keep using it. July 1st is the deadline to pay. If you don't pay by July 1st, your subscription stops working - that's what we mean by "expired."So, when we say a license is "expired," it means:

- The person had a valid license before
- They were supposed to renew it (like paying for another year)
- They didn't do this by July 1st
- Now their license isn't valid anymore, and they can't use it

It's important to renew on time to avoid having an expired license.

(k) "Inactive" means a licensee who is not authorized to conduct any real estate business and is not required to comply with any continuing education requirements.

(k) **"Inactive"** in real estate terms means:

- ► A person who has a real estate license but isn't allowed to do any real estate work right now.

They don't have to take any classes to keep their knowledge up-to-date. But you DO have to renew annually as "inactive" and pay the fee or you will expire!

(l) "License" means a license to act as a broker, associate broker or salesperson.

(l) A **"license"** in real estate is like an official permission slip that allows someone to work in certain jobs selling houses and other properties. There are three main types:

1. Broker license: This is the highest level. It lets you run your own real estate business and manage other agents.
2. Associate broker license: This is for someone who has a broker's license but works under another broker instead of running their own business.
3. Salesperson license: This is the entry-level license. It allows you to help people buy and sell properties, but you must work under a licensed broker.

Think of it like getting a driver's license, but for selling real estate. Just like you need a license to legally drive a car, these professionals need a license to legally help people buy and sell properties.

(m) "Licensee" means a person holding a license.

(m) **"Licensee"** is just a fancy word for someone who has a license. Think of it this way:

- If you have a driver's license, you're a licensee.
- If a bartender has a license to serve alcohol, they're a licensee.
- If a doctor has a medical license, they're a licensee.

Basically, whenever someone has an official permission slip (which is what a license really is) to do something, they can be called a licensee. It's just a more formal or legal way of saying "person with a license."

(n) "Member" means a commissioner of the Real Estate Commission.

(n) **"Member"** in this context means someone who is part of a special group called the Real Estate Commission. Think of it like being on a sports team, but instead of playing sports, these people make important decisions about real estate.

A **commissioner** is basically an official who is chosen to be part of this group. They have responsibilities and duties related to overseeing real estate matters in their area.

So when you hear "member of the Real Estate Commission," it's just a formal way of saying "one of the people who are officially part of this real estate decision-making group.

"It's kind of like how you might be a member of a club at school, but in this case, it's adults who are members of an important organization that deals with buying, selling, and regulating property.

(o) "Principal" means a person or entity that authorizes a licensee to act on his, her, or its behalf.

(o) In this context, a **"principal"** is like the boss or the main person in charge. It's someone who gives permission to another person (called a licensee) to do things for them. Think of it like this:

- The principal is the one calling the shots.
- They give someone else (the licensee) the okay to act on their behalf.
- This could be a single person, or it might be a company or organization.

For example:

- If someone hires a real estate agent to sell their house, they are the principal, and the agent is the licensee.
- When a company hires a lawyer to represent them in court, the company is the principal, and the lawyer is the licensee.

The principal is basically saying, "I trust you to handle this for me, and your actions will count as if I did them myself."

(p) "Property management" means the overseeing and management of commercial and residential real estate properties. This includes taking care of all the daily operations for a property which may include, but is not limited to, collecting rent, collecting or holding security deposits on behalf of the property owner, handling maintenance, paying vendors for repairs, and fielding tenant complaints. The amount of responsibilities the property manager has depends on their contract with the owner of the property.

(p) **Property management** is like being a caretaker for buildings that people live in or use for business. Imagine you're in charge of an apartment building or an office complex. Your job would be to:

- Collect rent from the people living or working there
- Keep the money safe that tenants give as a security deposit
- Make sure the building stays in good shape
- Call repair people when something breaks and pay them
- Listen to and help solve problems that the tenants have

The building's owner hires you to take care of these things so they don't have to worry about them. How much you actually do depends on what you and the building's owner agree on. Sometimes you might do all of these things, and sometimes just a few. It all depends on what the owner wants help with.

(q) "Real estate" means any interest or estate in land and anything permanently affixed to land.

(q) **"Real estate"** is a term that refers to:

- Land: This is the actual ground or earth that you can own or have rights to.
- Buildings and structures: These are things built on the land that don't move, like houses, office buildings, or barns.
- Anything permanently attached to the land: This includes things that are fixed to the ground or a building and aren't meant to be moved, such as:
  Trees
  Fences
  Built-in appliances (like a dishwasher in a kitchen)
  Underground pipes or cables

When we say "interest or estate in land," it means you don't always have to own the land outright. You could have different types of rights to use or control the land, even if you're not the full owner. So, in simple terms, real estate is basically land and anything that's permanently stuck to it, whether it's natural (like trees) or man-made (like buildings). When you buy or sell real estate, you're dealing with these fixed, unmovable things.

(r) "Salesperson" means a person employed or engaged by or on behalf of a broker to do or deal in any activity included in this article, in the name of and under the direct supervision of a broker, other than an associate broker: Provided, That for the purposes of receiving compensation, a salesperson may designate an entity to receive any compensation payable to the salesperson, including, but not limited to, a limited liability corporation or an S-corporation.

(r) This is most likely why you are studying this content. You want to be a salesperson: A **salesperson** is someone who:

- Works for a real estate broker
- Helps with buying, selling, or renting properties
- Does their job using the broker's name
- Is supervised by the broker

The main difference between a salesperson and an associate broker is that a salesperson has less responsibility and works under closer supervision. Now, here's an interesting part: When it comes to getting paid, a salesperson can choose to have their money sent to a company instead of directly to themselves. This company could be something like:

- A limited liability corporation (LLC)
- An S-corporation

This setup can sometimes help with taxes or organizing their finances. So, in simple terms, a salesperson is like an assistant to the broker, helping with real estate tasks, but always under the broker's watchful eye. And they have some flexibility in how they receive their pay.

(s) "Team" means any group of two or more associate brokers and/or salespersons, and other non-licensed professionals, affiliated with the same broker or company acting as one agent representative for the principal.

(s) A **"team"** in real estate is like a small group working together. It's made up of:

- At least two people who sell houses (they're called associate brokers or salespersons)
- Maybe some other people who help out but don't have a license to sell houses

All these people work for the same real estate company or boss (called a broker).

The important thing is that they act as one unit when they're helping someone buy or sell a house. The whole group is considered one representative for the client.

§30-40-5. SCOPE OF PRACTICE; EXCEPTIONS

(a) The practice of real estate brokerage includes acting in the capacity of a broker, associate broker, or salesperson as defined in §30-40-4 of this code.

Real estate brokerage is basically the job of helping people buy, sell, or rent properties. When we talk about "the practice of real estate brokerage," we're referring to the work done by three types of professionals:

1. **Brokers:** These are the top-level experts. They've got lots of training and experience, and they can run their own real estate businesses.
2. **Associate Brokers:** These folks have the same qualifications as brokers, but they work under a main broker instead of running their own business.
3. **Salespersons:** These are entry-level real estate professionals. They've completed some training but not as much as brokers. They also work under a main broker.

All these people are practicing real estate brokerage when they're doing their jobs. This definition comes from a specific part of the law (§30-40-4) that explains what each of these roles means and what they're allowed to do.

So, whether you're dealing with a broker, associate broker, or salesperson, they're all part of the real estate brokerage world, just at different levels of experience and responsibility.

(b) The practice of real estate brokerage does not include the activities normally performed by an appraiser, mortgage company, lawyer, engineer, contractor, surveyor, home inspector, or other professional who may perform an ancillary service in conjunction with a real estate transaction.

Real estate brokers have a specific job, and it's important to understand what they do and don't do. Their main role is to help people buy and sell properties. However, there are many other professionals involved in real estate transactions who have different jobs.:

1. **Real estate brokers:** They help connect buyers and sellers, negotiate deals, and guide people through the process of buying or selling a property.

2. **Other professionals involved in real estate:**

- **Appraisers:** Figure out how much a property is worth
- **Mortgage companies:** Help people get loans to buy houses
- **Lawyers:** Handle legal paperwork and make sure everything is done correctly
- **Engineers:** Check if buildings are structurally sound
- **Contractors:** Build or renovate properties
- **Surveyors:** Measure land and property boundaries
- **Home inspectors:** Check houses for problems before someone buys them

While these professionals might work on the same real estate deal, their jobs are different from what a real estate broker does. A broker doesn't do the specific tasks these other experts handle. Instead, they often work alongside these professionals to make sure everything goes smoothly in a property sale or purchase. So, when you're buying or selling a house, you'll probably work with a real estate broker, but you might also need help from some of these other professionals for different parts of the process.

(c) The provisions of this article do not apply to:

(1) Any person acting on his or her own behalf as owner or lessor of real estate.

(2) The regular employees of an owner of real estate, who perform any acts regulated by this article, where the acts are incidental to the management of the real estate: Provided, That the employee does not receive additional compensation for the act and does not perform the act as a vocation.

(c) This part of the law doesn't apply to:

(1) People who are dealing with their own property.

(2) Let's break this down into easier parts:

1. This is talking about **people who work for someone who owns real estate** (like apartments or houses).
2. These workers might do some tasks that are usually done by licensed real estate professionals.
3. However, these tasks must be:

- Small parts of their regular job of managing the property
- **Not something they get extra money for**
- Not their main job or career

For example:

Imagine you work as a maintenance person for an apartment complex. Sometimes, you might show an empty apartment to a possible new tenant. This is okay as long as:

- It's just a small part of your job
- You don't get a bonus or extra pay for doing it
- Your main job is still maintenance, not showing apartments

The key idea is that regular employees can do some real estate-related tasks without needing a special license, as long as it's not their main job and they're not making extra money from it.

(3) Attorneys-at-law: Provided, That attorneys-at-law shall be required to submit to the written examination required under §30-40-12 of this code in order to qualify for a broker's license: Provided, however, That an attorney-at-law who is licensed as a real estate broker prior to July 1, 1980, is exempt from the written examination required under §30- 40-12 of this code.

This is talking about lawyers (also called attorneys) who want to become real estate brokers.

The Main Points:

1. Lawyers usually need to take a written test to become real estate brokers.
2. This test is mentioned in a specific part of the law (§30-40-12).
3. There's an exception for some older lawyers.

The Exception Explained

If you're a lawyer who became a real estate broker before July 1, 1980, you don't have to take the written test. This is like a "grandfather clause" - it lets older professionals keep their licenses without new requirements.

In Simple Terms Basically, this law is saying:

- Most lawyers need to pass a test to become real estate brokers.
- But if you're a lawyer who's been a real estate broker since before July 1980, you're off the hook - no test needed!

This rule helps make sure that newer brokers have up-to-date knowledge, while respecting the experience of long-time professionals.

(4) Any person holding, in good faith, a valid power of attorney from the owner or lessor of the real estate.

Imagine you have a friend who owns a house. This friend is going on a long trip and wants someone to take care of their property while they're gone. So, they give you a special document called a "power of attorney." This document is like a permission slip that says you can make decisions about the house on your friend's behalf. Now, this rule is saying that if you have this power of attorney document, and you truly believe it's real and valid (that's what "in good faith" means), then you can act as if you were the owner of the house in certain situations.

You might be able to do things like:

1 Rent out the house to someone else
2 Make repairs or improvements
3 Deal with any issues that come up related to the property

The important parts are:

- You must actually have the document
- You must believe it's real and valid
- You're trying to do what's best for the property and its owner

This rule helps protect people who are given this responsibility and ensures they can take care of the property properly when the owner is away or unable to do so themselves.

(5) Any person acting as a receiver, trustee, administrator, executor, guardian, conservator, or under the order of any court or under the authority of a deed of trust or will.

This description is talking about people who are given special responsibilities to manage money, property, or important decisions for others. Let's break it down:

1. **Receiver:** Someone appointed by a court to take care of property or money during a legal dispute.
2. **Trustee:** A person who manages money or property for someone else's benefit.
3. **Administrator:** Someone who handles the affairs of a person who died without leaving a will.
4. **Executor:** A person named in a will to carry out the wishes of someone who has died.
5. **Guardian:** An adult who's legally responsible for taking care of a child or an adult who can't care for themselves.
6. **Conservator:** Similar to a guardian, but usually focuses on managing money and property for someone who can't do it themselves.
7. **Under court order:** This means the person is doing these tasks because a judge told them to.
8. **Under authority of a deed of trust or will:** This means the person is following instructions left in official legal documents.

Basically, all these roles involve being trusted to make decisions or manage things for other people, often in situations involving legal matters, money, or care for those who can't manage on their own.

(6) A public officer while performing his or her official duties.

A **public officer** doing their job. Imagine someone who works for the government or a public organization. This could be:

- A police officer
- A firefighter
- A teacher at a public school
- A mail carrier
- A city council member

These people have specific duties they're supposed to do as part of their job. When they're actively doing these duties, we call that "performing their official duties. "For example:

- A police officer patrolling the streets
- A firefighter putting out a fire
- A teacher teaching a class
- A mail carrier delivering letters
- A city council member attending a council meeting

When these people are doing their jobs, they're considered "public officers performing their official duties." This phrase is often used in legal contexts to describe situations where these workers are protected by special laws or have certain responsibilities while they're on the job.

(7) Any person acquiring or disposing of any interest in timber or minerals, or acquiring or disposing of properties for easements and rights of way.

Imagine you're playing a game where you can buy, sell, or trade different types of valuable things. In this case, we're talking about two specific valuable things: timber (which means trees that can be used for wood) and minerals (like gold, oil, or other stuff found in the ground). Now, let's break down the sentence:

1. **"Any person"** - This means anyone, including you, your friends, or even big companies.
2. **"Acquiring"** - This is just a fancy word for getting or buying some thing.
3. **"Disposing of"** - This means selling or getting rid of something.
4. **"Any interest in timber or minerals"** - This part means owning a share of trees that can be cut down for wood, or owning a share of valuable stuff found in the ground.
5. **"Acquiring or disposing of properties for easements and rights of way"** - This is about buying or selling land that lets people or companies use a part of your property. For example, letting a power company put electric lines across your land.

So, in simple terms, this sentence is talking about anyone who buys or sells:

- Trees that can be used for wood
- Valuable stuff found in the ground
- Permission to use part of their land for things like roads or power lines

It's basically about people or companies dealing with these specific types of property or land rights.

(8) Any person employed exclusively to act as the management or rental agent for the real estate of one person or entity.

A **property manager who only works for one owner**. Imagine you own an apartment building, but you're too busy to deal with all the tasks involved in running it. You might hire someone to handle everything for you. This person would:

- Find and screen new tenants
- Collect rent
- Handle repairs and maintenance
- Deal with tenant complaints or issues

If this person only works for you and doesn't manage properties for anyone else, they'd fit the description you mentioned. They're exclusively employed to manage or rent out the real estate (property) belonging to just one person or company. This arrangement is less common than property management companies that handle multiple properties for different owners. But for someone with a lot of properties or a large apartment complex, it might make sense to have a dedicated manager working only for them.

(9) Any person properly licensed pursuant to the provisions of §19-2C-1 et seq. of this code when conducting an auction, any portion of which contains any leasehold or estate in real estate, only when the person so licensed is retained to conduct an auction by:

Let's break this down into easier terms:

1. There are people called **auctioneers** who have special licenses to run auctions. These licenses are given out according to certain laws.

2. Sometimes, these auctions include selling or leasing real estate. Real estate means land or buildings.

3. This rule is talking about when these licensed auctioneers can conduct auctions that involve real estate.

4. The important part is that the auctioneer must be hired specifically to run the auction. They can't just decide to do it on their own.

So, in simple terms, this is saying: "Licensed auctioneers can run auctions that involve real estate, but only when someone hires them to do it. They need to have the proper license and be officially asked to conduct the auction. "This rule helps make sure that real estate auctions are run by qualified professionals who know what they're doing and have been properly hired for the job.

(A) A receiver or trustee in bankruptcy;

Imagine a company is in serious financial trouble and can't pay its debts. This is called bankruptcy. When this happens, someone needs to step in and take control of the situation. This person is called a receiver or trustee in bankruptcy. Think of this person like a financial superhero who comes in to save the day when a business is drowning in debt.

Their job is to:

1. Take control of the company's assets (things the company owns)
2. Figure out how much money the company owes and to whom
3. Try to sell off some of the company's stuff to raise money
4. Pay back as much of the debt as possible to the people the company owes money to

The **receiver or trustee** is usually appointed by a court or sometimes by the main people the company owes money to. They're not part of the company – they're an outsider who comes in to handle things fairly. Their main goal is to get the best possible outcome for everyone involved, especially the people who are owed money. Sometimes, if they're really good at their job, they might even be able to help the company recover and get back on its feet. In simple terms, a receiver or trustee in bankruptcy is like a financial doctor for very sick businesses, trying to cure them or at least make the best of a bad situation.

(B) A fiduciary acting under the authority of a deed of trust or will; or

A trustee is like a responsible grown-up who takes care of money or property for someone else. They're given this job by a legal document called a deed of trust or a will. **Think of it this way:**

1. Deed of trust: This is like a special agreement that says, "Hey, we trust you to look after this stuff for us."
2. Will: This is a document people write before they die to say who should get their things and who should be in charge of handling their affairs.

The trustee's job is to:

- Make sure the money or property is managed properly
- Follow the instructions given in the deed of trust or will
- Act in the best interest of the people who are supposed to benefit from the trust or will

It's a big responsibility, kind of like being a guardian for someone's money or property. The trustee has to be honest, careful, and make smart decisions to protect what they're in charge of.

(C) A fiduciary of a decedent's estate.

When someone passes away (the "decedent"), their money, property, and belongings (called their "estate") need to be managed and distributed according to their wishes or the law. The person responsible for handling this important task is called a "fiduciary. "Think of a fiduciary as a trusted helper who has a legal duty to act in the best interests of the deceased person and their estate. **This person could be:**

1 An executor named in the will

2 An administrator appointed by the court if there's no will

3 A trustee if the person left behind a trust

The fiduciary's main jobs include:

- Gathering all the deceased person's assets
- Paying off any debts or taxes the person owed
- Distributing what's left to the rightful heirs or beneficiaries

It's a big responsibility because the fiduciary must be honest, careful, and fair when dealing with the estate. They can get in trouble if they mishandle things or use the estate's money for themselves. In simple terms, a fiduciary of a decedent's estate is like a responsible caretaker who makes sure a deceased person's final affairs are handled properly and their wishes are carried out.

(10) Any person employed by a broker in a noncommissioned secretarial or clerical capacity who may in the normal course of employment, be required to:

Let's break this down:

1. We're talking about someone who works for a broker.
2. **This person has a job that doesn't earn commissions.** Instead, they probably get a regular salary or hourly wage.
3. Their main duties are secretarial or clerical. This means they do office work like:
    - Answering phones
    - Scheduling appointments
    - Filing papers
    - Typing documents
    - Organizing information
4. The phrase "in the normal course of employment" just means "as part of their regular job duties."
5. The word "may" tells us that what comes next isn't always required, but it could be sometimes.
6. The sentence ends with "be required to:" which means there are probably more duties listed after this part, but we can't see them here.

So, in simpler terms, this is talking about an office worker at a broker's company who might have some extra responsibilities beyond just basic office tasks.

(A) Disseminate brokerage preprinted and predetermined real estate sales and rental information;

Share ready-made real estate info. Real estate agents and companies often have pre-prepared information about houses and apartments for sale or rent. This information might include:

- Prices
- Photos
- Property details
- Neighborhood facts

Your job would be to pass out or send this information to people who might be interested in buying or renting. You'd be helping spread the word about available properties without having to create the materials yourself. It's like being a messenger for real estate listings!

(B) Accept and process rental reservations or bookings for a period not to exceed 30 consecutive days in a manner and procedure predetermined by the broker;

Rental Bookings: What You Can Do

As someone working for a real estate broker, you're allowed to:

1. Take and handle rental reservations
2. Process bookings for people who want to rent a place

But there are some rules you need to follow:

Time Limit

- **You can only book rentals for up to 30 days in a row**
- **This means no long-term rentals or leases**

Following the Boss's Rules

- Your broker (the person in charge) will tell you exactly how to handle these bookings
- You need to follow their instructions carefully

Why This Matters

This rule helps make sure that:

- Short-term rentals are handled properly
- Everyone follows the same process
- The broker stays in control of how rentals are managed

Remember, your job is to help people book short stays, but always within the rules set by your boss.

(C) Collect predetermined rental fees for the rentals which are to be promptly tendered to the broker;

Gather the agreed-upon rent money from people renting homes or apartments. Then, quickly give that money to the person or company in charge of managing the rentals (the broker). To break it down even further:

1. Collect rent: Get the rent money from tenants
2. Predetermined fees: The amount of rent was already decided before
3. Promptly tender: Give the money quickly to the broker: The broker is the person or company managing the rentals

This is typically a task for someone working in property management or as an assistant to a landlord or real estate company.

(D) Make appointments on behalf of the broker or licensed salesperson with buyers and sellers of real estate and potential buyers and sellers of real estate; or

An **unlicensed assistant** can: Set up meetings for real estate agents This means the assistant can:

• Schedule times for the real estate agent to meet with people who want to buy or sell homes

• Arrange appointments with folks who might be interested in buying or selling property in the future.

Basically, the assistant helps the real estate agent manage their calendar by booking times for them to talk with current and potential clients. This saves the agent time so they can focus on other important parts of their job. The assistant doesn't need a real estate license to do this task. They're just helping with scheduling, not giving real estate advice or handling any of the actual buying or selling process.

(E) Any combination thereof.

§30-40-6. COMMISSION CREATED; MEMBERSHIP; APPOINTMENT AND REMOVAL OF MEMBERS; QUALIFICATIONS; TERMS; ORGANIZATION.

(a) The West Virginia Real Estate Commission is hereby continued. The members of the commission in office on the date this section takes effect shall, unless sooner removed, continue to serve until their respective terms expire and until their successors have been appointed and qualified.

The West Virginia Real Estate Commission is staying in place. It's not going away or being replaced. The people who are currently members of this commission will keep doing their jobs until:

1. Their time in the position (called a "term") is finished, or
2. They are removed from their position for some reason

When a member's time is up or they leave, a new person will be chosen to take their place. This new person needs to be properly appointed and meet all the requirements for the job. This rule makes sure that there's always a group of people running the commission, even when members change. It helps keep things running smoothly without any gaps in leadership.

(b)(1) Commencing with the terms beginning with July 1, 2002, the commission shall consist of five persons appointed for terms of four years by the Governor with the advice and consent of the Senate. Four commissioners must be licensed under the provisions of this article and one commissioner must be a citizen member who is not licensed under the provisions of this article.

Starting July 1, 2002, a new group called a **commission** was created. Here's how it works:

1. The commission has five people in it.
2. The Governor chooses these five people, but the Senate has to agree with the choices.
3. Each person on the commission serves for four years.
4. Four of the five people must have a special license related to the work they do. This license is mentioned in some rules or laws.
5. One person on the commission is just a regular citizen. This person doesn't need the special license the others have.

This setup helps make sure that most of the commission members know a lot about the subject they're dealing with, but there's also one person who can give an outside perspective.

(2) Each licensed commissioner, at the time of his or her appointment, must have been licensed and practiced in this state as a real estate broker, associate broker or salesperson as his or her primary vocation for a period of not less than ten years immediately preceding the appointment. Each commissioner must have been a resident of this state for at least six years prior to his or her appointment and must remain a resident during the appointment term. No more than four commissioners shall belong to the same political party.

To become a **real estate commissioner** in this state, a person needs to meet certain requirements:

1. **Job experience:** They must have worked in real estate as their main job for at least 10 years right before being appointed. This could be as a real estate broker, associate broker, or salesperson.
2. **License:** They need to have had a valid real estate license during those 10 years.
3. **Residency:** They must have lived in the state for at least 6 years before being appointed and continue living there while serving as a commissioner.
4. **Political balance:** To keep things fair, no more than four commissioners can be from the same political party.

These rules help ensure that the commissioners have plenty of experience in the real estate field and understand the local market well. The political balance requirement aims to prevent one party from having too much control over real estate regulations

(3) The appointment of three licensed commissioners, whether for a full term or to fill a vacancy, shall be made by the Governor with the advice and consent of the Senate. The appointment of one licensed commissioner, whether for a full term or to fill a vacancy, shall be made by the Governor from among three nominees selected by the West Virginia association of realtors. If the appointment is for a full term, the nominations must be submitted to the Governor not later than three months prior to the date on which the appointment becomes effective. If the appointment is to fill a vacancy, the nominations must be submitted to the Governor within thirty days after a request for the nominations has been made by the Governor to the West Virginia association of realtors. If the association fails to submit nominations in accordance with the requirements of this section, the Governor may make the appointment without the nominations.

Imagine there's a group of people who make important decisions about real estate in West Virginia. This group needs four licensed commissioners. Here's how they're chosen:

1 The Governor picks three of these commissioners:

- The Governor chooses these people.
- The Senate has to agree with the Governor's choices.
- This applies whether it's for a full term or just to fill an empty spot.

2 For the fourth commissioner, it's a bit different:

- The West Virginia association of realtors suggests three people.
- The Governor then picks one of these three.

3 There are some time rules:

- If it's for a full term, the realtors' group needs to give their suggestions at least three months before the job starts.
- If it's to fill an empty spot, they have 30 days after the Governor asks for names.

4 What if the realtors'® group doesn't follow these rules?

- If they don't give their suggestions on time, the Governor can choose someone without their input.

So basically, the Governor has a big role in choosing these commissioners, but for one of them, they have to consider suggestions from the realtors' group, unless that group misses their deadline.

(c) Any commissioner immediately and automatically forfeits his or her membership on the commission if he or she has his or her license to practice as a real estate broker, associate broker or salesperson suspended or revoked by the board, is convicted of a felony under the laws of this state or of the United States, becomes a nonresident of this state, or holds any elective public office or becomes a member of any political committee.

A real estate commissioner will lose their position on the commission right away if any of these things happen:

1. The board takes away or suspends their license to work as a real estate broker, associate broker, or salesperson.
2. They are found guilty of a serious crime (called a felony) in this state or anywhere in the United States.
3. They move out of the state and no longer live there.
4. They get elected to any public office.
5. They join any political committee.

These rules are in place to make sure that commissioners stay qualified, unbiased, and focused on their job. If any of these things happen, the person automatically loses their position as a commissioner without any extra steps needed.

(d) No member of the commission may be removed from office by the Governor except for official misconduct, incompetency, neglect of duty, gross immorality or other good cause, but then only in the manner prescribed by law for the removal by the Governor of state elective officials.

The governor can't just fire members of the commission whenever they want. There are only a few specific reasons why a commission member can be removed from their job:

1. If they do something wrong while working (official misconduct)
2. If they're not capable of doing their job properly (incompetency)
3. If they're not doing their duties (neglect of duty)
4. If they behave in a way that's considered really unethical or im moral (gross immorality)
5. If there's another good reason that's similar to these

Even if one of these reasons applies, the governor still has to follow certain steps laid out by law to remove the person. It's the same process they'd use to remove other important government officials who were elected. This rule exists to protect commission members from being unfairly kicked out of their positions just because the governor doesn't like them or disagrees with them. It helps ensure that commission members can do their jobs without worrying about losing their positions for no good reason.

(e) No member of the commission may serve more than two consecutive full terms and any member having served two full terms may not be appointed for one year after completion of his or her second full term. A member shall continue to serve until his or her successor has been appointed and qualified.

This rule is about how long someone can be part of a commission. Let's break it down:

1 **Term limits:**

- A person can only serve two full terms in a row.
- After serving two full terms, they have to take a break for at least a year before they can be appointed again.

2 **Staying on until replacement:**

- Even if a member's term is over, they keep working until a new person is chosen and ready to take their place.

Think of it like this: Imagine you're on a school committee. You can be on it for two years straight, but then you have to step down and let someone else have a turn. You can't join again for at least a year. But if they haven't found your replacement when your time is up, you keep doing the job until the new person is ready to start. This rule helps make sure that:

- ► New people with fresh ideas get a chance to serve.
- ► No one person stays in power for too long.
- ► There's always someone doing the job, even when they're switching people.

(f) The Governor shall designate one member of the commission as chairman and the members shall choose a vice chairman and a secretary, each of whom shall continue to serve in their respective capacity until replaced.

The Governor picks one person from the group (called a commission) to be the leader. This person is called the

(1) chairman. The other people in the group then choose two more important roles:

(2) A vice chairman (like a second-in-command)

(3) A secretary (someone who keeps track of important information)

These three people (the chairman, vice chairman, and secretary) will keep doing their jobs until someone new takes over their position. It's kind of like how a school club might have a president, vice president, and someone to take notes. They stay in those roles until the next election or until they decide to step down

(g) Three members shall constitute a quorum for the conduct of official business.

To make decisions and get things done officially, at least three people from the group need to be present. This minimum number of people is called a "quorum. "

Think of it like this:

Imagine you're part of a school club with 10 members. The club has a rule that says at least 3 members must be there to make important decisions or vote on things. This way, decisions aren't made when only one or two people show up. It helps ensure that enough people are involved in the process. So, when they say "Three members shall constitute a quorum for the conduct of official business," they mean that three is the magic number needed to start making official decisions or doing important group work. Without at least three people, any decisions or actions wouldn't count as official.

(h) Each commissioner shall receive the same compensation as is paid to members of the Legislature for their interim duties as recommended by the citizens legislative compensation commission and authorized by law for each day or portion thereof engaged in the discharge of official duties. Each commissioner shall be reimbursed for his or her actual and necessary expenses for each day or portion thereof engaged in the discharge of official duties in a manner consistent with guidelines of the travel management office of the Department of Administration.

Compensation for Commissioners

Commissioners get paid the same amount as members of the Legislature do for their work between regular sessions. This pay is:

- Recommended by a special group called the citizens legislative compensation commission
- Approved by law
- Given for each day or part of a day they spend doing their official job

Reimbursement for Expenses

Commissioners also get money back for the expenses they have while doing their job. This includes:

- Actual costs they had to pay
- Necessary expenses related to their work
- Money for each day or part of a day they spend on official duties

The way they get paid back follows rules set by the Department of Administration's travel management office. This ensures everything is fair and properly managed. In simpler terms, commissioners get paid for their time and get reimbursed for work-related expenses, just like many other government officials do.

§30-40-7 GENERAL POWERS AND DUTIES

(a) May sue and be sued in its official name as an agency of this state;	Can take legal action and be legally challenged using its official name as a state agency
(b) Shall employ an executive director and shall fix his or her compensation subject to the general laws of this state. The commission shall determine the duties of the executive director as it shall consider necessary and appropriate to discharge the duties imposed by the provisions of this code;	Must hire a boss and decide their pay following state rules. The group decides what the boss does based on what the law says.
(c) Shall employ or contract with such other investigators, hearing examiners, attorneys, consultants, clerks and assistants as the commission considers necessary and determine the duties and ix the compensation of such investigators, clerks and assistants subject to the general laws of this state;	Can hire or work with other helpers like investigators, meeting leaders, lawyers, experts, office workers, and assistants. The group decides what these people do and how much they get paid, following state rules.
(d) Shall have the authority to issue subpoenas and subpoenas duces tecum through any member, its executive director or any duly authorized representative;	Can make people come or bring documents through any member, the boss, or anyone they choose
(e) Shall prescribe, examine and determine the qualifications of any applicant for a license;	Decides who can get a license by checking if they meet the requirements

(f) Shall provide for an appropriate examination of any applicant for a license;	Must set up a test for anyone who wants a license.
(g) May enter into agreements with other jurisdictions whereby the license issued by another jurisdiction may be recognized as successfully qualifying a nonresident for a license in this state;	Can make deals with other places to accept their licenses for people from outside the state
(h) Shall issue, renew, deny, suspend, revoke or reinstate licenses and take disciplinary action against any licensee;	Can give, renew, deny, pause, cancel, or restore licenses and punish license holders.

(j) Shall conduct hearings or cause hearings to be conducted upon charges calling for the discipline of a licensee or for the suspension or revocation of a license;

The commission will hold meetings or make sure meetings happen when someone with a license is accused of doing something wrong. These meetings are to decide if the person should be punished, have their license taken away for a while, or lose their license completely.

These meetings are important because they help make sure people with licenses are following the rules and doing their jobs properly.

(k) May examine the books and records relating to the real estate business of a licensee if the licensee is charged in a complaint of any violation of this article, commission rule or any order or final decision issued by the commission: Provided, That such examination shall not extend beyond the specific violation charged in the complaint;

What This Means:

Imagine you have a real estate license, which allows you to help people buy and sell houses. Now, let's break down what this rule is saying:

When Can Your Records Be Checked?

If someone files a complaint against you, saying you broke a rule related to your real estate work, the authorities can look at your business records. This includes things like:

- Your financial books
- Documents about houses you've sold or helped people buy
- Any other paperwork related to your real estate business

What's the Catch?

Here's the important part: **They can only look at records that are connected to the specific rule you're accused of breaking.** They can't just go through all your stuff for no reason.

An Example to Help Understand:

Let's say someone complains that you didn't tell them about a problem with a house they bought through you. The authorities can look at your records about that specific house sale, but they can't start digging into all your other deals that aren't related to this complaint.

In Simple Terms:

Basically, if you're accused of doing something wrong in your real estate job, the people in charge can check your work records, but only the ones that have to do with what you're accused of – not everything you've ever done.

(l) May impose one or more sanctions as considered appropriate in the circumstances for the discipline of a licensee. Available sanctions include, but are not limited to, denial of a license or renewal thereof, administrative fine not to exceed $1,000 per day per violation, probation, revocation, suspension, restitution, require additional education, censure, denial of future license, downgrade of license, reprimand or order the return of compensation collected from an injured consumer;

What This Means:

This rule is about how a licensing authority (like a government agency) can punish someone who has a professional license if they break the rules. It's like when you get in trouble at school, but for grown-ups in their jobs.

Possible Punishments:

The authority can choose one or more ways to discipline the person. Some **examples** are:

1 Not giving them a license or not letting them renew it
2 Making them pay a fine (up to $1,000 per day for each rule they broke)
3 Putting them on probation (like being watched closely)
4 Taking away their license completely
5 Suspending their license for a while
6 Making them pay back money to customers they hurt
7 Forcing them to take more classes or training
8 Giving them an official warning
9 Not letting them get a license in the future
10 Lowering the level of their license
11 Giving them a formal scolding
12 Making them return money they got from customers they harmed

The Bottom Line:

Basically, if someone with a professional license messes up, there are many ways they can be punished. The authority in charge can pick whatever punishment (or punishments) they think is right for the situation.

(m) Shall meet at least once each calendar year at such place and time as the commission shall designate and at such other times and places as it considers necessary to conduct commission business;

The rule is talking about **how often the commission needs to meet. Here's what it means:**

1. The commission has to meet at least once every year.
2. They can choose where and when to have this yearly meeting.
3. If they need to, they can also have extra meetings during the year.
4. These extra meetings can be held whenever and wherever the commission thinks it's necessary to get their work done.

Basically, it's saying that this group has to get together regularly to discuss important stuff, but they have some flexibility in deciding exactly when and where to meet.

(n) Shall publish an annual directory of licensees in compliance with the provisions of section thirteen, article one, chapter thirty of this code;

The law says that every year, a list of people who have special permits (called licenses) needs to be made public. This list is called a directory. To break it down further:

1. **"Shall publish"** means they have to make this list available for everyone to see.
2. **"Annual"** means it happens once every year.
3. **"Directory"** is like a big list or book with names and information.
4. **"Licensees"** are people who have official permission to do certain jobs or activities.

This rule is part of a bigger set of laws. It's mentioned in a specific part of those laws: section thirteen, article one, chapter thirty. The main idea is to keep track of who has these special permits and make sure this information is available to the public every year. This helps keep things organized and allows people to check if someone is officially allowed to do certain work.

(o) May sponsor real estate-related educational seminars, courses, workshops or institutes, may incur and pay the necessary expenses and may charge a fee for attendance;

The law says that certain organizations or companies can:

1. **Set up and run educational events about real estate. These events could be:**

- Seminars (like talks or presentations)
- Courses (longer, more in-depth classes)
- Workshops (hands-on learning sessions)
- Institutes (more formal, structured programs)

2. **Pay for all the stuff needed to make these events happen. This might include:**

- Renting a space
- Buying materials
- Paying speakers or teachers
- Providing refreshments

3. **Ask people to pay a fee to attend these events. This helps cover the costs of running them.**

Basically, it means that organizations can teach people about real estate, spend money to make it happen, and charge people who want to learn. This helps spread knowledge about real estate and allows the organizers to cover their expenses.

(p) May assist libraries, institutions and foundations with financial aid or otherwise in providing texts, sponsoring studies, surveys and programs;

The organization can help libraries, schools, and other groups by:

1. Giving them money to buy books and other reading materials
2. Paying for research projects or studies about important topics
3. Supporting programs that help people learn or improve their skills

Basically, they're like a helpful friend who can chip in with cash or other resources to make sure people have access to books, information, and educational opportunities. They might fund a new computer lab at a library, pay for a study about how to improve reading skills, or sponsor a summer reading program for kids. Their goal is to support learning and access to information in different ways.

(q) May perform compliance audits on real estate brokerage offices, education providers or any other person regulated by the commission;

The sentence is talking about something a real estate commission can do.

1. Compliance audits: These are like detailed checkups to make sure people are following the rules.

2. Who they can check up on:

- Real estate brokerage offices (places where real estate agents work)
- Education providers (people who teach real estate courses)
- Anyone else the commission regulates (controls or oversees)

3. What it means: The commission has the power to inspect these places or people to make sure they're doing everything correctly and legally.

In simpler terms, it's like how a teacher might check students' homework to make sure they're following instructions. The real estate commission can check on real estate businesses and schools to make sure they're following all the rules and laws about real estate

(r) May provide distance education courses for applicants for a license sufficient to meet the educational requirements contained in subsections (a) and (b), section fourteen of this article; and

The law says that an organization can offer online classes or remote learning courses for people who want to get a specific type of license. These online courses can help students complete the required education mentioned in parts (a) and (b) of section fourteen of the law.

This is about getting a license:

- To get this license, you need to complete some educational requirements.
- Instead of going to a physical school, you can take these classes online or through distance learning.
- The online courses are allowed to cover all the necessary topics that the law requires for getting the license.

This rule is helpful because it makes education more accessible to people who might not be able to attend in-person classes due to work, location, or other reasons.

(s) Shall take all other actions necessary and proper to effectuate the purposes of this article

"The person or group in charge should do whatever else is needed to make sure the goals of this section of the law are achieved."

1. "Shall take all other actions" means they should do anything else that's required, beyond what's already been listed.
2. "Necessary and proper" means these actions should be both needed and appropriate.
3. "To effectuate the purposes" means to make the goals or inten tions happen in real life.
4. "Of this article" refers to the specific section of the real estate law being discussed.

In everyday language, it's like saying, "Do whatever else you need to do to make sure this part of the law works the way it's supposed to." **This phrase is often included to cover any situations or actions that might not have been specifically mentioned but are still important for achieving the law's goals.**

§30-40-8. RULE-MAKING AUTHORITY.

(a) The commission may propose rules for legislative approval in accordance with the provisions of article three, chapter twenty-nine-a of this code which are necessary for the conduct of its business, the holding of hearings and for the general implementation, enforcement and administration of the provisions of this article, including, but not limited to, establishing, administering and governing the following:

The real estate commission has the power to suggest new rules. But don't worry, they can't just make these rules on their own!

How It Works

1. The commission comes up with ideas for new rules.
2. They present these ideas to lawmakers.
3. The lawmakers then decide whether to approve these rules or not.

What Kind of Rules?

The commission can suggest rules about:

- How they run their own business
- How they hold hearings
- How they put into action and enforce the laws they're responsible for

Some Examples

The commission might suggest rules about:

- How meetings are conducted
- How to handle complaints
- How to keep records

Important Points

- The commission doesn't have the final say - the lawmakers do.
- These rules must follow a specific part of the law (Article 3, Chapter 29-A).
- The rules can cover a wide range of topics, not just the ones listed.

Remember, this process helps ensure that the commission operates fairly and effectively, while still being accountable to elected officials.

(1) Fees for applications, examinations, licenses, renewal of licenses, changes to licenses requiring reissuance, courses, investigations, copies of records, license certifications and other fees considered necessary by the commission, none of which shall be prorated or refundable: Provided, That the fee schedule in effect prior to enactment of this article, enumerated in section nine, article twelve, chapter forty-seven of this code, shall continue to be effective until withdrawn, revoked or amended;

Understanding License Fees

The government has rules about fees for different things related to licenses. These fees cover:

- Applying for a license
- Taking tests
- Getting a new license
- Renewing your license
- Making changes to your license that require a new one
- Taking courses
- Investigations
- Getting copies of records
- Getting certifications for your license
- Other things the commission thinks are necessary

It's important to know that:

1. You must pay the full amount for these fees
2. You can't get a refund
3. The fees won't be divided up or reduced

What's Happening with the Current Fees

The fees that are in place right now will stay the same for a while. They're listed in a specific part of the law (section nine, article twelve, chapter forty-seven). These fees will continue to be used until the government decides to:

- Take them away
- Cancel them
- Change them

So, for now, you can expect to pay the same fees you've been paying. If there are any changes, the government will let everyone know

(2) The minimum requirements and qualifications necessary for approval by the commission of providers, instructors and the course content of any pre-license education course required in section fourteen of this article;

Understanding Commission Approval for Real Estate Education

The real estate commission (a group of experts) has to make sure that anyone teaching new real estate agents is qualified and knows their stuff. They also want to make sure the classes are teaching the right things. Here's what they look at:

1 Teachers (Instructors): The commission checks if the people teaching have enough knowledge and experience to teach others about real estate.

2 Schools or Companies (Providers): They make sure the places offering these classes are legit and can actually teach what they promise.

3 What's Being Taught (Course Content): The commission reviews the lessons to make sure they cover all the important stuff new real estate agents need to know before they can get their license.

These rules are there to make sure that when you take a class to become a real estate agent, you're learning from qualified people and getting all the information you need to do the job well

(3) The experience required of an applicant;

The experience required by the commission is explained in section 14 of their article. This is just a few pages away. This section points to where that info can be found. We will go over it in Article 30-40-14

(4) The minimum standards for licensure;

These "minimum" standards required by the commission are also explained in section 14 of their article. This statement points to where that info can be found. We will go over it in Article 30-40-14

(5) The standards for examinations;

The standards required by the commission for examinations are also explained in section 14 of their article. This statement points to where that info can be found. We will go over it in Article 30-40-14

(6) The minimum requirements and qualifications necessary for approval by the commission of providers, instructors and courses of continuing professional education required by section sixteen of this article;

The minimum requirements and what qualifications are needed to be approved by the commission are explained in section 16 of their article. This statement points to where that info can be found. We will go over it in detail in Article 30-40-16

(7) Continuing professional education requirements for licensees, including any exemptions;

This is a teaser of where you will find this info. This statement is written into the law code to say, you almost found the info you're looking for! Keep looking just a few pages away in article 30-40-16 and you've reached it.

(8) Renewal of licenses;

This statement is saying if you're seeking info on renewing your license it can be found later in article 30-40-16.

(9) Use of firm or trade name;

If you are looking for the real details as to how the commission deals with firm and trade names then look no further, eh hmmm. I mean, look further! And look at 30-40-16 to be exact

(10) Denying, suspending, revoking or reinstating a license;

Have you ever been curious about refusing to give someone a license? How about suspending it? Taking away a license from someone who already has one? Oh, the drama! How about reinstating the license after it has been taken away? Well, then we need to look at article 30-40-16

(11) Form and use of contracts used in a real estate transaction;

Curious about what forms and contracts we use? Look at 30-40-16

(12) Notification required to clients or customers of agency relationship;

This Notice of Agency relationship form I have seen abbreviated a lot as NOA. This form in particular has been in the news a lot lately because of the NAR settlement. You have probably heard of this. The WVREC is stating here that they do require you use a NOA and that this will be explained more in 30-40-16.

(13) Professional conduct requirements; and

Should Bob really be wearing a speedo at the meeting? Professional conduct that the WVREC requires will be explained in 30-40-16

(14) Any other purpose to carry out the requirements of this article or to protect the public interest.

This kind of statement is often included in legal documents or policies to cover situations that might not have been thought of when the rules were first written. It helps make sure that the overall goals of protecting people and following the rules can still be met, even if something unexpected comes up

(b) All rules in effect as of the passage of this article previously promulgated by the commission pursuant to article twelve, chapter forty-seven of this code will remain in effect until amended, modified, repealed or replaced, except that references to provisions of former enactments of this article are interpreted to mean provisions of this article.

This legal text is basically saying:

1. The rules that were in place before this new law was passed will stay in effect.

2. These rules will continue to be valid until someone decides to change them, get rid of them, or replace them with new rules.

3. If any of the old rules mention parts of the old law, we should now understand those mentions to be referring to the matching parts in the new law.

Why It Matters

This kind of language is important because:

- It ensures there's no gap in the rules when a new law is passed.
- It helps avoid confusion about which rules apply.
- It saves time and effort by not having to rewrite all the rules from scratch.

Think of it like updating the operating system on your phone. The new system (law) is installed, but your apps (rules) still work. They might just refer to the new system instead of the old one when they need to.

§30-40-9. FEES; SPECIAL REVENUE ACCOUNT; ADMINISTRATIVE FINES.

(a) All fees and other moneys, except administrative fines, received by the commission shall be deposited into the treasury of the state, daily, into a special revenue fund known as the "real estate license fund" which is continued.

There's a group called the "commission" that handles real estate stuff in your state. When people pay fees or give money to this commission for various reasons, here's what happens:

1 The commission collects all this money.
2 Every day, they take this money and put it into the state's big piggy bank (which is called the treasury).
3 But instead of mixing it with all the other money in the state's piggy bank, they put it into a special section called the "real estate license fund."
4 This fund already exists - it's not new. The law just says it will keep on going.
5 One important thing: If someone gets in trouble and has to pay a fine (called an administrative fine), that money doesn't go into this special fund. It goes somewhere else.

So basically, this rule makes sure that most of the money the commission gets goes to a specific place where it can be used for real estate-related stuff in your state.

(b) Except as may be provided in §30-40-10 of this code, the commission shall retain the amounts in the special revenue fund from year to year and no funds collected under this article may be used by the commission for any purpose other than the administration and enforcement of this article. No compensation or expense incurred under this article is a charge against the General Revenue Fund.

What This Law Means:

This law is about how a government commission handles certain money it collects.

Keeping the Money Separate

- The commission puts the money it collects into a special fund.
- This money stays in the fund from one year to the next.
- It's like having a separate piggy bank that's only for specific pur poses.

Using the Money

- The commission can only use this money for two things:
- To manage (or "administer") the rules related to this law
- To make sure people follow these rules

What the Money Can't Be Used For

- The commission isn't allowed to use this money for anything else.
- It's like having money in your lunch account at school - you can only use it for lunch, not for buying beer and video games.

(c) Any amounts received as administrative fines imposed pursuant to this article shall be deposited into the General Revenue Fund of the State Treasury.

Any money collected from fines given out for breaking the rules in this law will go into the state's main bank account. To break it down further:

1. When people or companies break certain rules, they sometimes have to pay fines.
2. These fines are called "administrative fines" because they're given out by government agencies, not courts.
3. All the money from these fines gets put together.
4. This money then goes into something called the "General Revenue Fund."
5. The General Revenue Fund is like the state's main piggy bank or checking account.
6. The state government uses this fund to pay for various things it needs to do.

So basically, instead of the money from fines going to a specific purpose, it all goes into one big pot that the state can use for different needs.

§30-40-10. CIVIL LIABILITY FOR COMMISSION MEMBERS; LIABILITY LIMITATIONS OF PERSON REPORTING TO COMMISSION

(a) Members of the commission shall be immune from individual civil liability for actions taken in good faith and without malice, within the scope of their duties as commission members.

This statement is about protecting the commission when they're doing their job. Here's what it means:

1. The members of this commission can't be personally sued (that's what "immune from individual civil liability" means) for the deci sions they make or actions they take as part of their job.

2. But this protection only applies if two things are true:

- They're acting "in good faith," which means they're honestly trying to do the right thing and not trying to cause harm.
- They're acting "without malice," which means they're not doing things out of spite or to purposely hurt someone.

3. The protection also only covers actions that are part of their job as commission members. If they do something outside of their job duties, this protection doesn't apply.

So basically, this rule is there to make sure the commission members can do their job without constantly worrying about being sued, as long as they're trying their best to do the right thing within the scope of their responsibilities.

(b) Any person who reports or otherwise provides evidence of violations of this article, the commission's rules, orders or final decisions to the commission or other law-enforcement agency, is not liable for making the report if it is made without malice and in the reasonable belief that the report is warranted by the facts known to him or her at the time.

If someone tells the authorities about rule-breaking, they're protected. Imagine you see someone breaking important rules or laws related to this specific area. You decide to report it to the people in charge or the police. This law says that you can't get in trouble for reporting it, as long as:

1. You're not lying or making things up to hurt someone (that's what "without malice" means)
2. Based on what you know at the time, you honestly believe that what you're reporting is true and needs to be reported

In other words, this law protects people who speak up about wrongdoing, if they're being honest and have good reasons to think something isn't right. It's like a safety net for people who want to do the right thing by reporting problems they see. This protection is important because it encourages people to come forward with information about rule-breaking without fear of getting in trouble themselves, as long as they're acting in good faith

§30-40-11. APPLICATION FOR LICENSE

The commission shall only issue an original license to an applicant if he or she:

To apply for the license from the West Virginia Real Estate Commission, you need to do a few things:

(a) Submits an application, in writing, on a form prescribed by the commission which shall contain, but is not limited to:

a) **Fill out an application form** (this form is online these days):

- This form is created by the commission, and you need to enter your answers on it.
- You'll need to provide some important information, including:

(1) The applicant's Social Security number;

1) Your Social Security number (that's your unique ID number from the government)

(2) A clear record indicating all jurisdictions where the applicant holds or has held any professional license;

2) A list of all the places where you currently have or used to have any professional licenses

(3) A clear record indicating if the applicant has been convicted of any criminal offense or if there is any criminal charge pending against the applicant, or a member or officer of the brokerage business, at the time of application;

3) Information about whether you've ever been found guilty of a crime or if you're currently being accused of one. This also applies to anyone who's a member or officer of the business you're working with.

Basically, they want to make sure you're being honest and that they have all the important info about you before they give you a license. It's like a background check to make sure you're qualified and trustworthy in the real estate profession

(b) Is at least 18 years of age

(b) This one's straight forward, however I will add something we get asked often enough. Students in high school who want to pursue this after graduation and are under 18 currently. You can take the pre licensing course we offer at any age so long as you plan on getting the license when you are 18. That said, if you are 17 and plan to work on the course we offer through the year, get started and then apply for the license when you are of legal age.

(c) Is a high school graduate or the holder of an equivalency diploma

(c) Again, this relates to the above statement about preparing to test and apply. You can take the class beforehand to prepare (and should if that's your plan to apply when you have graduated). So long as you graduate, or take your GED prior to applying for the license you are well on your way to getting your license.

(d) Is trustworthy, of good moral character, and competent to transact the business of a broker, associate broker, or salesperson;

In simpler terms, to work in real estate, you need to be honest, have strong values, and know your stuff. These qualities help ensure you'll do a good job for your clients and maintain a good reputation in the industry

(e) Has paid the appropriate fee, if any, which shall accompany all applications for original license or renewal;

These fees change so they have written this here to basically set you up to know there will be a fee to pay. Currently that fee is $75

(f) Has submitted to a state and national criminal history record check, as set forth in this subsection: Provided, That an applicant for a license who is an attorney at law may submit a letter of good standing from the West Virginia State Bar in lieu of submitting to a state and national criminal history record check;

To get this license, you need to do a background check. This means:

1. You have to let the state and national authorities look at your criminal record (if you have one).
2. They'll check to see if you've ever been in trouble with the law.
3. This is to make sure you're trustworthy and safe to give the license to.

But there's an exception:

- If you're a lawyer, you don't have to do this background check.
- Instead, you can just show a letter that says you're in good standing with the West Virginia State Bar (that's like a club for lawyers).
- This letter proves you're trustworthy without needing the full background check.
- It's also worth note that the state bar in WV makes applicants take a background check at a state and national level so honestly they have met the requirement already and this isn't a "loophole".

Basically, they want to make sure you're a good person before giving you the license. Lawyers get a shortcut because their job already requires them to be trustworthy.

(1) This requirement is found not to be against public policy.

This rule or condition is considered okay and allowed by law.

To break it down further:

- "Requirement" means a rule or something that's needed
- "Not to be against public policy" means it doesn't go against what society and the government think is good for everyone

Basically, it's saying that whatever rule or condition this law code is speaking of isn't harmful or unfair to people in general. The courts or lawmakers have decided it's acceptable and doesn't cause problems for society. For example, if there was a rule that said, "you must be 18 to vote," that would be considered okay and not against public policy. But if there was a rule that said, "only people with blue eyes can vote," that would probably be against public policy because it's unfair and discriminatory.

(2) The criminal history record check shall be based on fingerprints submitted to the West Virginia State Police or its assigned agent for forwarding to the Federal Bureau of Investigation.

When someone needs a criminal background check in West Virginia, here's what happens:

1. The person gets their fingerprints taken.
2. These fingerprints are sent to the West Virginia State Police.
3. The State Police (or someone they've chosen to help them) then sends these fingerprints to the FBI.
4. The FBI uses these fingerprints to search their records for any criminal history.

This process helps make sure that the background check is accurate and thorough. By using fingerprints, they can be sure they're checking the right person's history, since everyone's fingerprints are unique.

(3) The applicant shall meet all requirements necessary to complete the state and national criminal history record check, including:

When you apply for this license, you need to agree to a background check. This means:

(A) Submitting fingerprints for the purposes set forth in this subsection; and

1 You'll need to give your fingerprints.

(B) Authorizing the commission, the West Virginia State Police, and the Federal Bureau of Investigation to use all records submitted and produced for the purpose of screening the applicant for a license.

2 You're saying it's okay for the commission, the West Virginia State Police, and the FBI to look at your records to see if you qualify for the license.

(4) The results of the state and national criminal history record check may not be released to or by a private entity except:

The results of this background check are private. They can only be shared in three situations:

(A) To the individual who is the subject of the criminal history record check;

1 With you (since it's your information).

(B) With the written authorization of the individual who is the subject of the criminal history record check; or

2 If you give written permission for someone else to see it.

(C) Pursuant to a court order.

3 If a court orders the information to be released.

This process helps make sure that only qualified people get the license, while also protecting your privacy

(5) The criminal history record check and related records are not public records for the purposes of chapter 29B of this code.

Summary:

1. A criminal history record check is like a report card of someone's past run-ins with the law.
2. This report and any other papers connected to it are considered confidential.
3. The government has rules about what information can be shared with the public (these rules are in something called "chapter 29B").
4. This law is saying that criminal background checks are **NOT** part of the information that can be freely shared with just anyone who asks.

The main point is that this information is kept private to protect people's personal history and rights. It's not something that anyone can look up or access easily, unlike some other government records that are open to the public.

(6) The applicant shall pay the actual costs of the finger-printing and criminal history record check

This is not to be paid for by the WVREC. You pay it and there should be no extra costs associated with the process added on by the governing body, the WVREC.

(7) Before implementing the provisions of this subsection, the commission shall propose rules for legislative approval in accordance with §29A-3-1 et seq. of this code. The rules shall set forth the requirements and procedures for the criminal history record check and must be consistent with standards established by the Federal Bureau of Investigation and the National Crime Prevention and Privacy Compact as authorized by 42 U. S. C. A. §14611

This part of the law is talking about setting up rules for doing background checks on people. Here's what it's saying in simpler terms:

1. The commission (a group of people in charge) needs to create some rules.
2. These rules are about how to do criminal background checks on people.
3. Before these rules can be used, they need to be approved by law makers.
4. The rules need to explain:

- What's required for a background check
- How the background check will be done

5. These rules have to match up with what two important national organizations say:

- The FBI (Federal Bureau of Investigation)
- The National Crime Prevention and Privacy Compact

6. The law mentions some numbers (like §29A-3-1 and 42 U.S.C.A. §14611) - these are references to other laws that give more details about how this should work.

Basically, this law says that before they start doing background checks on people, they need to create clear rules about how it will work. These rules need to be approved by the government and follow national guidelines to make sure everything is fair and done properly

§30-40-12 QUALIFICATIONS FOR A BROKER'S LICENSE

(a) An applicant for a broker's license shall:

(1) Submit evidence satisfactory to the commission of either: (i) Real estate experience as a licensed real estate salesperson during the two years prior to the date of application showing the applicant's representation of a buyer or seller in a minimum of 20 closed transactions; if the applicant is engaged solely in the leasing or renting of real estate, representation of the landlord or tenant in a minimum of 20 closed transactions of at least one year in duration; or if the applicant is engaged solely in the management of a real estate brokerage company, active involvement in a minimum of 20 closed transactions; or (ii) regardless of the number of years as a licensed salesperson: a minimum of 40 closed transactions; if the applicant is engaged solely in the leasing or renting of real estate, representation of the landlord or tenant in a minimum of 40 closed transactions of at least one year duration;

To get a broker's license, you need to show:

You've been a licensed salesperson for 2 years and:

Helped in at least 20 house sales, or

Helped with 20 year-long (or longer) rentals, or

Been involved in 20 deals if you manage a real estate company

OR

No matter how long you've been a salesperson:

Helped in at least 40 house sales, or

Helped with 40 year-long (or longer) rentals, or

Been involved in 40 deals if you manage a real estate company

A "closed transaction" means:

A house was sold and you helped the buyer, seller, or both

A lease for at least a year was signed and you helped the landlord or tenant

or if the applicant is engaged solely in the management of a real estate brokerage company, active involvement in a minimum of 40 closed transactions. For the purposes of this section, a "closed transaction" means a transaction that resulted in the real estate being conveyed from seller to buyer in which the applicant represented the seller, buyer, or both, or a transaction that resulted in the consummation of a lease of no less than one year in duration in which the applicant represented either the landlord or tenant of the real estate;	
(2) Submit satisfactory evidence of having completed the required education course as provided for in §30-40-14 of this code; and	Show you've finished the required education course as stated in the law.
(3) Successfully pass the examination or examinations provided by the commission.	Pass the test or tests given by the commission.
(b) No broker's license shall be issued in the name of an entity except through one of its members or officers.	(b) A company can only get a broker's license through one of its members or officers.
(c) No broker's license may be issued in the name of an entity unless each member or officer who will engage in the real estate business, obtains a license as a real estate salesperson or associate broker.	(c) A company can't get a broker's license unless every member or officer who will work in real estate gets a license as a salesperson or associate broker.

§30-40-13. QUALIFICATIONS FOR SALESPERSON'S LICENSE

(a) An applicant for a salesperson's license shall:

Here's what someone needs to do if they want to get a license to be a salesperson:

(1) Submit satisfactory evidence of having completed the required education course as provided in §30-40-14 of this code; and

1. First, they need to take a special class or course. This isn't just any class, but a specific one that teaches them about being a salesperson. It's like training for the job.

2. After finishing the class, they need to prove that they actually completed it. This might mean showing a certificate or some other official document that says they passed the course.

3. The course they take isn't just any random class. It has to be one that's approved and follows the rules set out in "Section 30-40-14" of this very law code.

4. Once they have this proof, they need to give it to the people who hand out the licenses. This is called "submitting evidence."

5. The evidence they submit has to be "satisfactory," which means it needs to meet all the requirements and be good enough to convince the license-givers that the person really did complete the proper training.

So, in simple terms, if you want to be a licensed salesperson, you need to take an approved class, finish it successfully, and then show proof that you did it when you apply for your license.

(2) Successfully pass the examination or examinations provided by the commission

You must pass the real estate licensing examination.

(b) No salesperson's license may be issued in the name of an entity except through one of its members or officers.

No company or organization can get a salesperson's license on its own. Instead, the license has to be given to a specific person who works for that company or organization. This person needs to be either:

1. A member of the company (like someone who partly owns the business), or
2. An officer of the company (like a manager or executive)

So, if "Cool Gadgets Inc." wants to have a salesperson's license, they can't just get one for the whole company. They'd need to choose someone, like their sales manager Sarah or company president John, to hold the license in their name on behalf of the company. This rule helps make sure there's always a real person responsible for following the rules that come with having a salesperson's license.

(c) No salesperson's license may be issued in the name of an entity unless each member or officer, who will engage in the real estate business, obtains a license as a real estate salesperson or associate broker.

Here's what it means:

1. If a company or group (like a business) wants to get a license to sell real estate, they can't just get one license for the whole company.
2. Instead, every person in that company who will actually be doing the work of selling real estate needs their own personal license.
3. These people need to get either a "salesperson" license or an "asso ciate broker" license. These are two different types of real estate licenses.
4. This rule applies to all members or officers of the company who will be involved in selling real estate.
5. If even one person who will be selling doesn't have their own license, the company can't get a license either.

The main idea is that the government wants to make sure that every individual actually doing the work of selling real estate is properly trained and licensed, not just the company as a whole.

§30-40-14. PRE LICENSE EDUCATION

(a) Applicants for a broker's license shall provide evidence satisfactory to the commission that he or she has completed at least 180 clock-hours, equivalent to 12 college semester credit hours, in a course or courses approved by the commission: Provided, That an applicant for a broker's license who holds a salesperson's license in this state shall be required to provide evidence that he or she has completed an additional 90 clock hours, equivalent to six college semester hours, in a course or courses approved by the commission.

Getting a Broker's License: What You Need to Know

It's worth note, no one can start off applying for a brokers license, You must first be a salesperson and meet requirements laid out later in this code. I wanted to point this out now since the order of this is placed prior to the salesperson education requirements.

For First-Time Applicants

If you're applying for a broker's license for the first time, here's what you need to do:

1. Complete a training course approved by the real estate commission.
2. The course should be at least 180 hours long. This is about the same as taking 12 college credit hours, usually 4 classes.
3. After finishing the course, you need to show proof to the commission that you've completed it.

For Current Salespersons Applying for a Brokers License.

If you already have a salesperson's license in the state and want to become a broker:

1. You still need to take additional training.
2. The extra training should be 90 hours long. This is about the same as taking 6 college credit hours, usually 2 classes.
3. Like before, you need to show proof that you've completed this extra training.

Remember, all these courses must be approved by the real estate commission. They're designed to make sure you have the knowledge and skills needed to be a successful broker.

(b) Applicants for a salesperson's license shall provide evidence satisfactory to the commission that he or she has completed 90 clock hours, equivalent to six college semester credit hours, in a course or courses approved by the commission.

This is the section that goes over what a first time applicant needs to do in order to get a salesperson license. To become a licensed salesperson, you need to do some studying first. The commission wants to make sure you know enough about the job before they give you a license. Here's what you need to do:

1. Take classes that the commission approves. These aren't just any classes - they have to be ones that the commission says are okay. **Spruce School of Real Estate is fully approved to fulfill this requirement.**
2. Complete 90 clock hours of these classes. This means you need to spend about 90 hours in total learning the material.
3. These 90 hours are about the same as taking two college classes. In college terms, it's like taking 6 credit hours.
4. After you finish the classes, you need to show proof that you did them. This could be a certificate or some other document that the school gives you.
5. You'll give this proof to the commission when you apply for your license.

It's like training for a new job, but you have to do it before you can even apply for the license.

CLASS IS GOOD FOR 3 YEARS

(c) Any course required by subsection (a) or (b) of this section shall have been completed during the three-year period preceding the date of application to be accepted by the commission.

Any class you need to take for this program has to be pretty recent. Specifically:

- You can't use classes you took more than three years ago.
- The three-year calculation is based off your courses completion date (on your completion transcript) and when you apply for licensure.
- The people in charge (the commission) won't accept older classes.

For example:

- If you would theoretically apply on (October 16, 2025), they'll only accept classes you took after October 16, 2022.
- Classes from before that date won't count, even if they're the right subject.

This rule makes sure your knowledge is up-to-date when you apply.

§30-40-15. LICENSING BASED ON LICENSURE IN ANOTHER JURISDICTION.

(a) The commission may recognize a valid license issued by another jurisdiction as satisfactorily qualifying an applicant who is licensed to practice real estate brokerage in another jurisdiction to obtain a comparable license in this state: Provided, That the applicant has qualified for license in another jurisdiction by examination and by complying with all the provisions for obtaining a license in that jurisdiction and the jurisdiction affords the same privilege to licensees of this state.

The real estate commission in our state can accept a valid real estate license from another state or area. This means if you're already licensed to work as a real estate agent somewhere else, you might be able to get a similar license here without starting from scratch. But there are some conditions:

1. You must have passed a test to get your license in the other state.

2. You must have followed all the rules and requirements to get licensed there.

3. The other state must offer the same opportunity to people who are licensed in our state.

Basically, if you've done everything right to become a licensed real estate agent in another place, and that place would do the same for our agents, our state might let you transfer your license here more easily.

(b) In order to obtain a license in this state, an applicant under this section shall:

(1) Submit the application on a form prescribed by the commission and fee, if any;

(2) Pass the West Virginia state law portion of the licensure examination approved by the commission;

(3) Submit a certification of licensure showing that the applicant possesses an active license to practice real estate brokerage in another jurisdiction;

(4) Submit record(s) showing all disciplinary actions imposed against the applicant by any jurisdiction in which the applicant holds or held a license, if any; and

To get a real estate license in West Virginia, you need to do these things:

1. Fill out an application: The state has a special form you need to complete. You might also have to pay a fee, but that depends on the situation.

2. Take a test about West Virginia laws: You'll need to pass an exam that focuses on the state's real estate laws. This shows you understand how things work in West Virginia. **Did you realize THIS TEXTBOOK explains all the WV real estate law code? It does!**

3. Prove you're licensed elsewhere: You need to show that you already have an active real estate license in another state. This tells West Virginia that you have some experience in the field.

4. Share your record: If you've ever gotten in trouble with your real estate work in other states, you need to tell West Virginia about it. This includes any warnings or punishments you received while working as a real estate agent or broker elsewhere.

Basically, West Virginia wants to make sure you know what you're doing, understand their laws, and have been responsible in your work before giving you a license to practice real estate in their state.

(5) For non-resident applicants, submit an irrevocable written designation that appoints the executive director of the commission to act as the non-resident licensee's agent, upon whom all judicial and other process or legal notices directed to the licensee may be served. The designation shall stipulate and agree that service upon the executive director is equivalent to personal service upon the licensee. A copy of the designation of appointment, certified by the seal of the commission, may be admitted into evidence with the same force and affect as the original. The executive director shall mail a copy of any process or legal notice immediately upon receipt, by certified mail, to the last known business address of the licensee. No judgment by default may be taken in any action or proceeding until after 30 days of mailing and then only upon certification by the executive director that a copy of the judicial, other process or legal notice was mailed as required.

If you're applying for a license but don't live in the state, you need to do this:

1. Write a letter that can't be taken back. This letter does two things:

   (a) It makes the executive director of the commission your official representative.

   (b) It says that any legal papers or notices for you can be given to the executive director instead of directly to you.

2. The letter should clearly state that giving these papers to the exec utive director is the same as giving them to you personally.

3. If needed, a copy of this letter with the commission's official seal can be used in court just like the original.

4. When the executive director gets any legal papers for you, they'll mail a copy to your most recent business address right away using certified mail (which provides proof of mailing).

5. If you don't respond to a legal action, no default judgment (an automatic decision against you) can be made for at least 30 days after the executive director mails you the papers.

6. Even after 30 days, a default judgment can only happen if the executive director confirms that they mailed you the papers as required.

This process ensures that you'll be informed about any legal matters even if you're not in the state, and it gives you time to respond.

§30-40-16. CONTINUING PROFESSIONAL EDUCATION

(a) Every licensee shall complete seven hours of continuing professional education for each fiscal year, with each hour equaling 50 minutes of instruction. For brokers and associate brokers, three of the required seven hours shall be from the broker-level education curriculum approved by the commission.

Let's break down what this rule means for people who work in real estate:

1. Who does this apply to?
   This rule is for anyone who has a license to work in real estate, like real estate agents and brokers.
2. What do they need to do?
   They need to keep learning and improving their skills every year.
3. How much learning do they need to do?
   They have to complete 7 hours of education each fiscal year (which is like a business year, not necessarily January to December).
4. What counts as an hour?
   In this case, an "hour" is actually 50 minutes of learning time.
5. Is there anything special for brokers?
   Yes! If you're a broker or an associate broker, 3 out of those 7 hours need to be special broker-level courses.
6. Who decides what courses are okay?
   The real estate commission approves which courses count for the broker-level education.

So basically, it's like homework for grown-ups in the real estate business. They have to keep studying to make sure they're up-to-date with their job skills.

7 HOURS IS EASILY EXAM WORTHY

(b) Upon application for the renewal of a real estate license on active status, each licensee shall furnish satisfactory evidence, as established by the commission, that he or she has completed seven hours of approved continuing professional education during the term of the previous license.

When a real estate agent wants to keep their license active, they need to do a few things:

1. They have to apply to renew their license.
2. As part of this renewal process, they need to show proof that they've completed some extra education.
3. This extra education is called "continuing professional education."
4. They need to complete 7 hours of this education during the time their previous license was valid.
5. The education courses they take must be approved by the real estate commission (the group that oversees real estate agents).
6. The agent needs to provide evidence that they've done this educa tion, like certificates or course completion records.
7. The real estate commission decides what counts as acceptable proof.

Basically, this rule makes sure that real estate agents keep learning and stay up-to-date with their knowledge, even after they've gotten their initial license.

(c) When a licensee in an inactive status makes application to revert to an active status, he or she shall furnish satisfactory evidence to the commission that he or she has completed the approved continuing professional education that would have been required for active status at the time the license was renewed.

When someone with a professional license isn't actively using it (we call this "inactive status"), they might want to start using it again someday. To do this, they need to switch back to "active" status.

"But here's the thing: While their license was inactive, they probably missed out on some required education courses that active professionals have to take to keep their skills up-to-date.

So, when they apply to become active again, they need to prove to the licensing board (the "commission") that they've caught up on all the education they missed. They have to show they've completed the same courses that active professionals had to take during the time their license was inactive.

This rule helps make sure that everyone with an active license has the most current knowledge and skills in their field, even if they took a break from using their license for a while.

WHEN YOUR STATUS IS INACTIVE, YOU DO NOT NEED TO COMPLETE CONTINUING EDUCATION. HOWEVER, WHEN YOU REACTIVATE IT, YOU MUST COMPLETE A 7-HOUR COURSE

(d) Approval from the commission shall be obtained by each provider and instructor and for any course prior to any advertising or offering of the course.

(d) Before anyone can advertise or offer a real estate course, both the person teaching it and the course itself need to get an okay from the commission. This applies to everyone who wants to provide or teach these courses.

(e) Real estate-related continuing education courses provided by or approved by the real estate appraiser licensing and certification board, the Division of Highways, the West Virginia State Bar, or other agency of this state shall be recognized as approved by the commission.

(e) Some courses are automatically approved by the commission. These include real estate-related courses that are offered or approved by:

- The board that licenses and certifies real estate appraisers
- The Division of Highways
- The West Virginia State Bar
- Other official state agencies

(f) If approved in advance by the commission, distance education courses may be used to satisfy the continuing education requirement.

(f) Online courses or courses you can take from home (called distance education) can count towards your continuing education requirement. But here's the catch – the commission needs to approve these courses before you take them.

In simple terms, this is all about making sure that real estate professionals are getting good, approved education to keep their skills up-to-date. The commission wants to make sure everything is legit before people start learning or teaching.

(g) Any licensee holding a license on July 1, 1969, and continuously thereafter, shall be exempt from the continuing professional education requirement.

Wow, I wish I had my license prior to July 1, 1969 because if I did, I wouldn't need to do any continuing education. Granted if you were holding a real estate license this long I'd say you know what you're doing and thus, being exempt is fair.

§30-40-17. PLACE OF BUSINESS; BRANCH OFFICES; DISPLAY OF CERTIFICATES; CUSTODY OF LICENSE CERTIFICATES; CHANGE OF ADDRESS; CHANGE OF EMPLOYER BY A SALESPERSON OR ASSOCIATE BROKER; LICENSE CERTIFICATES; TERM OF LICENSE.

(a) Every person holding a broker's license under the provisions of this article shall:

(1) Have and maintain a definite place of business within this state, which shall be a room or rooms used for the transaction of real estate business and any allied business. The definite place of business shall be designated in the license certificate issued by the commission and the broker may not transact business at any other location, unless such other location is properly licensed by the commission as a branch office A broker who is a nonresident of this state may not be required to maintain an active place of business in this state if the nonresident broker's state of original licensure is party to an active reciprocity agreement with the commission that does not require West Virginia licensees holding licenses in that state to maintain an office in that state;

What a Licensed Real Estate Broker Must Do

If you're a licensed real estate broker in West Virginia, there are some rules you need to follow:

Have an Office in West Virginia

- You must have a specific place where you do your real estate busi ness in West Virginia.
- This office can be one or more rooms, but it has to be used for real estate and related work.
- The address of this office will be on your license.

Work Only from Licensed Locations

- You can only do business from the office listed on your license.
- If you want to work from another location, you need to get it ap proved as a branch office.

Exception for Out-of-State Brokers

- If you're a broker who lives in another state, you might not need an office in West Virginia.

  This is only if:

1. Your home state has an agreement with West Virginia.
2. This agreement doesn't require West Virginia brokers to have an office in your state.

The main idea is that the state wants to know where you're working from and make sure it's a proper business location. This helps protect customers and keeps everything organized and professional.

(2) Conspicuously display his or her branch office license in each branch office;

You must openly display your branch office license. For example, framed on the wall upon entry.

(3) Make application to the commission before changing the address of any office or within 10 days after any change;

You must notify the commission before you change the address. They will accept this notification as long as you do so within 10 days of changing it.

(4) Maintain in his or her custody and control the license of each associate broker and salesperson affiliated with him or her; and

The broker usually holds all these licenses in a filing cabinet or book. **The interesting thing is you do not hold your license as a salesperson or associate broker.** The broker you work under holds them.

The brokers office. NOT your home.

(5) Promptly return the license of any associate broker or salesperson whose affiliation with the broker is terminated.

If you have a license to work as an associate broker or salesperson in real estate, there are some important rules you need to follow:

There are a LOT of valuable concepts on this page that are test worthy. The significance of the broker and what you can and can't do can be applied many places.

(b) Every person holding an associate broker's or salesperson's license under the provisions of this article shall:

(1) Conduct real estate brokerage activities only under the direct supervision and control of his or her affiliated broker, which shall be designated in the license certificate; and

1. You can only do real estate work under the supervision of a licensed broker. This broker is like your boss, and their name will be on your license.

(2) Promptly make application to the commission of any change of employing broker: Provided, That it shall be unlawful to perform any act contained in this article, either directly or indirectly, after affiliation has been terminated until the associate broker or salesperson has made application to the commission for a change of affiliated broker and the application is approved.

2. If you want to change who you work for (your broker), you need to tell the real estate commission right away. It's really important to do this because:

- You're not allowed to do any real estate work after you stop working with your current broker.
- You can't start working with a new broker until you've applied to the commission and they've approved the change.

Basically, these rules make sure that you're always working under proper supervision and that the commission knows who you're working for. This helps protect both you and your clients

(c) The commission shall issue a license certificate which shall:

This is talking about **how the real estate commission gives out your real estate license**:

(1) Be in such form and size as shall be prescribed by the commission;

1 The license certificate will look a certain way, based on what the commission decides.

(2) Display the seal of the commission and shall contain such other information as the commission may prescribe: Provided, That a salesperson's and an associate broker's license shall show the name of the broker by whom he or she is affiliated;

2 It'll have the commission's official seal on it, plus other info they think is important. If it's for a salesperson or associate broker, it'll also show who their boss (main broker) is.

(3) If an active licensee, be mailed or delivered to the broker's main office address;

3 If the person with the license is actively working, they'll mail the certificate to the main office of the broker they work for.

(4) If an inactive licensee, be held in the commission office; and

4 If the person isn't currently working (inactive), the commission will keep the certificate at their office.

(5) Be valid for a period that coincides with the fiscal year beginning on July 1 and ending on June 30.

5 The license is good for one year, starting on July 1 and ending on June 30 the next year.

Basically, this is explaining how these licenses work - what they look like, what info is on them, where they're kept, and how long they last. It's kind of like how a driver's license has certain info on it and is good for a specific amount of time.

§30-40-18. TRUST FUND ACCOUNTS

(a) Every person licensed as a broker under the provisions of this article who does not immediately deliver all funds received, in relation to a real estate transaction, to his or her principal or to a neutral escrow depository shall maintain and reconcile one or more trust fund accounts in a recognized financial institution and shall place all funds therein: Provided, That nothing contained herein shall require a broker to maintain a trust fund account if the broker does not hold any money in trust for another party.

Let's break down this rule about real estate brokers and money:

1. First, this rule is about licensed real estate brokers - people who help buy and sell properties.

2. When a broker gets money related to a real estate deal, they have two choices:

- Give it right away to the person it belongs to (like the seller)
- Put it in a neutral holding account (called an escrow)

3. If they don't do either of those things right away, they need to:

- Open one or more special bank accounts called "trust fund ac counts"
- Put all the money they receive from deals into these accounts
- Keep track of the money and make sure everything adds up (that's what "reconcile" means)

4. These accounts need to be in a legit bank or financial institution.

5. But here's the catch: If a broker never holds onto money for other people, they don't need to have these special accounts.

Basically, this rule is to make sure brokers keep other people's money safe and separate from their own cash. It's like having a special piggy bank just for money that isn't yours yet.

(b) Funds that shall be deposited into a trust fund account include, but are not limited to, earnest money deposits, security deposits, rental receipts, auction proceeds, and money held in escrow at closing.

A trust fund account is like a special savings account that real estate agents or companies use to keep other people's money safe. This account holds different types of money, such as:

1. Earnest money: This is the deposit a buyer puts down to show they're serious about buying a house.
2. Security deposits: The money renters give landlords as a guarantee they'll take care of the property.
3. Rental receipts: The rent payments collected from tenants.
4. Auction proceeds: Money earned from selling property at an auction.
5. Money held in escrow at closing: Funds set aside during the final stages of a property sale to cover things like taxes or repairs.

These are just some examples of the money that goes into this special account. There could be other types of funds too. The main idea is that this account keeps people's money secure and separate from the real estate agent's or company's personal funds.

(c) Each trust fund account shall be established at a financial institution which is insured against loss by an agency of the federal government and the amount deposited therein cannot exceed the amount that is insured against loss.

A trust fund account is like a special savings account. This rule says:

- You have to open this account at a bank or credit union that has insurance from the government. This insurance protects your money if something goes wrong with the bank.

- You're not allowed to put more money into the account than what the government insurance covers.

For example, if the insurance covers up to $250,000, you can't put more than that amount in the account. This way, all your money in the account is protected. The main idea is to keep your money safe by using insured banks and not exceeding the insured amount

(d) Each trust fund account shall provide for the withdrawal of funds without notice.

Each savings account in the trust fund must allow you to take out your money whenever you want, without having to tell the bank ahead of time. In other words:

- You have a special savings account (called a trust fund account)
- If you need your money, you can go to the bank and get it
- You don't have to call or write to the bank first
- You don't have to wait for any specific time period
- You can just show up and ask for your money, and they have to give it to you

This rule is meant to make sure your money is always available to you when you need it, without any delays or extra steps.

(e) No trust fund account may earn interest or any other form of income, unless specifically authorized by commission rule

A trust fund account is like a special savings account used in real estate deals. Usually, these accounts aren't allowed to make money on their own, like earning interest or other types of income. The only way they can make money is if the real estate commission (a group that makes rules about real estate) says it's okay. Think of it like this: Imagine you have a piggy bank where you keep money for a specific purpose. Normally, this piggy bank doesn't grow your money on its own. It only changes if you add money to it or take money out. But if the people in charge of piggy bank rules say it's okay, then your piggy bank might be allowed to grow your money a little bit while it's just sitting there.

(f) The broker may not commingle his or her own funds with trust funds and the account may not be pledged as collateral for a loan or otherwise utilized by the broker in a manner that would violate his or her fiduciary obligations in relation to the trust funds: Provided, That nothing contained herein prevents the broker from depositing a maximum of $100 of his or her own money in the trust fund account to maintain a minimum balance in the account.

Imagine you're a broker and you're holding onto money for your clients. This rule is saying:

1. You can't mix your own money with your clients' money in the same bank account. It's like having separate piggy banks - one for you and one for your clients.
2. You're not allowed to use your clients' money as a guarantee to borrow money for yourself or use it in any way that goes against your promise to take care of their money.
3. However, there's one exception: You're allowed to put up to $100 of your own money into the clients' account. This is just to make sure there's always some money in there, kind of like making sure the piggy bank isn't completely empty.

The main idea is to keep your money and your clients' money separate and to make sure you're using your clients' money only for their benefit, not yours.

(g) The broker shall be the designated trustee of the account and shall maintain complete authority and control over all aspects of each trust fund account, including signature authority: Provided, That only one other member or officer of a corporation, association, or partnership, who is licensed under the provisions of this article, may be authorized to disburse funds from the account: Provided, however, That if disbursements from a trust fund account require two signatures, one additional member or officer may be a signatory as provided in this section.

Okay, so imagine you're in charge of a special bank account that holds money for other people. This is kind of what a real estate broker does with a trust fund account. Here's what the rule says:

1. The broker is like the boss of this special account. They're in charge of everything about it, including who can sign for the money.

2. The broker can let one other person help with the account, but this person needs to have a special license too. This helper can take money out of the account when needed.

3. Sometimes, the rules say you need two people to sign when taking money out. If that's the case, the broker can choose one more person to be a second signer. This extra person doesn't need the special license.

So basically, the broker is the main person responsible, but they can have one or two helpers depending on the situation. It's all about making sure the money is handled carefully and correctly.

(h) The broker shall, at a minimum, maintain records of all funds deposited into the trust fund account, which shall clearly indicate the date and from whom the money was received, date deposited, date of withdrawal, to whom the money belongs, for whose account the money was received, and other pertinent information concerning the transaction. All records shall be open to inspection by the commission or its duly authorized representative at all times during regular business hours at the broker's place of business

The rule is talking about how real estate brokers need to keep track of money they handle for their clients. Here's what it means in simpler terms:

1. The broker must keep detailed records of all money that goes into their special bank account (called a trust fund account).

2. These records need to show:

- When they received the money
- Who gave them the money
- When they put it in the bank
- When they took money out
- Who the money belongs to
- Why they received the money
- Any other important details about the transaction

3. The broker has to keep these records organized and up-to-date.

4. If someone from the real estate commission (the group that over sees brokers) wants to check these records, the broker must let them see everything during normal business hours.

5. The commission can send someone to the broker's office to look at these records at any time.

Basically, this rule makes sure that brokers are honest and careful with their clients' money, and that there's a way for officials to check if everything is being done correctly.

(i) The broker shall cause the financial institution wherein a trust fund account is maintained to execute a statement, prepared by the commission, which shall include, but is not limited to:

The real estate broker needs to get a statement from the bank where they keep their trust fund account. This statement is like a special form created by the real estate commission. It needs to include:

(1) Exact title of the account as registered by the financial institution;

1. The exact name of the account as it appears in the bank's records

(2) The account number of the trust fund account;

2. The account number

(3) Identification of all persons authorized to make withdrawals from the account;

3. A list of people who are allowed to take money out of the account

(4) Name and address of the financial institution;

4. The bank's name and address

(5) Title of the person executing the statement on behalf of the financial institution;

5. The job title of the person from the bank who signs the statement

(6) Date the statement was executed; and

6. The date when the statement was signed

(7) Certification that the financial institution will notify the Real Estate Commission if any checks drawn against the account are returned for insufficient funds and that the financial institution does not require a minimum balance in excess of the amount authorized in subsection (f) of this section.

7. The bank also has to promise two things:

a) They'll tell the Real Estate Commission if any checks from this account bounce due to not having enough money

b) They won't require the account to keep more money in it than what's allowed by the rules

This statement helps make sure the trust fund account is being managed properly and that the Real Estate Commission can keep an eye on things to protect everyone involved.

(j) The broker shall execute a statement authorizing the commission, or its duly authorized representative, to make periodic inspections of the trust fund account and to obtain copies of records from any financial institution wherein a trust fund account is maintained. A copy of any authorization shall be accepted by any financial institution with the same force and effect as the original.

Imagine you're a real estate broker, and you handle money for your clients. This money is kept in a special bank account called a trust fund account. The rule we're talking about says:

1. You, as the broker, need to sign a paper that gives permission to the real estate commission (a group that oversees brokers) to do a few things:

- Check your trust fund account from time to time
- Get copies of records about this account from your bank

2. This permission slip isn't just for show. When you give it to your bank, they have to treat it like it's a big deal. They can't ignore it or say it's not good enough.

3. The bank has to follow this permission slip just like they would if you were there in person asking them to share the information.

Basically, this rule makes sure that the people in charge of keeping an eye on brokers can actually see what's going on with the money brokers are handling for their clients. It's a way to make sure everything is being done properly and honestly.

(k) The broker shall notify the commission, within 10 days of the establishment of or any change to a trust fund account.

If the broker:

1. Opens a new trust fund account, or
2. Makes any changes to an existing trust fund account

They have to tell the commission about it within 10 days .So basically, it's saying that brokers need to keep the commission updated about these special bank accounts they use for their clients' money. They can't just open or change these accounts without letting anyone know.

§30-40-19. REFUSAL, SUSPENSION, OR REVOCATION OF A LICENSE.

(a) The commission may refuse a license for reasonable cause or revoke, suspend, or impose any other sanction against a licensee if the licensee:

The following are ways you can be rejected applying for a license or lose you're an existing license.

I like to light-heartedly call this section:

46 ways to lose a license

...until society figures out more

(1) Obtains, renews, or attempts to obtain or renew a license, for himself, herself, or another, through the submission of any application or other writing that contains false, fraudulent, or misleading information;

1. Submitting any application or document with false, misleading, or fraudulent information.

(2) Makes any substantial misrepresentation;

2. Making any big lie or misrepresentation.

(3) Makes any false promises or representations of a character likely to influence, persuade, or induce a person involved in a real estate transaction;

3. Making false promises or statements that could influence some one in a real estate deal.

(4) Pursues a course of misrepresentation or makes false promises or representations through agents or any medium of advertising or otherwise;

4. Consistently misrepresenting facts or making false promises through agents or advertising.

(5) Uses misleading or false advertising

5. Using misleading or false advertising.

(6) Uses any trade name or insignia of membership in any organization in which the licensee is not a member;

6 Using a name or symbol of an organization you're not actually a member of.

(7) Acts for more than one party in a transaction without the knowledge and written consent of all parties for whom he or she acts;

7 Working for more than one party in a deal without everyone knowing and agreeing in writing. *** This is a misleadingly small mention of a **massive concept called "notice of agency"** You will see more of this mentioned on page 200 and plenty of info on the concept within your presales class.

(8) Fails, within a reasonable time, to account for or to remit moneys or other assets coming into his or her possession, which belong to others;

8 Not promptly handling or returning money or assets that belong to others.

(9) Commingles moneys belonging to others with his or her own funds;

9 Mixing other people's money with your own funds.

(10) Advertises or displays a "for sale", "for rent", or other such sign on any property without an agency relationship being established or without the owner's knowledge and written consent

10 Putting up "for sale" or "for rent" signs on property without the owner's written permission or without having a proper agreement.

(11) Advertises any property on terms other than those authorized by the owner;	**11** Advertising property on terms the owner hasn't approved.
(12) Fails to disclose, on the notice of agency relationship form promulgated by the commission, whether the licensee represents the seller, buyer, or both;	**12** Not clearly stating on official forms whether you represent the seller, buyer, or both. **Take a look back at #7**
(13) Fails to voluntarily furnish copies of the notice of agency relationship, listing contract, sale contract, lease contract, or any other contract to each party executing the same;	**13** Not willingly giving copies of important documents to everyone who signs them.
(14) Pays or receives any rebate, profit, compensation, commission, or other valuable consideration, resulting from a real estate transaction, to or from any person other than the licensee's principal: Provided, That this subsection may not be construed to prevent the sharing of compensation or other valuable consideration between licensed brokers;	**14** Paying or receiving extra money from a real estate deal to anyone other than your client, except when sharing between licensed brokers.
(15) Induces any person to a contract to break the contract for the purpose of substituting a new contract with a third party;	**15** Convincing someone to break a contract so they can make a new one with someone else.
(16) Accepts compensation as a salesperson or associate broker for any act specified in this article from any person other than his or her broker;	**16** As a salesperson or associate broker, accepting payment for real estate work from anyone other than your broker.

(17) Pays compensation to any person for acts or services performed either in violation of this article or the real estate licensure laws of any other jurisdiction;

17 Paying someone for work that breaks this law or real estate laws in other places.

(18) Pays compensation to any person knowing that they will pay a portion or all of that which is received, in a manner that would constitute a violation of this article if it were paid directly by a licensee of this state;

18 Paying someone knowing they'll use part of that money in a way that would break this law if you did it directly.

(19) Violates any provision of this article, any rule, or any order or final decision issued by the commission;

19 Breaking any part of this law, any rule, or any decision made by the commission.

(20) Procures an attorney for any client or customer, or solicits legal business for any attorney-at-law;

20 Finding a lawyer for a client or customer, or trying to get legal business for a lawyer.

(21) Engages in the unlawful or unauthorized practice of law as defined by the Supreme Court of Appeals of West Virginia;

21 Doing legal work you're not authorized to do, as defined by the state's highest court.

(22) Commits or is a party to any material fraud, misrepresentation, concealment, conspiracy, collusion, trick, scheme, or other device whereby any other person relies upon the word, representation, or conduct of the licensee

22 Being involved in any kind of fraud, lie, or trick that others rely on. Working with or accepting services from a broker, associate broker, or salesperson who isn't properly licensed.

(23) Continues in the capacity of, or accepts the services of, any broker, associate broker, or salesperson who is not properly licensed;

23 Working with or accepting services from a broker, associate broker, or salesperson who isn't properly licensed.

(24) Fails to disclose any information within his or her knowledge or to produce any document, book, or record in his or her possession for inspection of and copying by the commission or its duly authorized representatives;

24 Not sharing information or documents when the commission asks for them.

(25) Accepts payment other than cash or its equivalent as earnest money or other deposit unless this fact is disclosed in the contract to which the deposit relates;

25 Accepting anything other than cash or its equivalent as a deposit without mentioning it in the contract.

(26) Accepts, takes, or charges any undisclosed compensation on expenditures made by or on behalf of the licensee's principal;

26 Taking or charging hidden fees on expenses made for your client.

(27) Discriminates against any person involved in a real estate transaction which is in violation of any federal or state antidiscrimination law, including any fair housing law;

27 Discriminating against anyone in a real estate deal, which goes against federal or state anti-discrimination laws.

(28) Fails to preserve for five years following its consummation, records relating to any real estate transaction;

28 Not keeping records of real estate deals for at least five years.

(29) Fails to maintain accurate records on the broker's trust fund account;

29 Not keeping accurate records of the broker's trust fund account.

(30) If a broker, fails to supervise all associate brokers and salespersons affiliated with him or her;

30 If you're a broker, not properly supervising the associate brokers and salespeople working under you.

(31) Breaches a fiduciary duty owed by a licensee to his or her principal in a real estate transaction;

31 Breaking the trust your client puts in you during a real estate deal.

(32) Directs any party to a real estate transaction in which the licensee is involved, to any lending institution for financing or to any affiliated business with the expectation of receiving a financial incentive, rebate, or other compensation, without first obtaining from his or her principal the signed acknowledgment of and consent to the receipt of the financial incentive, rebate, or other compensation: Provided, That this subsection may not be construed to prevent the sharing of compensation or other valuable consideration between licensed brokers;

32 Sending a client to a specific lender or affiliated business to get a kickback, without the client's written consent.

To those unfamiliar with this term a kickback in real estate is a reward given to someone for referring business or influencing a transaction, often hidden from other parties involved.

(33) Represents to any lending institution, or other interested party either verbally or through the preparation of false documents, an amount in excess of the true and actual sale price of the real estate or terms differing from those actually agreed upon;

33 Lying to a lender or interested party about the real sale price or terms of a deal.

(34) Fails to disclose to an owner the licensee's true position if he or she directly or indirectly through a third party, purchases for himself or herself or acquires or intends to acquire any interest in or any option to purchase the property;	34	Not telling an owner if you plan to buy their property yourself, directly or indirectly
(35) Lends a broker's license to any person, including a salesperson, or permits a salesperson to operate as a broker;	35	Letting someone else use your broker's license or allowing a sales person to act as a broker.
(36) Has been convicted in a court of competent jurisdiction in this or any other jurisdiction of forgery, embezzlement, obtaining money under false pretense, bribery, larceny, extortion, conspiracy to defraud, any other similar offense, a crime involving moral turpitude, or a felony;	36	Being convicted of crimes like forgery, embezzlement, fraud, bribery, larceny, or other serious offenses.
(37) Engages in any act or conduct which constitutes or demonstrates bad faith, incompetency, untrustworthiness, or dishonest, fraudulent, or improper dealing;	37	Behaving in a way that shows bad faith, incompetence, untrust worthiness, or dishonesty.
(38) Induces any person to alter, modify, or change another licensee's fee or commission for brokerage services, without that licensee's prior written consent;	38	Trying to get someone to change another agent's fee without that agent's written permission.
(39) Negotiates a real estate transaction directly with any person that is represented exclusively by another broker, unless the conduct is specifically authorized by the other broker;	39	Negotiating directly with someone who's exclusively represented by another broker, unless that broker allows it.

(40) Obtains, negotiates, or attempts to obtain or negotiate a contract whereby the broker is entitled to a commission only to the extent that the sales price exceeds a given amount, commonly referred to as a net listing;

40 Making a deal where you only get paid if the sale price is above a certain amount (called a net listing).

(41) Fails or refuses, on demand, to furnish copies of a document to a person whose signature is affixed to the document;

41 Not giving copies of a document to someone who signed it when they ask for it.

(42) In the case of an associate broker or salesperson, represents or attempts to represent a broker other than his or her employing broker;

42 As an associate broker or salesperson, trying to represent a broker other than the one who employs you.

(43) Fails to reduce a bona fide offer to writing;

43 Not putting a genuine offer in writing.

(44) Guarantees, or authorizes or permits another licensee to guarantee, future profits which may result from a real estate transaction;

44 Promising future profits from a real estate deal, or letting another agent make such promises.

(45) Is disciplined by another jurisdiction if at least one of the grounds for that discipline is the same as or equivalent to one of the grounds for discipline in this article; or

45 Being disciplined in another area for reasons similar to those in this law.

(46) Engages in any other act or omission in violation of professional conduct requirements of licensees established by legislative rule of the commission.

46 Doing anything else that goes against the professional conduct rules set by the commission.

(b) The provisions of this section shall be liberally construed in order to carry out the objectives and purposes of this article.

This part of the law says that when people read and apply this section, they should interpret it in a way that's open-minded and flexible. The goal is to make sure that the main ideas and goals of this part of the law are achieved. In other words, it's like telling people: "Don't be too strict or narrow when you're trying to understand what this law means. Instead, think about what we're really trying to accomplish here, and use that to guide how you interpret and apply these rules." This approach helps ensure that the law can be used effectively to solve problems and achieve its intended purpose, rather than getting stuck on technicalities or overly narrow interpretations.

(c) As used in this section:

Here's a simpler explanation:

(1) The words "convicted in a court of competent jurisdiction" mean a plea of guilty or nolo contendere entered by a person or a verdict of guilt returned against a person at the conclusion of a trial;

1. When we say someone is "convicted in a court of competent jurisdiction," it means one of these things has happened in a proper court:

- The person said they were guilty
- The person said, "no contest" (which is like saying "I won't fight the charges")
- A trial happened, and at the end, the jury or judge decided the person was guilty

(2) A certified copy of a conviction order entered in a court is sufficient evidence to demonstrate a person has been convicted in a court of competent jurisdiction.

2. To prove that someone was convicted in a proper court, all you need is an official copy of the conviction order from that court. This official copy is called a "certified copy," and it's enough evidence to show that the conviction really happened.

In simpler terms, being convicted means you've been found guilty in an official court, and there's an official document to prove it.

(d) Every person licensed by the commission has an affirmative duty to report, in a timely manner, any known or observed violation of this article or the rules, orders, or final decisions of the commission.

Every person who has a license from the commission must:

1. Keep an eye out for anyone breaking the rules
2. Report any rule-breaking they see or know about
3. Do this reporting quickly
4. This includes violations of:

- This specific set of rules (called an "article")
- Any other rules the commission has made
- Orders given by the commission
- Final decisions made by the commission

In other words, if you have a license, it's your job to speak up when you notice someone not following the rules. You can't just ignore it - you have to tell the proper authorities about it as soon as you can. This rule exists to help keep everyone honest and make sure the rules are being followed by all license holders.

(e) The revocation of a broker's license shall automatically suspend the license of every associate broker and salesperson affiliated with the broker: Provided, That the commission shall issue a replacement license for any licensee so affected to a new broker, without charge, if a proper application is submitted to the commission during the same license term.

When a real estate broker loses their license, it affects everyone working under them. Here's what happens:

Automatic Suspension

If a broker's license is taken away (revoked), all the people working for them - like associate brokers and salespeople - will have their licenses suspended right away. This means they can't work in real estate until they fix the situation.

Getting Back to Work

The good news is that these affected workers aren't totally out of luck. They have a chance to keep working in real estate by doing the following:

1. Find a new broker to work for
2. Apply for a replacement license with the commission (the group that oversees real estate licenses)
3. Submit this application during the same license term (before their current license expires)

If they do these things, the commission will give them a new license for free. This allows them to continue their real estate career under a different broker without having to pay for a new license.

Why This Matters

This rule exists to protect consumers and maintain professional standards in real estate. It ensures that all real estate professionals are working under a properly licensed broker who is responsible for overseeing their work. Remember, in the real estate world, brokers are like team leaders. When a leader loses their ability to lead, the whole team is affected, but there's a way for team members to quickly join a new team and keep working.

§30-40-20. COMPLAINTS; INVESTIGATION.

(a) Upon the initiation of a complaint by the commission or the filing of a complaint by another person, the commission may ascertain the facts and if warranted hold a hearing for the suspension or revocation of a license, or the imposition of sanctions against a licensee: Provided, That no disciplinary action may be brought against a licensee upon any complaint that is filed more than two years after the acts or omissions alleged in the complaint or, where the licensee is alleged to have engaged in fraud, deceit, or misrepresentation, more than two years after the date at which the complainant discovered, or through reasonable diligence should have discovered, the alleged unprofessional conduct. Time limits for the filing of a complaint shall be tolled during any period in which material evidence necessary for the commission's evaluation or use is unavailable to the commission due to an ongoing criminal investigation or prosecution.

When someone does something wrong in their job, the WVREC can look into it. This is how it works:

Starting an Investigation

The commission can start looking into a problem in two ways:

1. They can decide to investigate on their own
2. Someone else can file a complaint

What Happens Next

If the commission thinks there's a good reason, they might:

- Hold a hearing (like a meeting to discuss the problem)
- Suspend or take away the person's license to work
- Give the person some kind of punishment

Time Limits

There are some rules about when complaints can be made:

- Usually, complaints must be made within 2 years of when the problem happened
- If the person is accused of lying or tricking someone, the complaint must be made within 2 years of when the problem was dis covered (or should have been discovered)

Special Circumstances

Sometimes, the 2-year time limit can be paused. This happens if:

- There's important evidence that the commission needs
- But they can't get that evidence because of an ongoing criminal investigation

In these cases, the "clock" for the 2-year limit stops until the commission can get the evidence they need.

(b) All complaints shall be submitted in writing on a form prescribed by the commission, and shall fully describe the acts or omissions constituting the alleged violation(s) of this article or rules promulgated thereunder.

If you want to report someone for breaking the rules, you need to do it in a specific way:

1. You have to write down your complaint. You can't just tell some one about it.
2. There's a special form you need to use. The people in charge (the commission) have created this form, and you have to use it.
3. On this form, you need to explain exactly what happened. Be clear about what the person did wrong.
4. You should describe how their actions broke the rules. The rules could be from this specific set of laws (called an "article") or from other rules that were created because of these laws.
5. Make sure you include all the important details. Don't leave any thing out.

Basically, they want you to put your complaint in writing, use their official form, and give a complete picture of what happened and how it broke the rules. This helps them understand and deal with the problem properly.

(c) Upon initiation or receipt of the complaint, the commission shall provide a copy of the complaint to the licensee for his or her response to the allegations contained in the complaint. The accused party shall file an answer within 20 days of the date of service. Failure of the licensee to file a timely response may be considered an admission of the allegations in the complaint: Provided, That nothing contained herein may prohibit the accused party from obtaining an extension of time to file a response, if the commission, its executive director, or other authorized representative permits the extension.

Understanding Complaint Procedures

When someone files a complaint against a licensed professional, the following process takes place:

1. The commission sends a copy of the complaint to the accused professional.
2. The accused has 20 days to respond to the allegations.

Important points to remember:

- If the accused doesn't respond in time, it might be seen as admit ting to the allegations.
- The accused can ask for more time to respond if needed.
- The commission, its executive director, or another authorized person can approve an extension.

Think of it like this: If someone accuses you of something, you're given a chance to explain your side of the story. It's important to do this quickly, or people might think you're admitting to the accusation. But if you need more time to prepare your response, you can ask for it.

(d) The commission may cause an investigation to be made into the facts and circumstances giving rise to the complaint and any person licensed by the commission has an affirmative duty to assist the commission, or its authorized representative, in the conduct of its investigation.

The WVREC can decide to look into why someone made a complaint. This is called an investigation. It's like when detectives try to figure out what happened in a crime. If you have a license from this commission (which means they gave you permission to do a certain job), you have to help them with their investigation. This isn't optional - it's your responsibility to assist them. For example, let's say you're a hairdresser and the Hairdressing Commission is investigating a complaint about unsafe hair dyes. If they ask you questions or need information, you have to cooperate and provide what they need. You can't just ignore them or refuse to help. This rule exists to make sure the commission can do its job properly and protect people who use the services of licensed professionals.

(e) After receiving the licensee's response and reviewing any information obtained through investigation, the commission shall determine if probable cause exists that the licensee has violated any provision of this article or the rules.

After the commission gets the licensee's side of the story and looks into any other information they've found, **they'll decide if there's a good reason to believe the licensee might have broken any rules.** To break it down further:

1. The licensee (someone with a license) gives their explanation about what happened.
2. The commission investigates and gathers more information.
3. They look at everything they've learned.
4. Then, they decide if it seems likely that the licensee did something wrong or broke any rules.
5. This decision is called determining if there's "probable cause," which basically means there's enough evidence to make them think the licensee might have messed up.

This process is like when a teacher suspects a student of cheating. They'll listen to the student's explanation, look for more evidence, and then decide if they think the student actually cheated or not.

(f) If a determination that probable cause exists for disciplinary action, the commission may hold a hearing in compliance with §30-40-21 of this code or may dispose of the matter informally through a consent agreement or otherwise.

If there's enough evidence to suggest someone might have done something wrong, the commission has two options:

1. Formal Hearing: They can hold an official meeting to discuss the issue. This meeting follows specific rules set by law (§30-40-21).

2. Informal Resolution: They can handle the matter in a less formal way. This could involve:

- Making an agreement with the person involved
- Finding another solution that doesn't require a formal hearing

Basically, the commission can choose to either have a serious, official discussion about the problem or try to solve it in a more relaxed, unofficial manner.

§30-40-21. HEARINGS; JUDICIAL REVIEW; COST OF PROCEEDINGS.

(a) Hearings shall be conducted in accordance with the provisions of §29A-5-1 et seq. of this code and the commission's rules.

Understanding Legal Hearings
What are hearings?

Hearings are formal meetings where people present information and arguments about a specific issue or case.

How are hearings conducted?

Hearings must follow certain rules to make sure they're fair for everyone involved. In this case, there are two main sets of rules:

1. The law: Specifically, the rules found in section 29A-5-1 and the sections that follow it in the legal code.
2. The commission's rules: These are additional guidelines set by the group in charge of the hearing.

Why is this important?

Following these rules helps ensure that:

- Everyone gets a chance to be heard
- The process is consistent and fair
- Decisions made during the hearing are legally valid

Think of it like a sports game. Just as games have specific rules to make sure they're played fairly; hearings have rules to make sure they're conducted properly, and everyone is treated equally.

(b) Hearings shall be held at a time and place determined by the commission, but in no event less than 30 days after the notice of hearing is given.

When they need to have a hearing, which is like a formal meeting to discuss important issues, they have to follow some rules:

1. The commission gets to decide when and where the hearing will happen.
2. However, they can't just schedule it right away. They have to give people enough time to prepare.
3. So, the rule says that the hearing can't happen sooner than 30 days after they tell everyone about it.

This means that if the commission sends out a notice about a hearing on October 20, the earliest they could hold that hearing would be November 19. This gives everyone involved at least a month to get ready for the meeting. The purpose of this rule is to make sure the process is fair and that people have enough time to prepare their information or arguments before the hearing takes place.

(c) Any member has the authority to administer oaths and to examine any person under oath.

Any person who is part of this group has the power to:

1. Make someone promise to tell the truth officially (that's what "ad minister oaths" means)
2. Ask questions to someone who has made this promise to tell the truth

It's like in courtroom TV shows when the witness puts their hand on a book and swears to "tell the truth, the whole truth, and nothing but the truth." After that, lawyers ask the witness questions. In this case, any member of the group can do both parts - make someone promise to be truthful and then ask them questions. This rule gives members the ability to get honest answers from people they're questioning, kind of like how police or lawyers might do it, but in this specific group or organization.

(d) If, after hearing, the commission determines the licensee has violated any provision of this article, or the commission's rules, a formal decision shall be prepared which contains findings of fact, conclusions of law, and specifically lists the disciplinary actions imposed.

After the commission listens to all the information about a case, they decide if the person with the license broke any rules. If they did break rules, here's what happens:

1. The commission writes up an official decision.
2. This decision includes:

- Facts they found out during the hearing
- What laws or rules apply to the situation
- A clear list of punishments or consequences for the person who broke the rules

3. They write all this down in a formal way, kind of like a report card but more serious.
4. The punishments listed could be things like fines, having to take classes, or even losing their license for a while or forever.

Basically, it's like when you get in trouble at school. The principal decides if you really broke a rule, writes down what happened, and then tells you what your punishment is – all in an official way.

(e) The commission may elect to have an administrative law judge or hearing examiner conduct the hearing. If the commission makes this election, the administrative law judge or hearing examiner, at the conclusion of a hearing, shall prepare a proposed order which shall contain findings of fact and conclusions of law. The commission may request that disciplinary actions imposed be a part of the proposed order, or the commission may reserve this obligation for its consideration. The commission may accept, reject, or modify the decision of the administrative law judge or hearing examiner.

Imagine the commission is like a group of judges who make important decisions. Sometimes, they might ask another person (called an administrative law judge or hearing examiner) to listen to a case and gather information. An administrative law judge (ALJ) is a special kind of judge who handles specific types of legal cases outside of regular courts.

How They're Different from Regular Judges

1. Specialized knowledge: ALJs focus on specific areas of law related to government rules and regulations.
2. Less formal proceedings: Hearings with ALJs are often more relaxed than traditional courtrooms.
3. Dual role: ALJs act as both the judge and the jury, making decisions on facts and law

After listening to everything, this person writes up a report. In this report, they:

1. Explain what they found out (findings of fact)
2. Say what they think the law means in this situation (conclusions of law)

The commission can also ask this person to suggest what should happen next, like a punishment if someone did something wrong. Or the commission might want to decide that part themselves. When the commission gets this report, they have three choices:

- They can agree with everything and use it as is
- They can say "no thanks" and not use it at all
- They can change some parts of it to fit what they think is right

So basically, the commission has the final say, but they're getting help from someone else to make their decision easier and more informed.

(f) Any person adversely affected by any decision or final order made by the commission, after a hearing, is entitled to judicial review pursuant to the provisions of §29A-5-4 of this code.

If you're not happy with a decision made by the commission after they've held a hearing, you have the right to ask a court to look at that decision again. This is called "judicial review." To break it down further:

1. The "commission" is a group of people who make official decisions about something.

2. They hold hearings where they listen to different sides of an issue before making a decision.

3. If you think their decision negatively affects you in some way, you can challenge it.

4. You do this by asking a judge to review the commission's decision.

5. This process is outlined in a specific law, which is mentioned at the end of the original text (§29A-5-4).

This right to ask for a judicial review is important because it allows people to question decisions made by official bodies if they think those decisions are unfair or incorrect.

(g) In addition to any other sanction imposed, the commission may require a licensee to pay the costs of the proceeding.

When a real estate agent gets in trouble with the real estate commission, they might face some consequences. These consequences are called "sanctions." One of the things the commission can do, on top of any other punishment, is make the real estate agent pay for the costs of the investigation and hearing process. This means the agent might have to cover expenses like:

1. Paperwork and filing fees
2. The time spent by commission members reviewing the case
3. Any travel costs related to the hearing
4. Costs for witnesses or experts who had to testify

Basically, it's like saying, "Not only are you in trouble, but you also have to foot the bill for us figuring out that you were in trouble." This rule helps discourage bad behavior and ensures that the cost of dealing with problematic agents doesn't fall entirely on the commission or taxpayers.

§30-40-22. PENALTIES FOR VIOLATIONS.

(a) In addition to the sanctions imposed by the commission pursuant to this article, any person violating a provision of this article or the commission's rules is guilty of a misdemeanor. Any person convicted of a first violation shall be fined not less than $1,000 nor more than $2,000, or confined in jail not more than 90 days, or both fined and confined;

If you break the rules set by the commission, you can get in trouble in two ways:

1. The commission itself can punish you (these are called sanctions).
2. **You can also be charged with a crime called a misdemeanor.**

If it's your **first time** breaking these rules, and you're found guilty:

- You'll have to pay a fine. **The fine will be at least $1,000 but no more than $2,000.**
- **You might have to go to jail for up to 90 days.**
- **Or you might have to both pay a fine AND go to jail.**

In simple terms, breaking these rules can result in you having to pay money, spend time in jail, or both. It's serious stuff, so it's important to follow the rules set by the commission.

KNOW THESE FINES FOR ALL OF 30-40-22
(THE NEXT FEW PAGES)
THEY ARE EASILY TEST WORTHY

(b) Any person convicted of a second or subsequent violation shall be fined not less than $2,000 nor more than $5,000, or confined in jail for a term not to exceed one year, or both fined and confined;

If someone **breaks this law more than once**, here's what can happen:

1. They'll have to pay a fine. The fine will be:
   - **At least $2,000**
   - **But no more than $5,000**

2. They might have to go to jail:
   - **For up to one year**

3. Or, they might face both punishments:
   - **Pay the fine AND go to jail**

This is more serious than the first time they broke the law. The idea is to discourage people from repeating the same mistake. Remember, the exact punishment can vary within these limits. It's up to the judge to decide based on the specific situation.

(c) Any corporation, association, or partnership convicted of a first violation of this article or the commission's rules, shall be fined not less than $2,000 nor more than $5,000;

This rule is about businesses getting in trouble for breaking the law for the first time. It applies to:

- Companies (also called corporations)
- Groups of people working together (associations)
- Business partnerships

If one of these gets caught breaking this specific law or rule for the first time:

1. They'll have to pay a fine
2. The fine will be at least $2,000
3. But it won't be more than $5,000

So, the punishment is a money penalty. The exact amount will be somewhere between $2,000 and $5,000. It's like a serious warning to the business, telling them "Hey, you messed up, and there are consequences." The idea is to make sure businesses take the law seriously and follow the rules. It's a way to hold them accountable for their actions, just like individual people can get in trouble for breaking laws.

(d) Any corporation, association, or partnership convicted of a second or subsequent violation, shall be fined not less than $5,000 nor more than $10,000;

This rule is about what happens when **businesses break the same law more than once.** It applies to:

- Companies (also called corporations)
- Groups working together (associations)
- Business partnerships

If one of these gets caught breaking this law again:

1. They'll face a bigger fine than the first time
2. The fine will be at least $5,000
3. But it won't be more than $10,000

So, the punishment is a more serious money penalty this time. The exact amount will be somewhere between $5,000 and $10,000.Think of it like this:

- First time: "Okay, you messed up. Here's a smaller fine."
- Second time or more: "You didn't learn your lesson. Now you're in bigger trouble."

The higher fine is meant to:

- Show that repeat offenses are taken very seriously
- Encourage businesses to follow the rules more carefully
- Make sure they understand that breaking the law repeatedly has tougher consequences

It's like how in sports, a player might get a warning for the first foul, but if they keep doing it, they'll face harsher penalties.

(e) Any officer, member, employee, or agent of a corporation, association, or partnership, shall be subject to the penalties herein prescribed for individuals;

This rule is about who can get in trouble when a business breaks the law. It says:

1. It's not just the business itself that can be punished.
2. Specific people within the business can also face consequences.

These people include:

- Officers (like the CEO or president)
- Members (people who are part of the organization)
- Employees (anyone who works there)
- Agents (people who act on behalf of the business)

The key point is:

- These individuals can get the same punishments that a regular person would get for breaking this law.

Think of it like this:

- In a sports team, if there's cheating, it's not just the team that gets in trouble. The players, coaches, or managers involved can also face penalties.

This rule is important because:

- It stops people from hiding behind the business name
- It makes sure that the actual decision-makers face consequences
- It encourages everyone in a business to follow the rules, not just the business as a whole

So, if you're working for or running a business, remember that you can be held personally responsible for breaking the law, even if you did it as part of your job.

(f) Each day a violation of this article continues constitutes a separate offense;

This rule is about how breaking the law is counted **when it happens over time**. Here's what it means:

1. If someone breaks this law, it's not just counted as one big violation.
2. Instead, **each day the law is broken counts as a separate offense**.

Think of it like this:

- Imagine you're playing a video game where you lose points for breaking rules.
- If you break a rule and don't fix it, you don't just lose points once.
- You keep losing points every day until you start following the rules again.

In real life, this means:

- **If you break this law on Monday, keep breaking it until Friday, that's 5 separate offenses.**
- Each of these offenses could potentially get its own punishment.

Why is this rule important?

- It encourages people to fix their mistakes quickly
- It makes the punishment bigger for those who ignore the law for a long time
- It's a way to say, "The longer you break the law, the more trouble you're in"

So, if you ever find yourself in a situation where you've broken a law like this, remember that fixing it fast is really important. Each day you don't fix it, you're basically breaking the law all over again.

(g) In addition to the penalties herein provided, if any person receives compensation for acts or services performed in violation of this article, he or she shall also be subject to a penalty of not less than the value of the compensation received nor more than three times the value of the compensation received, as may be determined by a court of competent jurisdiction. Any penalty may be recovered by a person aggrieved as a result of a violation of this article;

This rule is about extra punishments for people who make money by breaking this law. Let's break it down:

1. **The main point:**

If someone gets paid for doing something that breaks this law, they can face an additional penalty.

2. **How much is the extra penalty?**

- At least as much as the money they made
- But it could be up to three times that amount

3. **Who decides the penalty?**

A judge in a proper court will decide the exact amount.

4. **Who can claim this penalty?**

Anyone who was hurt or affected because of this law being broken can try to get this money.

Think of it like this:

Imagine someone cheats to win a $1000 prize in a contest. They might have to:

- Give back the $1000 they won
- Pay a fine for cheating
- And now, pay an extra penalty that could be anywhere from $1000 to $3000

Why does this rule exist?

- To make sure people don't profit from breaking the law
- To discourage others from trying to make money illegally
- To help make things right for people who were harmed

The big takeaway:

If you break this law and make money from it, you could end up losing way more than you gained. It's a strong warning to play by the rules, especially when money is involved

(h) The penalties provided in this section do not apply to a violation of the duties or obligations of a financial institution under the certification required by §30-40-18(j)(7) of this code by a financial institution providing trust fund account services to a broker.

This rule is about an exception to the penalties we've been talking about. It's a bit specific, but let's break it down:

1. **The main point:**

Some people don't have to worry about these penalties we've discussed.

2. **Who doesn't have to worry?**

Banks or other financial institutions that handle special accounts for real estate brokers.

3. **What are they doing?**

They're providing a service called "trust fund account services" to brokers (people who help buy and sell property).

4. **What's the specific thing they're off the hook for?**

There's a certain certification they need to provide, mentioned in another part of the law (§30-40-18(j)(7)).

Think of it like this:

Imagine a bank is like a referee holding onto money for a real estate game. If the referee makes a mistake with some paperwork, they don't get in trouble the same way a player (broker) would for breaking the game's rules.

Why does this exception exist?

- It recognizes that banks have a different role than brokers
- It might be unfair to punish banks the same way as people directly involved in real estate deals
- There are probably other rules that apply to banks in these situations

The big takeaway:

If you're working at a bank and dealing with real estate brokers' accounts, you have different rules to follow. But if you're a broker or working in real estate directly, all those other penalties we talked about still apply to you. Remember, laws can be complicated, and there are often exceptions for specific situations or types of businesses.

§30-40-23. SINGLE ACT EVIDENCE OF PRACTICE.

One act by any person in consideration of receiving compensation, or with the expectation or intention of receiving such compensation, or upon the promise of receiving compensation for any act or service contained in this article shall constitute and consider the person a broker, associate broker or salesperson subject to the provisions of this article.

If someone does something related to real estate and:

1. Gets paid for it, or
2. Expects to get paid for it, or
3. Is promised payment for it

Then that person is considered a broker, associate broker, or salesperson under the law. This means they must follow all the rules and regulations that apply to these jobs in real estate.

In other words, if you're doing real estate work and money is involved (or expected to be involved), the law sees you as a professional in that field. This means you have certain responsibilities and must follow specific rules, even if you don't officially call yourself a broker or real estate agent.

§30-40-24. INJUNCTIONS; CRIMINAL PROCEEDINGS.

(a) Whenever the commission or other interested person believes that any person has engaged, is engaging or is about to engage in any act that constitutes a violation of this article, the commission or other interested person may make application to any court of competent jurisdiction for an order enjoining the acts or services. Upon a showing that the person has engaged in or is about to engage in any act which violates this article, an injunction, restraining order or another appropriate order may be granted by the court without bond.

If this commission or anyone else who cares about these rules thinks someone is:

1. Breaking these rules
2. Currently breaking these rules
3. About to break these rules

They can do something about it. What can they do?

They can go to a judge and ask for help. They'll explain to the judge why they think someone is breaking or about to break the rules. If the judge agrees that there's a good reason to believe this person is causing trouble, they can do a few things:

1. Tell the person to stop what they're doing (that's called an injunction)
2. Warn the person not to start doing the bad thing (that's a restraining order)
3. Come up with another way to solve the problem

The cool thing is, the judge can do this without asking for any money or security (that's what "without bond" means). Basically, it's a way to stop people from breaking rules before they cause too much trouble. It's like a grown-up version of "time out" but for following important rules!

(b) Whenever the commission, its executive director or its authorized representative has reason to believe that any person has knowingly violated a provision of this article, the commission or its authorized representative may bring its information to the prosecuting attorney in the county where the violation has occurred who shall cause appropriate criminal proceedings to be brought.

Now, let's say this commission, their boss (the executive director), or someone they've chosen to represent them thinks that someone has broken these rules on purpose. What can they do about it? Here's what happens:

1. They gather all the information they have about the rule-breaking.
2. They take this information to a special kind of lawyer called a prosecuting attorney. This lawyer works in the same area where the rule was broken.
3. The prosecuting attorney's job is to look at the information and decide if it's serious enough to take to court.
4. If the prosecuting attorney thinks it's a big deal, they'll start what's called "criminal proceedings." This basically means they'll take steps to have the person who broke the rules answer for what they did in court.

It's kind of like if you knew someone cheated in a big game at school. You'd tell the teacher or principal, and they'd decide if the cheating was bad enough to punish the person who did it. The main point is that if someone breaks these important rules on purpose, there are people whose job it is to make sure they face consequences for their actions. It's all about keeping things fair and making sure everyone follows the rules.

(c) Whenever any other interested person has reason to believe that any person has knowingly violated a provision of this article, such person may bring its information to the attention of the appropriate law-enforcement officer who may cause an investigation to be made in order for appropriate criminal proceedings to be brought.

Imagine you're part of a community with some important rules that everyone is supposed to follow. These rules are written down in something called an "article." Now, here's what this legal stuff is saying in simpler terms: If you or anyone else who cares about these rules (that's what "interested person" means) thinks someone has broken these rules on purpose, you can do something about it. Here's how it works:

1. You notice someone breaking the rules, and you're pretty sure they knew what they were doing.

2. You don't have to keep it to yourself or handle it alone. Instead, you can tell someone whose job it is to deal with rule-breakers.

3. The person you tell is called a "law-enforcement officer." Think of them like a referee in a game, but for real-life rules.

4. When you tell the officer what you saw or know, they don't have to just take your word for it. They can look into it themselves. This is called an "investigation."

5. If the officer finds enough evidence that the person really did break the rules on purpose, they can take it further. They might start what's called "criminal proceedings," which is basically a formal way of holding the rule-breaker accountable.

It's kind of like if you saw someone shoplifting at a store. You're not expected to confront them yourself, but you can tell a security guard or store manager. They'll then check it out and decide if they need to call the police. The main idea here is that everyone in the community can help make sure the rules are followed. If you see something wrong, you have the power to speak up and let the right people know about it.

§30-40-25. COLLECTION OF COMPENSATION.

No person may bring or maintain any action in any court of this state for the recovery of compensation for the performance of any act or service for which a broker's license is required, without alleging and proving that he or she was the holder of a valid broker's license at all times during the performance or rendering of any act or service: Provided, That an associate broker or salesperson may institute suit in his or her own name for the recovery of compensation from his or her affiliated broker for acts or services performed while affiliated with the broker.

Imagine you're playing a game where you need a special license to earn points. This law is like a rule for that game, but in real life. It's about people who help buy and sell houses, called real estate brokers. Here's what it means:

1. If you want to get paid for doing a broker's job, you need to have a valid license.
2. If you don't have a license and try to get money for doing broker work, you can't go to court to fight for that money.
3. When you go to court, you have to prove that you had a valid license the whole time you were doing the work.
4. There's one exception: If you're a helper (like an associate broker or salesperson) working under a licensed broker, you can go to court to get money from that broker for work you did while helping them.

Basically, this law makes sure that only people with proper licenses can get paid for doing real estate broker work. It's like making sure only certified lifeguards can work at a pool – it's for everyone's protection.

§30-40-26. DUTIES OF LICENSEES.

Every broker, associate broker, and salesperson owes certain inherent duties to the consumer which are required by virtue of the commission granting a license under this article. The duties include, but are not limited to:

(a) At the time of securing any contract whereby the broker is obligated to represent a principal to a real estate transaction, every licensee shall supply a true legible copy of the contract to each person signing the contract.

When you're buying or selling a house, you'll probably work with a real estate agent. These agents have to follow certain rules because they have a special license. Here are some of the things they must do:

1. Be honest and fair with you.
2. Explain things clearly so you understand what's happening.
3. Look out for your best interests.

One specific rule is really important When you agree to work with an agent (by signing a contract), they have to give you a copy of that contract right away. This copy needs to be:

- Real (not fake)
- Easy to read
- Given to everyone who signs it

This rule helps make sure you know exactly what you're agreeing to when you start working with a real estate agent. It protects you and keeps everything clear and open between you and the agent.

(b) Any contract in which a broker is obligated to represent a principal to a real estate transaction shall contain a definite expiration date, and no provision may be included in any contract whereby the principal is required to notify the broker of his or her intention to cancel the contract after the definite expiration date.

When you sign a contract with a real estate agent to help you buy or sell a house, there are two important things you need to know:

1. **End Date**

   The contract must have a clear end date. This is like an expiration date on food - after this date, the agreement is over unless you choose to renew it. For example, the contract might say it lasts for 3 months, ending on December 31st.

2. **No Tricky Renewal Clauses**

   The contract can't include any sneaky language that forces you to tell the agent if you don't want to continue working with them af ter the end date. Once the contract expires, it's done - no strings attached.

Why is this important?

- It protects you from being stuck with an agent forever.
- It gives you the freedom to choose a new agent or stop looking for a house without any hassle when the contract ends.
- It keeps things fair and straightforward between you and the agent.

Remember, if anything in a contract seems confusing, it's okay to ask questions or have someone else look it over before you sign.

(c) No provision may be inserted in any contract for representation that would obligate the person signing the contract to pay a fee, commission, or other valuable consideration to the broker, after the contract's expiration date, if the person subsequently enters into a contract for representation with a different broker.

When you sign a contract with a real estate agent to help you buy or sell a house, there's an important rule you should know about: The contract can't include any sneaky clauses that would make you pay the agent after the contract has ended, especially if you decide to work with a different agent later. Let's break this down:

1. Your contract has an end date (like we talked about before).
2. After that end date, you're free to do whatever you want. You can:

- Stop looking for a house
- Keep looking on your own
- Work with a different agent

3. The important part: If you choose to work with a new agent after your contract ends, your old agent can't force you to pay them anything.

Why is this rule important?

- It protects you from unfair charges
- It gives you the freedom to change agents if you're not happy
- It keeps the relationship between you and the agent clear and fair

Think of it like a gym membership. When your membership ends, you can join a different gym without owing anything to the old one. The same idea applies here - when your contract with an agent ends, you're free to "work out" with a new agent without any penalties. Remember, if you see anything in a contract that looks like it might go against this rule, it's a good idea to ask questions or get some advice before signing.

(d) Every licensee shall disclose in writing, on the notice of agency relationship form promulgated by the commission, whether the licensee represents the seller, the buyer, the seller and the buyer, the landlord, the tenant, or the landlord and the tenant. The disclosure shall be made prior to any person signing any contract for representation by a licensee or a contract for the sale or purchase of real estate.

It's worth mentioning that all of the news you've heard recently about the National Association of REALTORS® settlement could be broken down into how this form explains how a real estate salesperson represents a buyer or seller. When you're buying, selling, or renting a place, you'll work with a real estate agent. There's an important rule these agents have to follow:

The "Who's Who" Form

Before you sign any contracts, the agent must give you a special form. This form is like a "Who's Who" in your real estate deal. It clearly states who the agent is working for. Here's what you need to know:

1. The form is official - it's created by a special commission that oversees real estate agents.
2. It must be in writing - no verbal agreements here!
3. The agent has to fill it out before you sign any other paperwork.

THE NOTICE OF AGENCY FORM

What the Form Says

The form will tell you if the agent is representing:

- The seller (if you're buying)
- The buyer (if you're selling)
- Both the seller and buyer (this is called dual agency)
- The landlord (if you're rent ing)
- The tenant (if you're the landlord)
- Both the landlord and tenant

Why This Matters

This form is important because:

1. It helps you understand whose side the agent is on.
2. It prevents any confusion about who the agent is working for.
3. It protects you from potential conflicts of interest.

Think of it like sports teams. You want to know which jersey your agent is wearing before the game starts. This form tells you exactly that. Remember, if you don't get this form or don't understand it, speak up! It's your right to know who's representing who in your real estate deal.

(e) Every licensee shall promptly deliver to his or her principal, every written offer received.

When you're working with a real estate agent to buy or sell a house, there's an important rule they have to follow:

The "No Hiding Offers" Rule

Your agent (also called a licensee) must give you every written offer they receive as soon as possible. This applies whether you're:

- Selling a house and getting offers from buyers
- Buying a house and someone else makes an offer on the same property

What This Means for You

1. Quick Updates: Your agent can't sit on offers. If someone makes an offer, you should know about it fast.
2. See Everything: You get to see all offers, not just the ones your agent thinks are good.
3. No Filtering: Your agent can't decide which offers to show you. They have to show you all of them.
4. In Writing: This rule applies to written offers. Verbal offers don't count here.

Why This Rule Exists

This rule is in place to:

- Keep things fair
- Make sure you have all the information to make good decisions
- Prevent agents from playing favorites or hiding offers

Think of it like this: If you're selling cookies at a bake sale, you'd want to know about every person interested in buying, right? It's the same with houses. Your agent has to tell you about everyone who wants to buy (or sell), so you can make the best choice for yourself.

(f) Every licensee shall make certain that all the terms and conditions of a real estate transaction are contained in any contract prepared by the licensee.

When a real estate agent (called a "licensee") helps with buying or selling property, they have an important job to do. They need to make sure that everything important about the deal is written down in the contract. This means:

1. All the details about the sale should be in the contract.
2. Any agreements made between the buyer and seller must be included.
3. Nothing important should be left out or just talked about verbally.

The agent is responsible for putting all this information in the contract if they're the one writing it up. This rule helps protect everyone involved in the sale and makes sure there are no misunderstandings later.

Think of it like this: If you're making a big trade with a friend, you'd want all the details written down so you both remember exactly what you agreed to. It's the same idea, but for something as big and important as buying or selling a house or other property

(g) At the time of securing the signature of any party to a contract, the licensee shall deliver a true copy of the contract to the person whose signature was obtained.

When a real estate agent (also called a "licensee") gets someone to sign a contract for buying or selling property, they have to do something important right away:

1. The agent must give that person a copy of the contract they just signed.
2. This copy has to be a true and exact copy - not changed or differ ent in any way.
3. The person gets this copy right after they sign, not later.

Think of it like this: Imagine you're making a deal with a friend to trade something valuable. After you both sign an agreement, you'd want a copy of what you just agreed to, right? It's the same idea here, but for something much bigger, like a house. This rule is important because:

- It helps the person who signed remember exactly what they agreed to.
- It prevents any confusion or arguments later about what was in the contract.
- It's a way to make sure everything is fair and open.

So, in simple terms, if you sign a real estate contract, the agent must give you your own copy of it right then and there. This way, you have proof of what you agreed to, and you can look it over anytime you want.

(h) Upon the final acceptance or ratification of any contract, the licensee shall promptly deliver a true copy to each party that has signed the contract.

When a real estate deal is finally agreed upon by everyone involved, the real estate agent (also called a "licensee") has an important job to do:

1. They need to give a copy of the final contract to each person who signed it.
2. This needs to happen quickly - not days or weeks later, but as soon as possible.
3. The copy has to be a "true copy," which means it's exactly the same as the original, with no changes.

Think of it like this: Imagine you and your friends are planning a big group trip. Once everyone agrees on the plan and signs off on it, you'd want a copy of the final plan for yourself, right? It's the same idea with a real estate contract, but it's even more important because it involves a lot of money and legal stuff. Why is this important?

- It makes sure everyone knows exactly what they agreed to.
- It helps avoid confusion or disagreements later.
- It gives each person their own record of the deal.

So, in simple terms, once a real estate deal is fully agreed upon, the agent must quickly give each person who signed the contract their own copy to keep. This way, everyone has the same information and can refer back to it if they need to.

§30-40-27. DURATION OF EXISTING LICENSES.

Repealed

"Repealed" means that a law, rule, or regulation has been officially canceled or removed. It's no longer in effect or valid.

REPEALED

§30-40-28.

Repealed

"Repealed" means that a law, rule, or regulation has been officially canceled or removed. It's no longer in effect or valid.

THE SECOND HALF

YOU MADE IT SO FAR!
Onward, to title 174

The remaining part of the legal documents that pertain to WV Real Estate Licensing are contained in what is referred to as Title 174. It's worth note that this content will be highlighted in blue to give a visual reminder that this is technically not law code 30-40 anymore. For testing purposes I'm not so confident it matters but I like to visually separate things in my brain so that explains the colors. One might ask, or at least I do, why is this stuff not placed in the law code we reviewed in article 30-40 (the yellow portions)?

Well, the answer is these law portions are put into official reality by two different groups of people. One funny thing that jumped out at me is that Article 30-40 is written by legislature and the "Legislative rule" is not. Ha. The irony here is memorable. Let that sink in: The legislative rule is NOT authored by the state legislature.

The legislative rule is authored by the WV Real Estate Commission and is added onto the law code because they can change and edit this without bothering, well, a legislative body (34 senators and 100 delegates who meet every year for 60 days) every time they want to revise something. The remaining differences of these legal documents are separated as follows for the curious mind:

West Virginia Code Chapter 30 Article 40 (WV Code §30-40):

This is the primary statutory law passed by the West Virginia Legislature that establishes the Real Estate Commission and outlines the state's basic requirements for real estate licensing and regulation. It is part of the West Virginia Code, which contains all the state's statutory laws.

Title 174 Legislative Rule Real Estate Commission Series 1:

This administrative rule was created by the West Virginia Real Estate Commission to implement and enforce the statutory law. Administrative rules provide more detailed regulations and procedures that expand upon the broader statutory framework.

The key differences are:

1. Origin: The statute (WV Code §30-40) is created by the legislature, while the legislative rule (Title 174) is created by the Real Estate Commission.

2. Level of detail: The statute provides the general framework, while the legislative rule offers more specific guidelines and procedures.

3. Amendment process: Changing the statute requires legislative action, while the Commission can modify the legislative rule through a rule-making process (subject to legislative review).

4. Authority: The legislative rule derives its authority from the statute and must stay within the bounds set by the statutory law.

This separation allows for more flexibility in regulating the real estate industry, as the Commission can update rules more easily than changing state law, while still operating within the statutory framework established by the legislature.

Without further ado, the lovely title 174.

USER FRIENDLY INDEX

Who are these rules laid out for?

YOU MADE IT SO FAR!
Onward, to title 174

★ = study for salesperson

TITLE 174
LEGISLATIVE RULE
REAL ESTATE COMMISSION

SERIES 1 - INDEX

Index

Section 1. General.	(the overview)
Section 2. Definitions.	(more terms!!!)
Section 3. License Year and Fee	(Fees, everyone cheers)
Section 4 Licensure; Examination Required; Application and Licensure Fees.	(Why you took that exam! Why you pay those fees!)
Section 5. Background Checks.	(Somebody's watching you. Big brother and all that, not so much conspiracy stuff.)
Section 6. Qualifications for Broker's License.	(You can't just be a broker without doing a lot beforehand.)
Section 7. Licensing Non-Residents.	(You're out of state and want a WV License?)
Section 8. Renewal of License; Continuing Education Requirement; Late Fees; Failure to Renew; Cancellation.	(The education never ends. The fun never ends. More fees, not renewing your license and eventually losing it because of that)
Section 9. License Certificates: Issuance, Cancellation and Transfer.	(OooOooh your pretty certificate and rules about it)
Section 10. Special Provisions for Brokers.	(Brokers are special in more ways than one)
Section 11. Deceased or Incapacitated Responsible Broker.	(I want to be empathetic, but this begs for the summary of "Your broker kicks it") P.S. If you're experiencing loss, I do retract the statement and will accept text messages and emails to actually listen.

Section 12. Trade and Franchise Names.	(Guidelines to naming yourself that)
Section 13. Office Signs.	(Guidelines to hanging that sign!)
Section 14. Branch Offices.	(Rules about the office)
Section 15. Trust Funds and Accounts.	(Rules about the trust account holding clients' money)
Section 16. Agency Consent and Disclosure.	(Rules about who you represent)
Section 17. Advertising.	(Rules about your Facebook posts and all kinds of things you could get into trouble over)
Section 18. Offer of Consumer Rebates, Inducements and Other Discounts.	(More ways you could get into trouble on social media and elsewhere)
Section 19. Investigations and Complaints.	(You got into trouble on social media, and someone complained)
Section 20. Licensee's Duty to Report Other Actions.	(Your duties to police the situations you see)

LEGISLATIVE RULE
REAL ESTATE COMMISSION

SERIES 1 LEGISLATIVE RULE REAL ESTATE COMMISSION

LICENSING REAL ESTATE BROKERS, ASSOCIATE BROKERS, AND SALESPERSONS AND THE CONDUCT OF BROKERAGE BUSINESS

§174-1-1. GENERAL.

1.1. Scope. -- This legislative rule establishes general rules for the filing of applications for real estate licenses and the requirements necessary to renew licenses and for the enforcement and administration of the provisions of W. Va. Code §§30-40-1 et seq.

This rule sets up the basic guidelines for two main things related to real estate licenses in West Virginia:

1. Getting a License: It explains how to apply for a real estate license.
2. Keeping Your License: It outlines what you need to do to renew your license and keep it active.

Why It Exists

This rule helps make sure that the real estate laws in West Virginia (specifically, the ones found in W. Va. Code §30-40-1 and the sections that follow) are properly followed and enforced. Think of it as a rulebook that helps keep everything fair and organized in the real estate world. It makes sure that everyone who wants to work in real estate knows what they need to do to get started and how to stay in the business legally.

1.2. Authority. -- W. Va. Code §30-40-8.

The West Virginia Real Estate Commission isn't just making up rules without being told they can. If you look back at §30-40-8 you will see that the WV State Legislature officially wrote into the law that they could do this.

1.3. Filing Date. - April 10, 2024

This particular edit of this legislative rule was put into a proper filing cabinet somewhere deemed as the official place to put that document on April 10, 2024

1.4. Effective Date. -- April 10, 2024

The rules explained in this version of legislative rule went into effect on April 10, 2024

1.5. Sunset Provision. - This rule shall terminate and have no further force or effect upon August 1, 2029.

The main purposes of sunset provisions are to:

- Ensure periodic review and reassessment of laws or agreements
- Prevent outdated or ineffective laws from remaining in effect indefinitely
- Provide an opportunity to modify terms based on changing circumstances

How Sunset Provisions Work

When a sunset provision is included in legal paperwork:

1. It specifies an expiration date or triggering event
2. Upon reaching that date or event, the relevant law, regulation, or contractual term automatically becomes void
3. To keep the provision in effect, legislative action or agreement between parties is required to extend or renew it
4. In the case of this document, it expires on August 1, 2029. All evil doers, put a calendar event for August 2nd 2029 when you can wreak havoc. Granted, chances are they meet and renew this before it expires.

§174-1-2. DEFINITIONS.

2.1. "Advertise, advertisement, advertising" or similar means print media, yard signs, billboards, radio, television, internet, social media, or any other advertising medium utilized by anyone engaged or employed by a brokerage;

"**Advertise**," "**advertisement**," or "**advertising**" means any way a real estate company or its workers try to get people's attention and share information about their services or properties. This can include:

- Things you can read, like newspapers or magazines
- Signs in yards or on big boards along roads
- Radio shows or commercials
- TV shows or commercials
- Anything on the internet, including websites and apps
- Posts or ads on social media platforms like Instagram or Facebook
- Any other creative way they might come up with to spread the word about what they're selling or offering

Basically, it covers all the different methods real estate people use to tell the public about their business and the properties they're trying to sell or rent.

2.2. "Applicant" means any person who is making application to the Commission for a license.

You are an **"applicant"** if you are filling out the forms the WVREC has to apply for a real estate license.

2.3. "Commingling," "commingle," or similar means the mixing of trust funds with non-trust funds by a fiduciary or other person entrusted with the management of another's funds.

"**Commingling**" or "to **commingle**" means mixing money that isn't yours with your own money when you're supposed to be taking care of it for someone else.

Imagine you're babysitting and the parents give you $50 to order pizza for the kids. If you put that $50 in your own wallet with your personal money, that's commingling. You're supposed to keep it separate because it's not your money - it's meant for a specific purpose (buying pizza) and belongs to someone else (the parents).

In real estate or business, it's the same idea but usually with larger amounts of money. If someone trusts you to manage their money (like a real estate agent holding a deposit for a house), you're not supposed to mix it with your own cash or use it for your personal stuff. It should be kept in a separate account, often called a trust account, to make sure it's used only for its intended purpose.

Commingling is generally considered unethical and, in many cases, illegal because it can lead to misuse of funds that don't belong to you.

2.4. "Commission" means the West Virginia Real Estate Commission as authorized by W. Va. Code §30-40-6.

Pretend the word **commission** is slang for the West Virginia Real Estate Commission. Pretty cool, right? Heh. We're talking about legal stuff here so even slang needs clearly described

2.5. "Responsible broker" means the designated broker as defined in W. Va. Code §30-40-4 or the broker doing business as a sole proprietor who employs or engages and supervises other licensees.

A "**responsible broker**" is like the team captain or manager in a real estate company. They're the person in charge who oversees all the other real estate agents (called licensees) working for that company. There are two types of responsible brokers:

1. The "**designated broker**": This is the main boss chosen by a real estate company to be in charge. They're responsible for making sure everyone follows the rules and does their job correctly.
2. The "**sole proprietor broker**": This is someone who runs their own small real estate business. They're the boss and may hire other agents to work for them.

In both cases, the responsible broker has important duties:

- They hire and supervise other real estate agents
- They make sure everyone follows the laws and rules of real estate
- They're ultimately responsible for what happens in their company

Think of it like this: If a real estate company were a ship, the responsible broker would be the captain. They're in charge of steering the ship, making sure everyone does their job, and taking responsibility if anything goes wrong.

2.6. "Employing broker" means the responsible broker regardless of whether the licensees are working as independent contractors or employees.

An "**employing broker**" is basically the boss of a real estate company. They're called this whether they actually hire people as regular employees or work with agents who are more like independent contractors. To break it down:

- This person is the same as the "responsible broker" we talked about before - the one in charge of the whole operation.
- They're called an "employing broker" because they're the one who brings real estate agents into the company to work.
- It doesn't matter if these agents are:

1. Regular employees (who get a steady paycheck and benefits)
2. Independent contractors (who work more flexibly and handle their own taxes)

The key point is that this broker is responsible for all the agents working under their company's name, no matter how those agents are classified in terms of employment. Think of it like this: If you're running a lemonade stand and you get your friends to help, you'd be the "employing" person whether you pay them hourly or give them a cut of the profits. You're still the one in charge, and you're responsible for making sure everything's done right.

2.7. "Licensee" means a broker, an associate broker, or a salesperson as defined in W. Va. Code §30- 40-4.

You will learn, or have already learned in the course, the proper designation of legal wordings ending in "ee", or "or". They are basically laying out that the term "**licensee**", ending in "ee" can refer to a few person types.

You could be a broker holding a license, an associate broker (holding a license) or a salesperson (holding a license). In all cases you would hold a license and thus, the term ends in the "ee", reflecting they receive something. In this case, the license.

2.8. "Usual place of business" means the physical location from which a broker carries on his or her business and which the broker holds forth to the public as his or her usual place of business.

The "**usual place of business**" is just a fancy way of saying "the main office" or "headquarters" of a real estate broker. It's basically where they do most of their work and where people can find them if they need to. Think of it like this:

- It's the physical location - a real building or office, not just a web site or phone number.

- It's where the broker does most of their business stuff, like meet ing clients or keeping important documents.

- It's the address they give out to the public, like on business cards or advertisements.

2.9. "Team" includes any group of two or more associate brokers and/or salespersons, and other non- licensed professionals, affiliated with the same broker or company acting as one agent or representative for the principal.

A "**team**" in real estate is like a squad or crew working together. It's a group of people who join forces to help buy or sell properties. Here's what you need to know:

- It's made up of at least two people but can be more.
- The team members are usually:
- Associate brokers (like senior real estate agents)
- Salespersons (regular real estate agents)
- Sometimes other professionals who aren't real estate agents (like marketers or assistants)
- They all work for the same real estate company or boss (called a broker).
- When they work together, they act like one big super-agent for their client.

Think of it like a sports team:

- Different players have different roles (like how a quarterback and receiver have different jobs in football)
- They all wear the same jersey (work for the same company)
- They work together to win the game (help their client buy or sell a property)

The main idea is that instead of just one agent helping you buy or sell a house; you get a whole group of people with different skills all working together to help you out.

§174-1-3. LICENSE YEAR AND FEES.

3.1. License year. -- The license year begins on July 1 and ends June 30. The Commission may issue licenses on an annual or biannual basis. Fees are not prorated.

Think of it this way. Your year begins on January 1 and ends December 31st. The license year does not. It's funky that way. **The license year starts on July 1 and ends on June 30th**. Befriend a commissioner and go to a new years party on June 30th.

Here's how it works:

- Real estate licenses can be given out for one year or two years at a time. *Worth note regarding this two year thing. Although the law code states this is possible, I have never seen this option in the renewal or application.

- The fees you pay for these licenses are fixed, meaning they don't get reduced if you get your license partway through the year.

So, if you're getting a real estate license, just remember that it follows this specific timeline, and you'll pay the full fee no matter when during the year you apply.

3.2. Proper fee. -- Each application for a license shall be accompanied by a separate check or money order for the proper fee for that particular application as set forth in Series 2 of the Commission's rules. When a licensed salesperson desires to be licensed as a broker, his or her responsible broker shall surrender his or her salesperson's license certificate to the Commission before a broker's certificate is issued. He or she shall pay the fee for the broker's license as set forth in Series 2 of these rules. The Commission shall not give credit for the fee paid for the salesperson's license.

When you apply for a real estate license, you need to include a separate check or money order to pay the fee that goes with your application. The exact amount you need to pay is listed in the Commission's rules.

If you're already a licensed real estate agent and want to become a broker (which is a higher level), your current boss (the responsible broker) has to give up your agent license to the Commission before you can get your broker license. You'll also have to pay the fee for the broker license, which is different from the agent fee.

It's important to know that you won't get any money back or credit for what you paid for your agent license when you switch to becoming a broker.

§174-1-4. LICENSURE; EXAMINATION REQUIRED; APPLICATION AND LICENSURE FEES.

4.1. Application. -- To apply for a real estate license, an applicant shall utilize forms prescribed by the Commission and comply with the following:	When you want to apply for a real estate license, you need to use the specific forms that the Commission provides. You also have to follow these steps:
4.1.1. The commission shall only issue an original license to an applicant if he or she:	
4.1.1.a. Submits an application in writing, on a form prescribed by the commission which shall contain, but is not limited to:	This application is done online these days. So in writing basically means filling out the forms on their website. You will need to include:
4.1.1.a.1. The applicant's Social Security number;	1 Your Social Security number.
4.1.1.a.2 A clear record indicating all jurisdictions where the applicant holds or has held any professional license;	2 A list of all the places where you currently have or previously had any kind of professional license.
4.1.1.a.3. A clear record indicating if the applicant has been convicted of any criminal offense or if there is any criminal charge pending against the applicant, or a member or officer of the brokerage business, at the time of application;	3 Information about whether you've ever been convicted of a crime or if there are any criminal charges against you or someone in your real estate business when you apply.
4.1.1.b. Is at least 18 years of age;	Also, you need to be at least 18 years old to apply

4.1.1.c. Is a high school graduate or the holder of an equivalency diploma;	You finished High School, right? If not, you got a GED or equivalent, right?
4.1.1.d. Is trustworthy, of good moral character, and competent to transact the business of a broker, associate broker, or salesperson	You're a good person, right? This cracks me up as to the open ended reality of interpretation that can be applied here
4.1.1.e. Has paid the appropriate fee, if any, which shall accompany all applications for original license or renewal;	You paid the fee, right?
4.1.1.f. Has submitted to a state and national criminal history record check, as set forth in this subsection: Provided, That an applicant for a license who is an attorney at law may submit a letter of good standing from the West Virginia State Bar in lieu of submitting to a state and national criminal history record check;	You must go through a state and national criminal background check. However, if you're a lawyer, you can provide a letter of good standing from the West Virginia State Bar instead of doing this background check.
4.1.1.f.1. This requirement is found not to be against public policy.	It's considered "ok" to require this.

4.1.1.f.3. The applicant shall meet all requirements necessary to complete the state and national criminal history record check, including:	You have to do a background check.
4.1.1.f.3.A. Submitting fingerprints for the purposes set forth in this subsection; and	You have to submit your fingerprints. No if's, no buts, no coconuts.
4.1.1.f.3.B. Authorizing the commission, the West Virginia State Police, and the Federal Bureau of Investigation to use all records submitted and produced for the purpose of screening the applicant for a license.	You need to give permission for the Commission, the West Virginia State Police, and the FBI to use all the information and records you provide. This is so they can check your background and make sure you're eligible for the license.
4.1.1.f.4. The results of the state and national criminal history record check may not be released to or by a private entity except:	The results of your state and national criminal background check can't be shared with or by private companies, except in specific situations.
4.1.1.f.4.A. To the individual who is the subject of the criminal history record check;	The results of your criminal background check can be shared with you, the person who the check is about.

4.1.1.f.4.B. With the written authorization of the individual who is the subject of the criminal history record check; or	The results of your criminal background check can be shared with others if you give written permission for it to happen.
4.1.1.f.4.C. Pursuant to a court order.	A court would order it to be shared. This is pretty unlikely, but you need to know that it's possible in extreme cases. I've personally never seen this or even heard of it happening.
4.1.1.f.5. The criminal history record check and related records are not public records for the purposes of chapter 29B of this code.	Your criminal background check and any related documents are private and aren't considered public records, so they can't be accessed by just anyone.
4.1.1.f .6. The applicant shall pay the actual costs of the fingerprinting and criminal history record check.	You pay the actual costs to the company doing the check. The WVREC will not add some sort of package where they upcharge anything.
4.1.1.f.7. Before implementing the provisions of this subsection, the commission shall propose rules for legislative approval in accordance with §29A-3-1 et seq. of this code. The rules shall set forth the requirements and procedures for the criminal history record check and must be consistent with standards established by the Federal Bureau of Investigation and the National Crime Prevention and Privacy Compact as authorized by 42 U.S. C. A. §14611, et seq.	Before starting the process of doing criminal background checks, the Commission has to create rules and get them approved by the legislature. These rules will explain how the background check will work and must follow the standards set by the FBI and other national guidelines.

4.2. Third-party provider. -- The Commission may contract with an independent testing service provider to develop and/or administer any required examination(s), in which case the examination fee shall be paid directly to the provider.

The Commission can hire an outside company to create and give any tests you need to take. If they do, you'll pay the test fee directly to that company.

After finishing the pre-approved 90 hour course you will sign up to get a check currently through the company Identogo. This is the background check company that the WVREC has contracted to work with them on this task and no other company suffices while this working relationship is in place.

I often get asked by students who have already had a background check done for another job if they can use that and the answer is no, it can't. A new one has to be done through Identogo.

4.3. Valid duration of approval; re-application. -- An approval for taking the examination shall only be valid for three (3) months from the date of approval and for no more than two (2) attempts at passing the examination. Upon the expiration of three (3) months or the examinee's second unsuccessful attempt at passing the examination, whichever comes first, the examinee will be required to submit a new application which shall be valid for three (3) months and for two (2) more examinations.

When you're approved to take the real estate exam, you have three months to take it and you can try up to two times. If three months pass or you fail twice, whichever happens first, you'll need to apply again. With the new application, you'll get another three months and two more chances to pass the exam.

Rinse and repeat.

You can technically take the exam as many times as you want but you have to do so in that pattern of

2 fails or 3 months = apply to test again.

4.4. Examination Rules. -- The following rules apply to all examinations, and violation of any rule is grounds for disqualification of the applicant from taking the test and may be grounds for further disqualification:

When you take the real estate exam, there are certain rules you have to follow. If you break any of these rules, you might not be allowed to take the test, and it could also affect your chance to take it in the future.

4.4.a. Examinees may not refer to any notes, books or memoranda.	During the exam, you can't look at any notes, books, or written reminders.
4.4.b. The examinee must show all computations on paper provided at the examination site	If you need to do any calculations during the exam, you have to write them down on the paper they give you at the test location.
4.4.c. The copying of questions or the making of notes is prohibited.	You can't copy down their questions or make notes of what you see to carry out of there.
4.4.d. All examinees must present identification which contains a current recognizable photograph and their signature. Any examinee who does not present the required identification will be prohibited from taking the examination.	When you go to take the exam, you need to bring an ID that has your photo and signature on it. If you don't have this ID, you won't be allowed to take the test.
4.4.e. All examinees must pay the required examination fee at the time of registering for the examination.	You can't say, "I'll pay you later." Granted where in life does that exist? Ha.
4.5. Reexamination. -- An examinee who fails to attain a passing grade on the examination will receive a notice of failure and a score report containing diagnostic scoring information. Reexamination is available in accordance with this section.	If you don't pass the exam, you'll get a notice telling you that you didn't pass and a report showing how you scored in different areas. Kind of funny, but if you pass they don't tell you your scores like they do if you fail. They only tell you your score if you fail. This has always been the case for as long as I am aware so if anyone tells you they "aced the exam" they're lying. If they passed it they have no idea their grade,
4.6. Review of examination. -- An examinee who fails the examination(s) after two (2) attempts may request a review to verify that everything was properly handled, by making written request to the testing service provider.	If you fail the exam twice, you can ask for a review to make sure everything was done correctly. To do this, you need to write to the company that gave the test.

4.7. Payment of license fee. -- An applicant for a real estate license, upon successfully passing the required examination(s) must pay the required license fee and submit all completed supporting documents within three (3) months from the date of passing the exam(s). The Commission will cancel the application of any applicant who does not pay the required license fee within three (3) months. Any applicant that fails to comply with this rule, will be required to reapply and successfully pass the examination(s). The Commission may grant a one-time extension up to three (3) months to pay the license fee if good cause to do so is demonstrated by the applicant. Each request for an extension will be considered on a case by case basis and shall be granted if extenuating facts or circumstances warrant.

After you pass the real estate exam, you have three months to pay the license fee and send in all the necessary paperwork. If you don't do this within three months, your application will be canceled, and you'll have to apply again and retake the exam.

If you have a good reason for needing more time, you can ask for an extra three months to pay the fee. Each request is looked at individually, and you'll get more time if your situation is considered special enough.

This is pretty huge in real life. This test is incredibly difficult so if you pass it **you do not want to have to test again because you made a silly mistake like forgetting to activate** and pay the license fee to the WVREC.

When in doubt, simply ask Spruce School of Real Estate for details on how to activate the license after you pass the licensing exam and we will happily congratulate you on your success and guide you through the activation process.

4.8. Multiple concurrent licenses. -- Licensees who choose to be affiliated with more than one brokerage must have a license and license certificate for each brokerage. These additional licenses have no additional requirements other than the payment of the appropriate license fee.

If you want to work with more than one real estate company at the same time, you need to have a separate license and certificate for each company. The only extra thing you need to do is pay the license fee for each one.

This comes off a little more confusing than it sounds. Some people work at multiple different companies because they serve different areas of the state that one broker is not in. If this is the case you need to have your license filed at each office which requires you to pay a fee to the WVREC so they can get that license to that other office.

There is not a whole other licensing process or test. This is just a matter of a printed copy of your license and the WVREC wanting to know where you work in each case.

§174-1-5. BACKGROUND CHECKS.

This is more reinforcement of the rules about background checks. Again, this Legislative Rule is separate from law code 30-40 and seems somewhat repetitive, but it is here so that there is more ease in editing by the WVREC when necessary.

5.1. Applicants for a broker, associate broker or salesperson license shall furnish fingerprints to the State Police, or its assigned agent, for the purpose of performing a national criminal history record checks by the Criminal Identification Bureau of the West Virginia State Police and the Federal Bureau of Investigation.

If you're applying to be a real estate broker, associate broker, or salesperson, you need to give your fingerprints to the State Police or the company they choose. These fingerprints will be used to do a background check on you. This check will be done by both the West Virginia State Police and the FBI to look at your criminal history across the whole country.

It is worth note that this is currently done through a company contracted with the WVREC. **Do NOT go and make an appt with your local police station, etc. without checking with the proper protocol** and who is to do this. Simply want to save you time and money because NOT all background checks are going to be used for this. **Spruce School of Real Estate or the WVREC will happily instruct you on which company is currently being used to avoid you time and frustration.**

5.1.a. The fingerprints shall be accompanied by a signed authorization for the release of information to the West Virginia Real Estate Commission by the Criminal Investigation Bureau and the Federal Bureau of Investigation.

When you give your fingerprints, you also need to sign a form. This form gives permission for the Criminal Investigation Bureau and the FBI to share the results of your background check with the West Virginia Real Estate Commission.

5.1.b. The applicant shall furnish any additional information required to complete the criminal history records checks.

If they need any more information to finish your background check, you'll need to provide it. This could be things like extra details about your past or clarification on something in your records.

5.2. The Applicant shall pay the associated fees for the fingerprinting and criminal history records check.

You'll have to pay for the fingerprinting and background check yourself. It's not free, and the cost isn't covered by anyone else.

5.3. The criminal history records required by this section shall have been requested no more than three (3) months prior to the application for license being filed with the Commission. The records expire three (3) months after the date the application is received by the Commission.

When you apply for your real estate license, your background check needs to be recent. You should request it no more than three months before you send in your application. Once the Commission gets your application, your background check is only good for three months. After that, it's considered expired and you will need to get a new one.

5.4. Applicants are solely responsible for reconciling with any reporting agency a challenge to the accuracy or completeness of information provided by the West Virginia State Police, the Federal Bureau of Investigation or other agencies reporting information to the Commission. The applicant is solely responsible for providing the Commission with proof of any error and correction thereof by any reporting agency.

If there's something wrong or missing in your background check report, it's up to you to fix it. You need to contact the agency that provided the information (like the West Virginia State Police or FBI) and work with them to correct any mistakes.

If you find an error, you have to prove to the Commission that it was fixed. The Commission won't do this for you - it's your responsibility to make sure all the information about you is correct.

5.5. If the applicant provides adequate proof of any error and correction thereof by any reporting agency, the Commission shall reconsider the application of that applicant.

If you find a mistake in your background check and get it fixed, you need to show proof to the Commission that it's been corrected. If you do this successfully, the Commission will look at your application again, taking the corrected information into account.

5.6. An applicant whose background check reveals a criminal history must provide additional information, which history and information will be reviewed by the Commission. Such applicants must be approved by the Commission in order to be eligible for the examination.

If your background check shows that you have a criminal record, you'll need to give the Commission more details about it. The Commission will look at your criminal history and the extra information you provide. You'll only be allowed to take the real estate exam if the Commission reviews all this and decides to approve your application.

What I don't particularly like about this addendum is it is open ended about what the commission sees as unacceptable or not regarding findings on someone's criminal record.

What I have been told in meetings with the WVREC is that they are looking for criminal behavior in the past that could hurt the public in the present. If your particular case has nothing worrisome to real estate transactions or the overall good of the community, they very likely go on to approve you. I have personally seen many people with minor incidents on their background checks go on to get licensed.

5.7. The Commission may deny licensure to an applicant who fails or refuses to submit to the criminal history records check.

If you don't agree to do the background check or if you start it but don't finish it, the Commission can say no to giving you a license. Basically, if you don't cooperate with the background check process, you might not be able to get your real estate license.

More vague statements in my opinion. Basically, says you could deny being background checked and possibly gain licensure. I highly doubt that reality, but this is written there for some reason and thus here it is.

5.8. The Commission shall maintain confidential records and reports pertaining to criminal record checks in a separate file which is only accessible to personnel authorized by the State Police to receive such records and reports.

The Commission keeps all the information from your background check private. They store these records and reports in a special file that's separate from everything else. Only certain people who have permission from the State Police are allowed to look at these files. This means that not just anyone can see your background check information - it's kept secure and confidential.

5.9. Records received as part of the criminal history record check shall be maintained by the Commission for a period of two (2) years subsequent to the Commission's final action on the application and then disposed of by shredding.

The WVREC will hold these background check results for two years and then destroys them to protect your privacy.

§174-1-6. QUALIFICATIONS FOR BROKER'S LICENSE.

For any of you who jumped in and IMMEDIATELY wanted to become a broker, only to find out that you have to be a salesperson first, these are the exact requirements to moving on to becoming a broker.

6.1 An applicant for a broker's license shall submit evidence satisfactory to the commission of either:

You need to show the commission that you have enough experience. You can do this in one of two ways:

(i) Real estate experience as a licensed real estate salesperson during the two years prior to the date of application showing the applicant's representation of a buyer or seller in a minimum of 10 closed transactions; if the applicant is engaged solely in the leasing or renting of real estate, representation of the landlord or tenant in a minimum of 10 closed transactions of at least one year in duration; or if the applicant is engaged solely in the management of a real estate brokerage company, active involvement in a minimum of 20 closed transactions; or

Option 1: Recent Experience

- **You've been a licensed real estate salesperson for the last two years**
- **During this time, you need to have completed at least 10 deals** where you helped someone buy or sell a house
- If you only do rentals, you need to have helped with 10 leases that lasted at least a year
- If you only manage a real estate company, you need to have been involved in at least 20 completed deals

(ii) regardless of the number of years as a licensed salesperson: a minimum of 20 closed transactions; if the applicant is engaged solely in the leasing or renting of real estate, representation of the landlord or tenant in a minimum of 20 closed transactions of at least one year duration; or if the applicant is engaged solely in the management of a real estate brokerage company, active involvement in a minimum of 30 closed transactions. "Closed transaction" means a transaction that resulted in the real estate being conveyed from seller to buyer in which the applicant represented the seller, buyer, or both, or a transaction that resulted in the consummation of a lease of no less than one year in duration in which the applicant represented either the landlord or tenant of the real estate.

Option 2: More Experience, No Time Limit

- **You've been a licensed salesperson** (doesn't matter for how long)
- **You've completed at least 20 deals** where you helped someone buy or sell a house
- If you only do rentals, you need to have helped with 20 leases that lasted at least a year
- If you only manage a real estate company, you need to have been involved in at least 30 completed deals

What counts as a "completed deal"?

- For buying and selling: When the property actually changes hands from the seller to the buyer, and you represented either the buyer, the seller, or both
- For rentals: When a lease of at least one year is signed, and you represented either the landlord or the tenant

Remember, **you need to provide proof of this experience that satisfies the commission's requirements.** This could be things like transaction records or other documentation showing your involvement in these deals. The next page goes over what qualifies as proper documentation of what you have done.

6.2. Written documentation of experience. -- In order for the Commission to determine the experience of an applicant or a broker's license, the applicant shall submit, on forms prescribed by the Commission, a complete list of all the real estate transactions in which the applicant has been involved. The information submitted must, at a minimum, cover a two year period prior to the date of application.

Here is how you prove what's required in 6.1

1. **Paperwork:** The Commission (the group that decides if you can be a broker) has special forms for you to fill out.

2. **List of Deals:** On these forms, you need to write down all the real estate deals you've been involved in. This includes houses you've helped people buy or sell, or apartments you've helped people rent.

3. **Time Period:** You need to include information about your deals for at least the last two years before you apply. If you've been working in real estate longer than that, you can include more, but you must cover at least the last two years.

4. **Details:** Make sure you include all the important information about each deal. The Commission wants to see that you really know what you're doing.

5. **Be Thorough:** Don't leave anything out! The more complete your list is, the better chance you have of showing the Commission that you're ready to be a broker.

If you're like me, you hate paperwork. Regardless, make it easy on yourself and keep a running word document, or something similar, to track these transactions as you progress through life and it will be a lot easier later. It's how the Commission figures out if you have enough experience to become a broker. So take your time, be accurate, and include everything you can think of about your real estate work over the past couple of years.

6.3. Broker Recommendation. -- Each and every responsible broker who has engaged or employed a salesperson applying for a broker's license shall furnish the Commission with an affidavit attesting to the applicant's experience and qualifications. Each such broker shall submit the affidavit on a form prescribed by the Commission. If a former responsible broker is deceased or for other good cause cannot submit the affidavit, the broker applicant may apply for a waiver of this requirement on the form prescribed by the Commission.

When you're trying to become a real estate broker, you need a recommendation from your boss (or bosses). Here's how it works:

1. **Boss's Recommendation:** Every broker you've worked for as a salesperson needs to write a recommendation for you.
2. **Official Form:** The Commission (the group that decides if you can be a broker) has a special form for this. Your bosses need to use this form.
3. **What's in the Recommendation:** Your bosses will write about your experience and skills. They're basically saying, "Yes, this person knows what they're doing and is ready to be a broker."
4. **Sworn Statement:** This recommendation is called an "affidavit." That means your bosses are swearing that what they're saying is true.
5. **Multiple Bosses:** If you've worked for more than one broker, you need a recommendation from each of them.
6. **What if You Can't Get a Recommendation:** Sometimes, you might not be able to get a recommendation from a former boss. Maybe they've passed away, or there's another good reason. If this happens, you can ask the Commission to waive (skip) this requirement. There's a special form for this too.

Probably a good idea to not have an awkward history of salesperson experiences with your broker if you seek this type of path. These recommendations are really important. They show the Commission that experienced brokers think you're ready for the job.

6.4. Education. An applicant for a broker's license shall submit satisfactory evidence of having completed the following:

6.4.1 Applicants for a broker's license shall provide evidence satisfactory to the commission that he or she has completed at least 180 clock-hours, equivalent to 12 college semester credit hours, in a course or courses approved by the commission: Provided, That an applicant for a broker's license who holds a salesperson's license in this state shall be required to provide evidence that he or she has completed an additional 90 clock-hours, equivalent to six college semester hours, in a course or courses approved by the commission.

6.4.2. Applicants for a salesperson's license shall provide evidence satisfactory to the commission that he or she has completed 90 clock-hours, equivalent to six college semester credit hours, in a course or courses approved by the commission.

6.4.3. Any course required by subsection (a) or (b) of this section shall have been completed during the three-year period preceding the date of application in order to be accepted by the commission.

If you want to become a real estate broker, you need to show that you've completed some education. Here's what you need to know:

For Broker's License:

Total Hours: You need to complete 180 hours of approved real estate courses. This is about the same as taking 12 college credit hours. (Usually three college classes)

Already a Salesperson?: If you're already a licensed salesperson in West Virginia, you only need to do an extra 90 hours (about 6 college credit hours) on top of what you did to become a salesperson.

For Salesperson's License:

If you're just starting out and want to be a salesperson, you need to complete 90 hours of approved courses. This is about the same as taking 6 college credit hours. (Usually two college classes)

Important Points for Both:

- Approved Courses: You can't just take any classes. They have to be courses that the real estate commission has approved.
- Time Limit: Here's a crucial detail - you need to have finished these courses within the last three years before you apply. So if you took the classes four years ago, they won't count.
- Proof: You'll need to show evidence that you've completed these courses. This could be certificates, transcripts, or other official documents.

Remember, education is a big part of getting your license. It helps make sure you know what you're doing in the real estate world. Make sure you are getting an approved class when you take it! Every class sold on the internet or around your hometown might not be formally approved. If it is not approved, it does not count. Spruce School of Real Estate has been approved with the WVREC since 1992!!! They are trusted and have a proven track record. Take your classes from Spruce School of Real Estate and you know you're in good hands!

6.5. Examination. An applicant for a broker's license shall pass the examination or examinations provided by the commission

No brainer moment:

Just like before when we discussed the salesperson exam, passing the brokers exam is also necessary in order to gain your brokers license.

§174-1-7. LICENSING BASED ON LICENSURE IN ANOTHER JURISDICTION.

7.1. The commission may recognize a valid license issued by another jurisdiction as satisfactorily qualifying an applicant who is licensed to practice real estate brokerage in another jurisdiction to obtain a comparable license in this state:

Provided, That the applicant has qualified for license in another jurisdiction by examination and by complying with all the provisions for obtaining a license in that jurisdiction and the jurisdiction affords the same privilege to licensees of this state.

You wouldn't believe how many times I'm asked "what states accept our license?" or "what states have a reciprocal agreement (reciprocity) with West Virginia?"

The short answer is "I don't know," which is NOT good of an authority on real estate! But here is why I don't know. It's a lengthy reason. It depends on the other states' acceptance of WV, which is an ever-changing state law across 49 other different states' legislature and their real estate commissions. So the real answer is "it depends." It depends on them. It seems childish and a potentially vicious circle of "if they do, I do," but that's the short answer. The rest of this explains the long answer

Imagine you're already a licensed real estate salesperson in one state, and you want to work in a different state. Here's how that might work:

1. License Recognition: The real estate commission in the new state might say, "Hey, we see you're already licensed in another state. That's cool, we might be able to use that."

2. Comparable License: If your current license matches up with what they offer in the new state, they might let you get a similar license there without starting from scratch.

But there are some conditions:

1. Exam Requirement: You need to have passed an exam to get your current license. They won't accept licenses that were just handed out.

2. Following the Rules: You must have followed all the rules and met all the requirements in your current state to get your license.

3. Fair Play: Here's the tricky part - the state where you're currently licensed needs to offer the same deal to people from the new state. It's like a "you scratch my back, I'll scratch yours" situation between states.

So, in simple terms, if you're a licensed salesperson in one state and want to work in another, you might be able to transfer your license if:

- You passed an exam for your current license
- You met all the requirements in your current state
- Your current state would do the same for brokers from the new state

This process can save you time and effort if you're moving or want to work across state lines. But remember, each state has its own rules, so always check with the new state's real estate commission for the exact details.

All of that said, I personally don't like the vague way this is phrased in law. It is written very open-ended and will be constantly changing because of this. Perhaps that's why they did that? Regardless, the state of WV basically takes a stance that if the other states commission is cool, then the state of WV will be cool back. I will go out on a limb here and say that during meetings with the commission they have said the states that are currently NOT cool. and that is Kentucky. This changes all the time. Used to be three states that "weren't cool".

Fill in your giggles of states that aren't cool but when we're dealing with real estate commissions apparently the list is short, and its currently Kentucky. I'm sure this will change numerous times as this book goes to be published.

I will update this as needed so take these few statements with a grain of salt, as it does change so pay attention to the age of the revision you are reading before you go quoting me and always check with the commissions of each state first, as they are the authority on the matter.

7.2. In order to obtain a license based on licensure in another jurisdiction, the applicant shall:

If you already have a real estate license in another state and want one here in WV here's what you need to do:

7.2.a. Submit the application on a form prescribed by the commission and fee, if any;

1 **Fill out an application:** You'll need to complete a form that the real estate commission provides. There might be a fee for this, so be prepared to pay if needed.

7.2.b. Pass the West Virginia state law portion of the licensure examination approved by the commission;

2 **Take the state portion of the test:** You'll have to pass a test about West Virginia's real estate laws. This is to make sure you understand how things work in this specific state.

7.2.c. Submit a certification of licensure showing that the applicant possesses an active license to practice real estate brokerage in another jurisdiction;

3 **Prove you have a license elsewhere:** You need to show that you have an active real estate license in another state. This proves you already know the basics of real estate.

7.2.d. Submit record(s) showing all disciplinary actions imposed against the applicant by any jurisdiction in which the applicant holds or held a license, if any; and

4 **Be honest about your past:** If you've ever gotten in trouble with your real estate license before, you need to tell them about it. They want to know about any disciplinary actions from other states.

7.2.e. For non-resident applicants, submit an irrevocable written designation that appoints the executive director of the commission to act as the non-resident licensee's agent, upon whom all judicial and other process or legal notices directed to the licensee may be served. The designation shall stipulate and agree that service upon the executive director is equivalent to personal service upon the licensee. A copy of the designation of appointment, certified by the seal of the commission, may be admitted into evidence with the same force and affect as the original. The executive director shall mail a copy of any process or legal notice immediately upon receipt, by certified mail, to the last known business address of the licensee. No judgment by default may be taken in any action or proceeding until after 30 days of mailing and then only upon certification by the executive director that a copy of the judicial, other process or legal notice was mailed as required.

Extra step for out-of-state applicants: If you don't live in West Virginia, you need to agree to let the head of the real estate commission receive legal papers for you. This means if someone needs to sue you or send you official documents, they can send them to this person instead of trying to track you down out of state. Don't worry - they'll mail you a copy of anything they receive.

The last part is just saying that if someone does sue you, they can't win automatically (called a "default judgment") until at least 30 days after the commission sends you the legal papers. This gives you time to respond to any legal issues.

Remember, this process is designed to make sure that real estate agents from other states meet West Virginia's standards before they can work there. It's all about protecting consumers and maintaining professional standards in the real estate industry.

7.3. The license status for every state in which the nonresident applicant was licensed or is currently licensed shall be evidenced by a certification of licensure obtained from the regulatory body of each state of licensure within 60 days prior to submitting an application for a license in West Virginia.

Here's what this rule is saying:

1. **You need to prove your license status:** The West Virginia real estate commission wants to know about your real estate career in other states.

2. **Show your history:** This includes both states where you used to have a license and states where you currently have one.

3. **Get official proof:** You can't just tell them about your licenses. You need to get an official document called a "certification of licensure" from each state where you've been licensed.

4. **It needs to be recent:** These certifications can't be old. They need to be obtained within 60 days before you submit your application to West Virginia.

5. **Every state counts:** If you've been licensed in multiple states, you need to get this certification from each one of them.

Basically, West Virginia wants to make sure you're in good standing as a real estate professional. They're asking for recent, official proof of your license status from every state you've worked in. This helps them verify your experience and check if you've had any issues in other states before they give you a license to work in West Virginia.

One of the main things to highlight from these particular rules is that this proof can't be attained at any time. Has to be within 60 days of application here in WV.

7.4. Applicants seeking a salesperson or broker license based on licensure in another jurisdiction, at a minimum the certification of licensure from each state shall show:

Yet again, more redundancy on the outline of things you must have when applying for a WV license when you have a license elsewhere.

When you apply, you need to get a document called a "**certification of licensure**" from each state where you've been licensed. This document needs to include:

7.4.a. Name and address of the licensee;

1. **Your basics:** Your name and address. Pretty straightforward, right?

7.4.b. Status of license (current, active, inactive, renewed, expired, etc.);

2. **License status:** Is your license currently active? Inactive? Expired? They want to know the current situation.

7.4.c. Type of license (salesperson, broker, associate broker);

3. **Type of license:** Are you a salesperson, broker, or associate broker? Each has different responsibilities and qualifications.

7.4.d. Date of initial license and expiration date;

4. **Important dates:** When did you first get your license, and when does it expire?

7.4.e. Period of time the license has been active and inactive;

5. **Active vs. Inactive time:** How long has your license been active? Has it ever been inactive, and for how long?

7.4.f. The way the license was obtained (by examination or by reciprocity);

6. **How you got it:** Did you take an exam to get your license, or did you get it through reciprocity (which means another state recognized your existing license)?

7.4.g. Type of examination(s) -- national and state or only state; 7.4.h. Record of any disciplinary actions against the licensee; and

7. **Exam details:** If you took an exam, was it just for that state, or did it include a national portion too?
8. **Any trouble?**: They want to know if you've ever been disciplined or had any issues with your license.

7.4.h. Any additional information the Commission may require.

9. **Extra info:** The commission might ask for additional information if they need it.

Think of this like a detailed report card for your real estate career. West Virginia wants to see your full history as a real estate professional before they decide to give you a license. They're checking to make sure you're qualified and have a good track record.

This helps protect consumers and maintains high standards in the real estate industry. It's a way for West Virginia to say, "Hey, we trust that you know what you're doing because we can see your experience and good standing in other states."

7.5. Applicants may apply only for the same level of license as the one they obtained by examination in their state of initial licensure.	You can't test for your brokers license in WV if you just have a salesperson license elsewhere. The same license type is what is honored. Salesperson license gets another salesperson license. Brokers can get another brokers license.
7.6. West Virginia-specific examination.	This all is basically regurgitating the same info we read about in 4.3 a few pages earlier.
7.6.a. Applicants are required to pass the state-specific portion of the licensing examinations for salesperson or broker.	You will have to pass the exam (In this case the state portion and not both the state and national portion like an unlicensed person)
7.6.b. An examination fee shall be paid for each scheduled examination unless the applicant reschedules in accordance with the policies of the examiner provider.	You will have to pay for the exam.
7.6.c. Applicants who fail the state-specific examination may retake it by following the procedures set forth in Section 4.3 of this rule.	If you fail the exam you follow the same rules as retaking it as an unlicensed person does, which are explained in 4.3.
7.7. Applicants under this section must submit a complete application and pay the required license fee within three (3) months of passing the exam(s).	This is the same as an unlicensed person taking the exam as well. If you do not pay the licensing fee after passing the exam you will have to retake the test again. No bueno. Pay the fee within 90 days or suffer the consequences.

§174-1-8. RENEWAL OF LICENSE; CONTINUING EDUCATION REQUIREMENT; LATE FEES; FAILURE TO RENEW; CANCELLATION.

8.1. Expiration; duty to renew. -- All licenses expire on June 30 regardless of the date the license was issued. It is the duty of all licensees to renew their licenses by paying the renewal fee for a license as set forth in Series 2 of these rules.

Expiring June 30th needs tattoed on you. This calendar year will forever be used and is massively worth remembering.

Imagine your real estate license is like a yearly subscription to your favorite streaming service. Here's what you need to know:

1. **Expiration date:** All real estate licenses in West Virginia expire on June 30th. It doesn't matter when you got your license - whether it was in July or May - they all end on the same day. The WVREC opens up their online renewal usually two months prior to this expiration date so you have plenty of time and can avoid glitches in website operation etc.

2. **Your responsibility:** It's up to you to renew your license. The state won't do it for you automatically.

3. **How to renew:** To keep your license active, you need to pay a renewal fee. It's like renewing your subscription to keep watching your shows.

4. **Where to find the fee:** The exact amount you need to pay is listed in another document called "Series 2" of the rules. You'll need to check that to see how much it costs and you can imagine this changes often.

5. **Why it matters:** If you don't renew, your license will expire, and you won't be able to work as a real estate professional legally.

Think of it like this: June 30th is the "New Year's Eve" for all real estate licenses in West Virginia. Everyone's license "clock" resets on July 1st, and you need to pay to keep your license going for another year.

It's extremely important to remember this date and make sure you renew on time. Set a reminder on your phone or mark it on your calendar. You don't want to accidentally let your license expire and have to go through the hassle of getting a new one!

8.2. Late fees. -- Upon payment of the appropriate renewal and late fees set forth in Series 2 of the Commission's rules, an expired license may be renewed on or before December 31 of the year in which the license expired. In addition to payment of a late fee, licensees who continue to practice while his or her license is expired, and brokers who accept the services of a licensee while that licensee's license is expired, may also be subject to disciplinary action by the commission.

Imagine you forgot to renew your driver's license on time. It's kind of like that, but for your real estate license. Here's what you need to know:

1. **Grace period:** If you miss the June 30th deadline, don't panic! You have until December 31st of the same year to renew your expired license.

2. **Extra costs:** But here's the catch - you'll have to pay more than just the regular renewal fee. There's also a late fee. It's like a penalty for being tardy.

3. **Where to find the fees:** The exact amounts for the renewal and late fees are listed later in what is called "Series 2." Which is part of this Title 174 (Commission's rules) and just a few pages away.

4. **Don't work with an expired license:** This is super important! If you keep working as a real estate agent after your license ex pires, you could get in big trouble. It's like driving with an expired driver's license - not a good idea!

5. **Brokers, watch out:** If you're a broker, and you let someone with an expired license work for you, you could also get in trouble.

6. **Consequences:** If you break these rules, the real estate commission might take disciplinary action against you. This could mean fines, suspension, or even losing your license altogether.

The main takeaway here is: try your best to renew on time (by June 30th). But if you mess up, you have a second chance until December 31st. Just be prepared to pay extra, and whatever you do, don't keep working with an expired license. It's not worth the risk!

Remember, being a professional means staying on top of these important deadlines. Set reminders, mark your calendar, do whatever you need to do to keep your license current and avoid these headaches!

8.3. Failure to renew; cancellation; examination required. -- The license of any licensee who does not renew his or her license on or before December 31 of the year in which the license expired shall be cancelled and the licensee shall be required to comply with all the requirements for obtaining a new license, including the examination requirement.

Imagine your real estate license is like a video game character. If you don't "recharge" it (renew it) in time, it's game over. Here's what this rule is saying:

1. **Last chance deadline:** December 31st is your absolute final opportunity to renew your expired license.

2. **What happens if you miss it**: If you don't renew by December 31st, your license gets cancelled. It's like your character in the game dying - game over!

3. **Starting from scratch:** If your license gets cancelled, you can't just pay a fee to bring it back to life. You have to go through the whole process of getting a new license, just like you did the first time.

4. **Back to school:** This is the worst penalty if you ask me and I'm not kidding. This means you'll have to take the real estate exam again. Yep, you'll need to study and pass that test one more time.

5. **Other requirements:** You'll also need to complete all the other steps for getting a new license, which might include things like background checks, education courses, and application fees.

The main point here is: don't let it get to this stage! It's much easier (and cheaper) to renew your license on time or even during the late period than to have to start all over again.

Think of it this way: June 30th is your first alarm clock, December 31st is your final snooze button. If you sleep through both, you're late for work and have to reapply for your job!

So, set those reminders, mark those calendars, and make sure you renew your license well before these deadlines. It'll save you a lot of time, money, and headaches in the long run!

8.4. Continuing education. -- Each licensee applying for the renewal of his or her license on active status shall complete seven

(7) hours of instruction in an approved real estate course for each year covered by the term of the previous license. It is the responsibility of the broker to confirm that all licensees under his or her supervision comply with this requirement prior to the submission of their license renewal application.

Imagine you're playing a video game where your character needs to level up regularly to keep playing. That's kind of like what's happening here with your real estate license. Here's the deal:

1. **Keeping your skills sharp:** To keep your real estate license active, you need to take some classes every year. It's like leveling up your character's skills in the game.

2. **How much learning?**: You need to complete 7 hours of approved real estate courses for each year your license was active.

3. **Approved courses:** You can't just take any class. It has to be a course that's approved for real estate education. Think of it like using the right power-ups in your game.

4. **Your responsibility:** It's up to you to make sure you complete these courses. Don't expect someone to remind you!

5. **Boss check**: If you work under a broker (think of them as your team leader), they're supposed to double-check that you've done your courses before they submit your license renewal application.

6. **Why it matters:** This continuing education keeps you up-to-date with the latest in real estate. It's like getting the newest upgrades for your game character.

The main point here is: to keep your real estate license active, you need to keep learning. It's not just a one-and-done deal when you first get your license. You need to stay on top of your game by taking these courses every year.

Pro tip: Don't wait until the last minute to do these courses. Spread them out over the year if you can. It's easier to do a little bit at a time than to cram it all in right before your renewal deadline!

Remember, staying educated isn't just about keeping your license. It also makes you better at your job, which can lead to more success in your real estate career. So think of it as an investment in yourself, not just a requirement!

8.5. Exemptions.

8.5.a. Recent Examinees. -- A licensee who qualified for licensure by passing both the national and state licensing examinations is exempt from the continuing education requirement for their first renewal if the licensee renews on or before June 30 of that fiscal year.

8.5.b. Inactive status. -- A licensee on an inactive status is not required to comply with the continuing education requirement. A licensee on an inactive status who desires to be placed on active status must furnish satisfactory evidence to the Commission that he or she has completed the approved continuing professional education that would have been required for active status at the time the license was renewed. The licensee must comply with this requirement prior to being placed on active status.

This is all about exceptions to the continuing education rule we just talked about. Think of it like cheat codes in a video game - they change the normal rules:

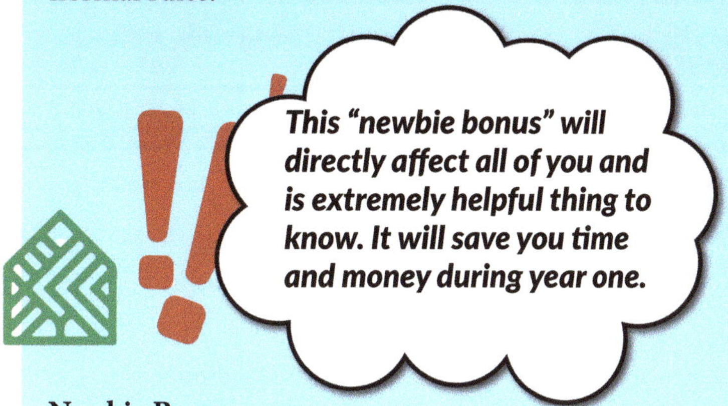

Newbie Bonus:

If you just passed your real estate exams (both national and state), you get a free pass on your first renewal.

But this only works if you renew by June 30 of that year.

It's like getting a "skip level" card in your first round of the game.

Inactive Status:

If your license is inactive (like putting your game character on pause), **you don't need to do the continuing education.**

But if you want to go back to active status, you'll need to catch up on all the education you missed.

It's like if you paused your game for a while - when you come back, you need to complete all the levels you skipped before you can play new ones.

8.5.c. Non-resident licensees. -- Non-resident licensees must comply with the continuing education requirement. However, if the non-resident's jurisdiction has a comparable continuing education requirement and recognizes West Virginia continuing education credits as fulfilling that jurisdiction's continuing education requirement, the Commission will accept continuing education credits earned in the other jurisdiction.

Out-of-State Players:

If you're licensed in West Virginia but live in another state, you still need to do continuing education.

1 But here's the cool part: if your home state has similar education requirements and accepts West Virginia's courses, West Virginia will accept your home state's courses too.

It's like if you're playing a game on a different console, but the achievements still count on your main account.

The main points to remember:

- New licensees get a one-time break on their first renewal.
- If you're inactive, you don't need to do the education, but you'll have to catch up if you want to go active again.
- Out-of-state licensees might be able to use their home state's education courses, but only if there's a reciprocal agreement.

These exceptions can save you time and effort, but make sure you qualify before you try to use them. It's always best to check with the real estate commission if you're not sure about your specific situation. Stay on top of these rules, and you'll keep your real estate career running smoothly!

8.6. The courses taken to satisfy the then-current continuing education requirement shall not be the same as courses taken for the previous license renewal.

You can't just keep retaking the same CE year after year. It has to be a different approved one.

Pro Tip: However, this is more of a lazy tip rather than bettering yourself tip. You can go back to the same CE after you skip it for a year. This can be a system hack where you probably can get through the CE easier however on a personal level, your job skills aren't growing so much. Use with caution.

8.7. The Commission may audit the continuing education of any licensee, at which time the licensee must provide proof of the continuing education completed for renewal.

You've heard of an IRS audit, correct? Well, the WVREC can request to see the paper trail of your real estate things. Keep your records. You're supposed to file these CE completions with your broker anyway but just to be safe keep a record for yourself as well.

The continuing education providers all issue certificates for completing their courses and most likely you have a record of them on your "ce-broker" account as well (This is a free online subscription the WVREC requires us (real estate salespeople) to have now that keeps our records orderly). You will find out a lot more about cebroker as your career moves along. If you want to go the extra mile, keep it in a special folder on your PC and back it up every now and then.

§174-1-9. LICENSE CERTIFICATES: ISSUANCE, CANCELLATION AND TRANSFER.

9.1 License certificate. -- The Commission shall issue to each licensee a license certificate in such form and size as shall be prescribed by the Commission. Each license certificate shall include the name of the brokerage for which the licensee is authorized to conduct real estate transactions and such additional information as may be deemed necessary by the Commission or required by law.

Imagine you've just leveled up in a video game and you get a cool badge to show off. That's kind of like what's happening here with your real estate license certificate. Here's the deal:

1. **Your official badge:** When you become a licensed real estate professional, the Commission (think of them as the game developers) gives you an official license certificate.

2. **Custom design:** The Commission decides what this certificate looks like and how big it is. It's like they're designing a unique badge for real estate pros.

3. **Your team name:** The certificate will show the name of the brokerage you work for. It's like displaying your team name on your player profile.

4. **Extra info:** The Commission might add other details they think are important or that are required by law. This could be things like your license number or the type of license you have.

5. **Proof of your skills:** This certificate is your official proof that you're allowed to do real estate work. It's like having a special pass that lets you play in the big leagues.

9.2. Inactive status. -- License certificates shall reflect when a license had been placed on inactive status, and all licenses on inactive status shall be maintained in the custody and control of the Commission.

You may or may not remember earlier in the law code it was stated that your broker held your license and that you never actually did. This is significant because it's an easy test question that some might not think of. As in, can you hang that thing you worked really hard for on your office wall at home? And the answer is no. Why? Because your broker has it on their office wall, or filing book, etc.

This takes it a step further and says that even when you go inactive you still don't get the license! They really don't like our grubby hands on these things apparently. The license gets sent back to the WVREC for them to hold while you are in inactive status. Again, an easy test question for them to catch you off guard if you haven't read this book!

9.3. Custody and return of inactive license certificates. -- The responsible broker shall maintain in his or her custody and control the active license certificates of each salesperson and associate broker. Upon the separation of a licensee from the current responsible broker, the responsible broker shall immediately return the license certificate to the Commission for appropriate action and notify the salesperson or associate broker of same.

Here's other test question material I have historically heard has made it on the test. They can ask a lot about the order of these events to try and trick you.

Imagine you're playing a team-based video game, and your team captain holds onto everyone's player cards. That's kind of what's happening here with real estate licenses. Here's the deal:

1. **Team Captain's Job:** The responsible broker (think of them as your team captain) is in charge of keeping all the active license certificates for their team members (salespeople and associate brokers).

2. **Safekeeping:** It's the broker's job to make sure these certificates are safe and accounted for. It's like they're holding onto your player ID cards.

3. **When Someone Leaves the Team:** If a salesperson or associate broker decides to leave or gets kicked off the team (separates from the broker), the broker has two important tasks:

a) Return the License: The broker must immediately send the license certificate **back to the Commission.**

b) Notify the Player: The broker also must let the salesperson or associate broker know that they've sent the license back.

Why It Matters: This process helps keep everything official and above board. It prevents people from using licenses they shouldn't be using anymore.

The main point here is that your broker is responsible for your license certificate while you're working with them. But if you stop working together, they have to give it back to the official authorities right away and let you know they've done so.

This system helps maintain order in the real estate world. It ensures that only active, properly affiliated agents have their licenses in use. It's a way of keeping track of who's allowed to play in the real estate game and with which team.

9.4. Change of responsible broker by salesperson or associate. -- In the event a salesperson or associate broker seeks to transfer from his or her current responsible broker to another responsible broker, he or she must first notify his or her current responsible broker in writing, submit a properly executed application for change of responsible broker on the form prescribed by the Commission, and pay the fee set forth in Series 2 of the Commission's rules.

CHANGE

BROKER

Here is another rather big one as far as real world application. A lot of you will change brokers over time if one doesn't fit you at first. Make note of these not only for the exam but because they clearly lay out the steps you need to take to change brokers.

Imagine you're playing for a sports team, and you want to switch to a different team. In the real estate world, it's kind of like that when you want to change brokers. Here's what you need to do:

1. **Tell your current coach:** First things first, you need to let your current broker (think of them as your team coach) know that you're planning to leave. You can't just ghost them - you have to tell them in writing. It's like giving your coach a formal resignation letter.

2. **Fill out the transfer form:** The real estate commission (think of them as the league officials) has a special form for when you want to switch teams. You need to fill this out correctly. It's like filling out official transfer papers in sports.

3. **Pay the transfer fee:** Just like there might be a fee to switch teams in a sports league, there's a fee to change brokers in real estate. The exact amount is listed in another document called "Series 2" of the Commission's rules.

4. **Wait for approval:** After you've done all this, you need to wait for the Commission to approve your transfer before you can start working with your new broker.

The main points to remember are:

- You can't just quietly slip away from your current broker. You need to formally notify them.
- There's official paperwork involved - make sure you fill it out correctly.
- There's a fee for making this change.
- Everything needs to be approved before you can start with your new broker.

This process helps keep everything official and above board. It ensures that everyone (your old broker, your new broker, and the Commission) knows what's happening and agrees to the change.

9.5. Sworn statement by new broker. -- In the event a salesperson or associate broker makes an application for change of responsible broker, the application shall include a sworn statement by the new responsible broker confirming the transfer.

This rule is also going over the same topic as above. So let's stick with the sports analogy. This is to make sure your new coach officially welcomes you to the team. Here's what it means:

1. **New team confirmation:** When you're trying to change from one real estate broker to another, it's not just about you saying you want to switch.

2. **Your new boss has to speak up:** The broker you want to work with (your new boss) has to make an official statement.

3. **It's a big deal:** This statement isn't just a casual "yeah, they can work here." It's a sworn statement, which means it's super serious and official.

4. **What's in the statement:** The new broker is basically saying, "Yes, I confirm that this person is transferring to work with me."

5. **It's part of your application:** This statement from your new broker needs to be included with your application to change brokers.

Why is this important?

- It proves that your new broker actually wants you on their team.
- It helps prevent any misunderstandings or false claims about where you're going to work.
- It makes the whole process more official and legitimate.

Think of it like this: If you were joining a new sports team, you'd want the coach to publicly say, "Yes, this player is joining our team." That's what's happening here, but in the real estate world.

The main point is that changing brokers isn't just about you deciding to move. Your new broker has to officially confirm that they're taking you on. It's a two-way street, and this rule makes sure both sides are on the same page.

Remember, in the professional world, especially in real estate, everything needs to be official and above board. This rule helps make sure that happens when you're making a big career move like changing brokers.

9.6. Change of licensee contact information. - Each licensee shall notify the Commission in writing of any change in name, personal address, and phone and email address of record within thirty (30) days of the change or prior to June 30, whichever comes first. A change of name must be submitted on the form prescribed by the Commission and accompanied with the fee set forth in Series 2 of the Commission's rules.

Imagine you're part of a big group chat for a game you play, and the admins need to be able to reach you. This rule is kind of like that, but for real estate. Here's what it means:

1. **Keep your info up-to-date:** If anything about your contact info changes, you need to let the Real Estate Commission know. This includes:

- Your name
- Where you live
- Your phone number
- Your email address

2. **Don't wait too long:** You've got to tell them about these changes pretty quickly. You have two deadlines to remember:

- Within 30 days of the change, OR
- Before June 30 (whichever comes first)

3. **Name changes are special:** If you're changing your name (maybe you got married or divorced), there's a bit more to do:

- You need to fill out a special form that the Commission provides
- You'll have to pay a fee (the amount is listed in another document called "Series 2" of the Commission's rules)

Why is this important?

- The Commission needs to be able to reach you if there's important info about your license
- It keeps everything official and up-to-date in their records
- It helps prevent any mix-ups or missed communications

Keep your email current with the WVREC or else how can they reach you!?

Think of it like updating your profile in a game or social media. You want people to be able to find and contact you easily, right? It's the same idea here, but for your professional real estate life.

The main point is: Keep the Commission in the loop about how to reach you. Don't ghost them! If anything changes, let them know ASAP. It's part of being a responsible professional in the real estate world.

Remember, staying on top of these little administrative tasks can save you big headaches down the road. It's all part of managing your real estate career like a pro!

Pro tip: It might not come as common routine to always let the WVREC know things like email address changes, but they really do need to know if you're going to stay informed and keep on track for holding your license. If you ditch an old email, be sure to update your new one with the WVREC so you're not surprised when you don't get an extremely important notification.

§174-1-10. SPECIAL PROVISIONS FOR BROKERS.

10.1. Designated broker. -- To be designated as a broker for a partnership, association, corporation, or other form of business organization, the governing body of the business organization must execute a subordination resolution which grants full authority to the partner/member/officer acting as the broker for the business organization. The subordination resolution must be submitted on a form prescribed by the Commission and be sworn to and notarized.

This rule is for real estate companies and assigning the companies (broker), not salespeople. Here's what it means:

1. **Picking a team leader:** A real estate company (like a partnership or corporation) needs to choose one person to be their main broker. This person is called the "designated broker."

2. **Giving them power:** The company can't just casually say, "Yeah, that's our leader." They need to make it official and give this person real authority.

3. **Official paperwork:** The company has to fill out a special form called a "subordination resolution." Think of it like a power-up card in a game that gives one player special abilities.

4. **What's in this form?**: This form basically says, "We're giving this person full authority to act as our broker." It's like telling everyone, "When this person speaks, it's like the whole company is speaking."

5. **Making it official:** This isn't just any form. It needs to be:

- Sworn to (which means they're promising it's true)
- Notarized (a special official has to witness and stamp it)

6. **Using the right form:** The real estate commission provides a specific form for this. You can't just write it on a napkin or make up your own form.

Why is this important?

- It makes it clear who's in charge of the real estate side of the business
- It gives one person the power to make decisions for the whole company in real estate matters
- It helps prevent confusion about who has the authority to do what

The main point is: When a company wants to do real estate business, they need to officially choose one person to be their main broker and give them full authority. This process needs to be done formally and officially to make sure everyone's on the same page.

10.2. Broker becoming licensed salesperson. -- The holder of a broker's license may, during the term of that license, request inactivation of the broker's license and upon filing the appropriate application and payment of the proper fee, be issued a salesperson's license. Under this procedure he or she need not qualify by taking the salesperson's examination. The former broker may reinstate the broker's license at any future date without taking the broker's examination upon filing the appropriate application and fee, as long as the broker applicant is the holder of an active salesperson's license.

Imagine you're playing a video game where you can be either a high-level character (like a boss) or a regular character. In this case, the broker is like the boss, and the salesperson is like the regular character. Here's what this rule is saying:

1. **Switching from boss to regular:**

- If you're a broker (the boss), you can choose to become a salesperson (regular character) if you want.
- You don't have to start the game over or pass any new tests to do this.

2. **How to make the switch:**

- You need to ask to make your broker license inactive (like putting it on pause).
- Fill out some paperwork and pay a fee.
- Then you'll get a salesperson license instead.

3. **No need for a new test:**

- Usually, you'd have to take a test to become a salesperson.
- But since you were already a broker, you get to skip this step. It's like having a free pass.

4. **Keeping your options open:**

- If you ever want to be a broker again, you can!
- You don't have to retake the broker test.
- You just need to fill out some forms and pay a fee.

5. **One important catch:**

- To switch back to being a broker, you need to have an active sales person license.
- It's like needing to maintain a certain level in the game to access the boss character again.

Why is this cool?

- It gives brokers flexibility in their career.
- It allows for easier career moves without losing progress.
- It recognizes that if you were qualified to be a broker, you're qualified to be a salesperson.

The main point is: If you're a broker and want to step back to being a salesperson for a while, you can do that pretty easily. And if you change your mind later, you can go back to being a broker without much hassle. It's all about giving you options in your real estate career!

10.3. Records. -- Every broker shall maintain all records required by the Commission for a minimum of five (5) years. Required records include but are not limited to books, contracts, closing documents, trust account records, and other documents necessary for the Commission to conduct its audits and investigations. These records may be kept in any electronic format that is accessible to the Commission. The records shall be provided to the Commission upon request and shall also be open to inspection by the Commission through its duly authorized representative(s) at the broker's usual place of business and at all times during regular business hours. The broker shall provide sufficient space to permit the Commission's inspection of the records without interference by other users of the property.

This rule is about record keeping.

1 **Keep everything for five years:**

- Brokers need to hang onto all their important paperwork for at least five years.
- It's like keeping all your old videos and contracts, just in case.

2 **What kind of stuff to keep:**

- Books (like financial records)
- Contracts (agreements with clients)
- Closing documents (paperwork from when a sale is completed)
- Trust account records (special accounts for holding client money)
- Basically, anything that shows how you're doing business

3 **Digital is cool:**

- You don't need to have stacks of paper everywhere.
- You can keep these records electronically, like on a computer or in the cloud.
- But make sure the Commission can access them if needed!

4 **Be ready for inspections:**

- The Commission might want to check your records anytime during normal business hours.
- It's like being ready for a surprise visit from YouTube to check if you're following their rules.

5 **Make space for inspections:**

- If the Commission comes to check, you need to give them enough room to look through your stuff.
- Don't make them squeeze into a tiny closet or something!

6 **Hand it over when asked:**

- If the Commission asks for specific records, you need to provide them.
- It's not optional - it's part of the deal of being a broker.

Why is this important?

- It helps keep brokers honest and accountable.
- It protects clients by ensuring there's a paper trail of all transactions.
- It allows the Commission to investigate any issues if they come up.

The main point is: As a broker, you need to be organized with your paperwork. Keep everything important for at least five years, be ready to show it to the Commission if they ask, and make sure they can easily access and review your records.

10.4. Change of address. -- Each broker shall notify the Commission in writing of any change of company address within ten (10) days after the change. The notice shall be made on a form prescribed by the Commission and accompanied by the license certificate and the fee set forth in Section 2 of the Commission's rules. The Commission shall issue a new certificate with the new address.

Imagine you're running a popular online store, and you need to keep your customers updated on where to find you. This rule is kind of like that, but for real estate brokers. Here's what it means:

1. **Moving? Tell the Commission ASAP:**

- If your real estate company changes its address, you've got to let the Real Estate Commission know.
- You've only got 10 days to do this after you move. It's like updating your shipping address, but for your business.

2. **Use the official form:**

- You can't just send a text or an email. The Commission has a specific form you need to fill out.
- It's like using an official change of address form at the post office.

3. **Send in your old license:**

- You need to include your current license certificate when you notify them.
- Think of it like trading in your old ID for a new one with your updated address.

4. **Pay a fee:**

- There's a cost for this change. The exact amount is listed in another document called "Section 2" of the Commission's rules.
- It's like paying for expedited shipping to make sure your new info gets processed quickly.

5. **Get a shiny new certificate:**

- Once you've done all this, the Commission will send you a new license certificate with your updated address.
- It's like getting a new, updated profile for your business.

Why is this important?

- It keeps the Commission's records up-to-date.
- It ensures that important information or notices can reach you.
- It maintains the official record of where you're authorized to do business.

10.5. Notice of payment to co-brokers. -- A broker shall provide written notice to all parties prior to paying a portion of his or her compensation to a broker representing another party to the transaction.

Imagine you're playing a team video game, and you decide to share some of your in-game rewards with a player from another team who helped you win. This rule is kind of like that, but for real estate brokers. Here's what it means:

1. **Sharing the prize:**

- Sometimes in real estate deals, brokers from different companies work together.
- One broker might decide to share some of their commission (their payment) with the other broker.

2. **No secret handshakes:**

- If a broker wants to do this, they can't just quietly slip the other broker some cash under the table.
- They have to tell everyone involved in the deal that they're doing it.

3. **Put it in writing:**

- The broker needs to write down that they're sharing their commission.
- It's like announcing in the game chat that you're sharing your loot with another player.

4. **Tell everyone:**

- This written notice needs to go to all parties in the transaction.
- That means the buyers, sellers, and anyone else officially involved in the deal.

5. **Do it before paying:**

- The broker needs to send out this notice before they actually hand over any money to the other broker.
- It's like announcing your intentions before you actually transfer any in-game items.

Why is this important?

- It keeps everything transparent and honest.
- It prevents any suspicions of secret deals or unfair advantages.
- It helps all parties understand how the money is being distributed.

The main point is: If you're a broker and you want to share your commission with another broker, you need to be upfront about it. Tell everyone involved in writing, before you do it.

10.6. Broker's right to earnest money. -- When for any reason a seller fails, refuses, neglects or is unable to consummate the transaction as provided for in the contract and, through no fault or neglect of the purchaser, the real estate transaction cannot be completed, the broker has no right to any portion of the earnest money paid by the purchaser except by agreement of the parties or by court order.

Imagine you're trying to buy a cool collectible item online, and you put down a deposit to hold it. But then the seller backs out of the deal. This rule is kind of like that, but for real estate. Here's what it means:

1. **The deal falls through:**

- Sometimes, a house sale doesn't work out.
- In this case, it's because the seller can't or won't complete the sale.
- It's like if the person selling that collectible suddenly says, "Oops, can't sell it after all!"

2. **Not the buyer's fault:**

- This rule applies when the buyer (that's you in this scenario) didn't do anything wrong.
- You were ready to buy, but the seller messed things up.

3. **Earnest money:**

- This is like a deposit you put down to show you're serious about buying the house.
- It's similar to paying a bit upfront to reserve that collectible item.

4. **Broker can't keep the money:**

- Even though the deal fell through, the real estate broker (the person helping with the sale) can't just pocket your deposit.
- They don't automatically get to keep any of that earnest money.

5. **How to split the money:**

- The only way the broker can get any of that earnest money is if:
  a) You and the seller both agree to give some to the broker, or
  b) A court decides the broker should get some

Why is this important?

- It protects buyers from losing their deposit unfairly.
- It ensures that brokers don't profit from deals that fall through.
- It keeps the earnest money safe until everyone agrees on what to do with it.

The main point is: If a house sale falls apart because of the seller, and it's not your fault as the buyer, your deposit (earnest money) is protected. The broker can't just keep it – they only get a share if everyone agrees or if a court says so.

Remember, in real estate deals, **your earnest money is meant to show you're serious about buying, not to pay the broker if things go wrong.** This rule helps make sure that money is handled fairly if a deal doesn't work out. It's all about protecting you as a buyer and keeping things fair for everyone involved!

§174-1-11. DECEASED OR INCAPACITATED RESPONSIBLE BROKER.

11.1. In the event of death or other incapacity of the responsible broker:

Imagine you're part of a sports team, and suddenly your coach can't lead the team anymore (maybe they got sick or passed away). This rule is about what happens in a similar situation with real estate brokers. Here's what it means:

11.1.a. Sole proprietor broker. -- The Commission may, in its discretion based upon the specific circumstances, permit an associate broker or a designated salesperson licensed with the sole proprietor broker to complete and close the then-existing business of that broker, including taking contracts then signed to closing, for a temporary period not to exceed six (6) months from the date of Commission approval of a non-broker licensee to serve in that capacity. The sole proprietor's licensees may also transfer to a new broker.

1. **For a solo broker** (sole proprietor):

- If a broker who works alone can't do their job anymore (like if they die or get really sick), the Commission has a plan.
- They might let one of the broker's team members (an associate broker or experienced salesperson) take over temporarily.
- This person can finish up any ongoing deals and close any con tracts that were already signed.
- This temporary arrangement can last up to 6 months.
- The other team members (licensees) can also choose to join a different broker's team if they want.

This is about the death of a broker but it can honestly be applied to many things that all show the importance of the broker. For testing you will see a lot of questions about how you act under your brokers orders and who you work for etc. It is extremely noteworthy to understand the brokers importance and when you can and can't work.

11.1.b. Designated broker. -- The partnership, association, corporation, or other form of business organization, the governing body of the business organization must execute a new subordination resolution which names a successor broker for the business organization. The subordination resolution must be submitted on a form prescribed by the Commission and be sworn to and notarized prior to the transaction of any real estate business.

2. **For a broker who leads a company** (designated broker):

- If this happens to a broker who's in charge of a real estate company, the company needs to act fast.
- They have to officially choose a new leader (successor broker).
- This is done by filling out a special form called a "subordination resolution."
- This form needs to be sworn to (like making a promise) and notarized (made official by a special witness).
- The company can't do any real estate business until they've done this.

Why is this important?

- It ensures that ongoing deals don't fall apart if something happens to the broker.
- It protects the clients who are in the middle of buying or selling property.
- It gives the real estate team a way to keep working even if their leader can't continue.

The main point is: There's a plan in place if something happens to the person in charge of a real estate business. For solo brokers, someone can temporarily take over. For company brokers, the company needs to quickly appoint a new leader.

Remember, in the real estate world, it's crucial to have a backup plan. This rule makes sure that even if something unexpected happens to the broker, the business can continue, and clients aren't left hanging. It's all about being prepared and professional, no matter what happens!

§174-1-12. TRADE AND FRANCHISE NAMES.

12.1. Use of trade or franchise name. -- An individual broker may use a trade name which is the name of the brokerage and not the name of the broker's business organization. Any broker who operates under a trade name must include the trade name in the broker license application and, upon approval by the Commission, the trade name will be placed upon the broker's license certificate in addition to the business organization's name. The trade name shall not be the same as that currently being used by another broker in the same locality unless such restriction is prohibited by law. A broker shall not use any trade name not set forth on the license certificate. The Commission does not require brokers who choose to operate under a franchise agreement to register the name of the franchise organization.

Here's what it means:

1. **Choosing a business name:**

- A broker can use a special name for their business, called a trade name.
- It's like picking a catchy channel name instead of just using your real name.

2. **It's not the company name:**

- This trade name is different from the official name of the broker's company.
- Think of it like having a YouTube channel name that's different from your legal name.

3. **Getting permission:**

- The broker needs to tell the Real Estate Commission about this trade name.
- They put it in their license application, like registering your channel name with YouTube.
- If the Commission says okay, the trade name goes on the broker's official license.

4. **No copycats allowed:**

- You can't use a trade name that another broker in your area is already using.
- It's like not being allowed to use the same channel name as another YouTuber in your city.
- (But sometimes there might be laws that say this rule doesn't apply.)

5. **Stick to what's approved:**

- Brokers can only use trade names that are on their license.
- It's like only being allowed to use the channel name YouTube approved for you.

6 **Franchise names are different:**

- If a broker is part of a big franchise (like being part of a popular YouTube network), they don't have to register that franchise name.
- The Commission doesn't require this extra step for franchise names.

Why is this important?

- It helps brokers create a unique identity for their business.
- It prevents confusion by not allowing multiple brokers to use the same name in the same area.
- It keeps everything official and on record with the Real Estate Commission.

The main point is: Brokers can use a special business name (trade name) if they want, but they need to get it approved and put on their license. They can't just make up names as they go along or copy other brokers' names.

12.2. In the event a broker uses a licensed trade name, the company name required on all advertising must be the trade name which appears on the broker's license.

Here's what it means:

1 You've got a cool business name:

- Let's say you're a broker and you've chosen a catchy trade name for your business.
- You've done it the right way - you've registered it and it's on your official license.

2 Stick to that name in your ads:

- Whenever you make any kind of advertisement, you HAVE to use this official trade name.
- It's like always using your YouTube channel name in your videos, not your real name.

3 No switching it up:

- You can't decide to use a different name just because you think it sounds better for an ad.
- The name on your ads must match the trade name on your license. No exceptions!

4 Consistency is key:

- Whether it's a newspaper ad, a website, a billboard, or a social media post, that official trade name needs to be there.
- It's like using your channel name consistently across all platforms - YouTube, Instagram, TikTok, etc.

Why is this important?

- It prevents confusion: People always know which business they're dealing with.
- It's honest advertising: You're using the name that's officially registered and approved.
- It builds your brand: Consistently using one name helps people remember your business.

The main point is: If you've gone through the trouble of getting an official trade name for your real estate business, you've got to use that exact name in all your advertising. No ifs, ands, or buts!

12.3. Change of trade name. -- Each broker shall notify the Commission in writing of any change in the name of the broker's business organization name or trade name within thirty (30) days of such change. The notice shall be made on a form prescribed by the Commission and accompanied by the license certificate and the fee set forth in Section 2 of the Commission's rules. The Commission shall issue a new certificate with the new trade name.

If you change your business name as a real estate broker, you need to tell the Commission right away using their official process. It's not just about updating your business cards or website - it's about keeping your official records current and accurate

§174-1-13. OFFICE SIGNS.

13.1. Sign requirement. -- All brokers holding an active license shall erect and maintain a sign on or about the entrance of their principal office and each branch office, which shall be easily observed and read by persons about to enter any of the offices. Every sign shall prominently display the name of the broker, the term "Broker" and the company name, if any, all in letters not less than 1 inch in height. If the broker so desires, the names of the salespersons or associate brokers may be placed below the name of the broker.

This is the rule for signage at a real estate office:

1. **Put up a sign:**

- If you're a real estate broker with an active license, you need to have a sign for your office.
- This applies to your main office and any other offices you might have.

2. **Make it easy to spot:**

- The sign needs to be where people can easily see it when they're about to enter your office.
- It's like having your food truck's name and menu clearly visible to customers.

3. **What needs to be on the sign:**

- Your name (the broker's name)
- The word "Broker" (so people know what you do)
- Your company name (if you have one)

4. **Size matters:**

- All these words need to be in big letters - at least 1 inch tall.
- Think of it like using a font size that's easy to read from a distance.

5. **Optional extras:**

- If you want, you can also put the names of your team members (salespersons or associate brokers) on the sign.
- But their names should go below yours.
- It's like listing your food truck crew, but making sure your name as the owner is the most prominent.

Why is this important?

- It helps people find your office easily.
- It clearly shows who's in charge (the broker).
- It makes your business look professional and official.

The main point is: As a real estate broker, you need to have a clear, visible sign that tells people who you are and what you do. It's all about making your business easy to identify and looking professional.

13.2. Brokers who rent desk space in an office. -- A broker who rents desk space within an office and whose own brokerage business is conducted separate from whom the desk space is rented shall maintain a sign on the main entrance door or on a wall or window immediately adjacent to the door, and comply with all other requirements of holding a broker's license.

This rule is for real estate brokers who are renting a space in a larger space. Here's what it means:

1 **Renting a workspace:**

- Some brokers don't have their own office. Instead, they rent a desk in someone else's office.

2 **Running your own show:**

- Even though you're in someone else's space, you're still running your own separate business.

3 **You need your own sign:**

- You can't just rely on the main office's sign. You need your own.
- Think of it like having your own YouTube channel name displayed in the studio, not just the studio's name.

4. **Where to put your sign:**

- You have a few options:

a) On the main entrance door
b) On the wall right next to the door
c) On a window right next to the door

5. **Follow all the other rules:**

- Just because you're renting space doesn't mean you can skip other broker requirements.
- You still need to follow all the rules that apply to brokers with their own offices.

Why is this important?

- It helps clients find you specifically, even in a shared office.
- It shows that you're running your own business, separate from the office you're renting in.
- It keeps everything professional and clear, even in a shared space.

The main point is: If you're a broker renting desk space, you still need to have your own visible sign and follow all the regular broker rules. You're running your own show, even if you're sharing space with others.

§174-1-14. BRANCH OFFICES.

14.1. License required; exception. -- Every licensed broker who desires to conduct brokerage transactions at any location other than his or her principal place of business under the same brokerage name must make application for a branch office license and pay the required fee in order to receive a license certificate for each branch office. A temporary shelter in a subdivision being sold by the broker, for the convenience and protection of licensees, clients and customers and at which transactions are not closed and licensees are not permanently assigned, is not considered to be a branch office. The permanence, use and character of activities conducted at the office or shelter shall determine whether it must be registered.

Imagine you're running a successful food truck business and want to expand. This rule is kind of like that, but for real estate brokers who want to expand with a branch office. Here's what it means:

1. **Main office vs. branch offices:**

- You've got your main food truck (your principal place of business).
- Now you want to set up additional food trucks in different locations (branch offices).

2. **You need a license for each location:**

- For each new "food truck" (branch office), you need to get a special license.
- You can't just open up shop anywhere you want without telling anyone.

3. **How to get the license:**

- You need to apply for each branch office license.
- There's a fee you have to pay for each one.
- Once approved, you'll get a license certificate for each branch.

4. **Using the same brand name:**

- These branch offices will operate under your main business name.
- It's like having multiple food trucks, all with your original brand name.

5. **Exception for temporary setups:**

- Let's say you set up a small stand at a festival to promote your food truck. That's not considered a branch.
- For real estate, if you have a temporary shelter in a new housing development you're selling, just to keep your team and clients comfortable, that's not a branch office.
- These temporary spots aren't where you do all your business or permanently assign your team.

6. **What makes it a branch office?:**

- The Commission looks at how permanent the setup is, how it's used, and what kind of activities happen there.
- If it looks and acts like a full office, it probably needs to be registered as a branch.

Why is this important?

- It helps the Real Estate Commission keep track of where brokers are doing business.
- It ensures that all locations meet professional standards.
- It protects clients by making sure all offices are official and regulated.

The main point is: If you're a broker and want to open additional offices beyond your main one, you need to get them licensed. But don't worry about temporary setups - those usually don't count as full branches.

14.2. Manager of branch office. -- Every broker who obtains a license for a branch office must designate one associate broker or salesperson as manager of each branch office. A broker may act as the manager of a branch office if the broker is capable of adequately supervising all associate brokers and salespersons assigned to that branch office. If the broker chooses to appoint a manager of a branch office, the licensee must be an active licensee and have at least two (2) years actual experience.

Imagine you're running a successful chain of coffee shops. This rule is kind of like that, but for real estate offices. Here's what it means:

1. **Branch office boss:**

- For each new coffee shop (branch office) you open, you need to pick someone to be in charge.
- In real estate terms, this person is called the manager of the branch office.

2. **Who can be the boss?:**

- You have a few options:

  a) An associate broker (like an experienced barista who knows how to run things)

  b) A salesperson (like a skilled coffee shop employee)

  c) You, the main broker (like the owner of the coffee shop chain)

3. **If you want to be the boss:**

- You can manage the branch yourself, but only if you can keep an eye on everyone working there.
- It's like being able to run multiple coffee shops and still make sure each one is doing a good job.

4. **If you pick someone else to be the boss:**

- They need to be actively working in real estate (no picking your retired uncle who used to sell houses).
- They should have at least 2 years of real experience in the field.
- It's like choosing a manager for your new coffee shop who's been making lattes and running shifts for at least a couple of years.

Why is this important?

- It ensures that each branch office has someone responsible and experienced in charge.
- It helps maintain quality and professionalism across all locations.
- It makes sure there's always someone looking out for the team and the clients.

The main point is: When you open a new branch office, you need to put someone in charge who knows what they're doing. Whether it's you or another experienced team member, make sure they're up for the job of running things smoothly.

§174-1-15. TRUST FUNDS AND ACCOUNTS.

15.1. Commingling Prohibited. -- In order to prevent the commingling of trust funds with other funds, brokers are required to deposit all trust funds into one or more trust accounts established in accordance with W. Va. Code §30-40- 18, which accounts may be audited by the Commission through its authorized representative.

A lot of these rules you've already seen by now earlier in this textbook when we went over their establishment in 30-40. Remember Title 174 just adds to, or clarifies points already made in 30-40. Title 174 exists so the WVREC can make modifications more easily. That said:

If you're a broker handling other people's money (like deposits or payments), you need to keep it completely separate from your own money or your business money. Put it in special accounts that are just for client funds.

15.2. Funds received by salesperson or associate broker. -- Every salesperson and associate broker who receives any trust funds shall immediately or by the next business day following receipt pay over or deliver the trust funds to the responsible broker. No salesperson or associate broker shall collect any money in connection with any real estate transaction, whether as a commission, deposit, payment, rental, or otherwise, except in the name of and with the consent of the responsible broker.

If you're a real estate salesperson or associate broker and you receive any money related to your job, you need to give it to your boss (the broker) right away. You can't collect or handle money without your boss knowing and agreeing to it.

"ASAP" here means either right away or by the next business day at the latest.

15.3. Deposit of trust funds. -- Unless otherwise directed or allowed in the signed purchase agreement, every broker who receives any trust funds shall immediately or by the next business day following receipt deposit the trust funds in the broker's trust account.

If you're a broker and someone gives you money that's part of a real estate deal, you need to put it in a special bank account right away. Don't wait around or mix it with other money.

> It's worth note that this handling is by a broker and not the salesperson. Your job as the salesperson is to get it to the broker ASAP, as defined in 15.2.

15.4. Interest bearing trust account. -- Trust funds may be transferred from a non-interest-bearing trust account into an interest-bearing trust account only under the following conditions:

15.4.a. The broker must obtain, from all parties to the transaction, a written agreement which must contain, at a minimum:

15.4.a.1. Authorization to remove the funds from the trust fund account for the express purpose of depositing the funds into an interest-bearing trust fund account;

15.4.a.2. Identification of the financial institution and the type of account to be opened;

15.4.a.3. Identification of who will earn the interest on the funds; and

15.4.a.4. How and when the interest will be disbursed.

15.4.b. No interest, privilege, or other compensation received or obtained by virtue of establishing or maintaining any interest-bearing trust account shall benefit the broker or any other licensee.

15.4.c. Upon closing any interest-bearing trust account established in compliance with this sub- section, the total proceeds of the account must be deposited in the broker's trust fund account prior to any disbursements being made.

Imagine you're running a savings club for your friends. This rule is kind of like that, but for real estate brokers handling other people's money. Here's what it means:

1. **Moving money to earn interest:**

- Sometimes, brokers want to put client money in an account that earns interest.
- It's like moving your friends' savings from a regular piggy bank to one that grows their money.

2. **You need everyone's okay:**

- Before doing this, the broker needs to get written permission from everyone involved in the deal.
- It's like getting all your friends to sign off on moving their savings to a different bank.

3. **What the permission slip needs to say:**

a) "Yes, you can move our money to earn interest."
b) Where exactly the money is going (which bank and what kind of account).
c) Who gets to keep the interest earned.
d) How and when the interest will be paid out.

4. **No personal benefit:**

- The broker (or any other real estate agent) can't keep the interest or get any perks from this account.
- It's like you, as the savings club manager, not being allowed to keep any of the interest your friends' money earns.

5. **Closing the account:**

- When it's time to close this interest-earning account, all the money (including the interest) has to go back into the regular trust account first.
- It's like putting all your friends' savings, plus the extra they earned, back into the main club piggy bank before giving it back.

Why is this important?

- It protects clients' money and ensures transparency.
- It makes sure everyone agrees on how interest is handled.
- It prevents brokers from personally profiting off clients' funds.

The main point is: Brokers can put client money in interest-earning accounts, but they need clear permission, can't benefit personally, and must handle the funds carefully.

15.5. Sweep accounts. -- For brokers with excess funds, which means trust account funds in excess of the amount that is insured against loss by the broker's financial institution, the federal insurance requirement set forth in West Virginia Code §30-40-18(c) may be complied with either through the use of multiple trust accounts at various financial institutions or the use of a cash sweep account established at a financial institution for which a Trust Fund Account Statement and Consent to Examine is on file with this Commission in accordance with the following requirements:

This is directed at real estate brokers handling lots of client money. Here's what it means:

1 **Too much money in one place:**

- Sometimes, brokers end up with a ton of client money in their trust account.
- If it's more than what the bank can insure (protect if something goes wrong), it's called "excess funds."
- It's like having so much lemonade money that it won't all fit in your piggy bank safely.

2 **Keeping the money safe:**

- law (West Virginia Code §30-40-18(c)) says brokers need to make sure all this money is insured..

3 **Two ways to handle it:**

a) Multiple accounts: Open several trust accounts at different banks. It's like having multiple piggy banks at different friends' houses.

b) Use a "sweep account": This is a special type of account that moves money around automatically to keep it safe. Think of it like a robot that takes your extra lemonade money and puts it in different safe spots every night.

4 **If using a sweep account:**

- The broker needs to file some paperwork with the Real Estate Commission.
- This paperwork says it's okay for the Commission to check on this account.
- It's like telling your parents exactly where all your lemonade money is and giving them permission to check on it.

Why is this important?

- It protects large amounts of client money from being lost if a bank fails.
- It helps brokers manage lots of funds safely and efficiently.
- It ensures that the Real Estate Commission can oversee these funds properly.

The main point is: When brokers have more client money than a single bank account can safely hold, they need to spread it out or use a special account to keep it all protected.

15.5.a. Addendum required.

15.5.a.1. An addendum in the form prescribed by the Commission must be signed by the broker and the financial institution and made a part of the Trust Fund Account Statement and Consent to Examine; and

15.5.a.2. A copy of the Addendum must be submitted to the Commission within ten (10) business days of entering into the agreement to establish the cash sweep account.

Imagine you've got a super fancy piggy bank system for your lemonade stand money. This rule is about setting up and using that system. Here's what it means:

1. **Special agreement needed:**

- If you want to use this fancy "sweep account" system, you need to sign a special form.
- Both you (the broker) and the bank need to sign it.
- It's like you and your parents signing a contract about how to handle your lemonade money.

2. **Tell the authorities:**

- You need to send a copy of this agreement to the Real Estate Commission within 10 business days.
- It's like telling your school principal about your new lemonade money system within two weeks.

15.5.b. Ability to advance funds required. The broker's relationship institutions, which are (1) the financial institution where the broker has both a trust fund account and a cash sweep account and (2) the financial institution serving as the custodian of the cash sweep account, must agree to advance funds on any check drawn against the broker's trust fund account for which there are sufficient funds in the cash sweep account unless prohibited by applicable law or court order or they cannot by reason of force majeure or circumstances beyond the relationship banks' control. Inasmuch as the advanced payment is not a loan and the funds in the cash sweep account are not collateral for a loan, the anticipated debit of the funds in the cash sweep account does not breach the broker's fiduciary obligations in relation to the broker's trust fund account and does not violate West Virginia Code §30-40-18(f) and this rule

3 Banks need to play nice:

- You'll be dealing with two banks: one where you keep your regular trust account and the sweep account, and another that watches over the sweep account.
- These banks need to agree to cover your checks if you have enough money in the sweep account.
- It's like your parents agreeing to cover your lemonade stand expenses if you have enough money in your special savings jar.

4 Exceptions to covering checks:

- The banks don't have to cover your checks if:

  a) It's illegal
  b) A court says they can't
  c) Something crazy happens that's out of their control like a natural disaster.

5 It's not a loan:

- When the bank covers your check using money from the sweep account, it's not lending you money.
- It's just moving your own money around.
- This means you're not breaking any rules about borrowing money or using client funds as collateral.

Why is this important?

- It makes sure everyone understands how this fancy money system works.
- It keeps the Real Estate Commission in the loop.
- It ensures that client money is always available when needed, even if it's spread across different accounts.

The main point is: If you want to use this special system for handling lots of client money, you need to set it up properly, tell the authorities, and make sure the banks agree to work together smoothly

.

§174-1-16. AGENCY CONSENT AND DISCLOSURE.

16.1. Agency form required.

-- The notice of agency relationship and consent form prescribed by the Commission discloses the party or parties the licensee is representing to all parties to the real estate transaction. A notice of agency relationship and consent form shall be signed by the licensee and the client at the time the agency relationship is created.- Prior to the initiation of negotiations, each licensee's agency form shall be signed by all parties. The broker shall provide a copy to each person executing an agency form and shall maintain a copy of each signed form in the transaction file. All members of a team must be listed on or attached to any Notice of Agency Relationship form signed by a team member.

It's worth note that THIS CONTENT is literally what the whole NAR settlement and "shakedown of the industry" you have heard about in the news is over:

1 **The "Who's Who" form:**

- There's a special form that says who the real estate agent is working for.
- It's like wearing a team jersey in sports, so everyone knows which side you're on.

2 **Sign it early:**

- The agent and their client (the person they're working for) need to sign this form when they first start working together.
- It's like picking your Monopoly piece before the game starts.

3 **Everyone needs to sign:**

- Before any serious talk about buying or selling starts, all the people involved in the deal need to sign these forms.
- It's like all players agreeing on the rules before rolling the dice.

4 **Copies for everyone:**

- The broker (think of them as the game master) needs to give a copy to everyone who signs.
- They also need to keep a copy for their records.
- It's like everyone getting a rulebook and the game master keeping one too.

5 **Team players:**

- If the agent is part of a team, all team members' names need to be on the form.
- It's like listing all your teammates on the back of your jersey.

Pro tip: Avoid a messy audit. At meetings with the WVREC they stated the importance of having these agreements dated earlier than contract offer dates. No white out or scratching things out

Why is this important?

- It makes sure everyone knows who's working for whom.
- It prevents confusion about whose interests the agent is representing.
- It keeps everything clear and above board from the start.

The main point is: Before any real estate deal gets going, everyone needs to sign a form that clearly shows which agent is working for which person. This helps avoid any misunderstandings later on.

16.2. Dual agency. -- A licensee may not be the agent for both the buyer and the seller without first obtaining the written consent of both the buyer and the seller.

Imagine you're playing a game of basketball, and someone wants to be the referee and a player on both teams at the same time. Sounds tricky, right? This rule is kind of like that, but for real estate agents. Here's what it means:

1 **Two teams:**

- In a real estate deal, you usually have a buyer (someone who wants to buy a house) and a seller (someone who wants to sell a house).
- They're like two different teams in a game.

2 **The referee/player situation:**

- Sometimes, a real estate agent might want to work for both the buyer and the seller in the same deal.
- This is called "dual agency."
- It's like trying to play for both teams and be the referee at the same time.

3 **You can't just do it:**

- An agent can't just decide to work for both sides without asking.
- It's not allowed unless they get special permission.

4 **Getting permission:**

- The agent needs to ask both the buyer and the seller if it's okay.
- And not just ask - they need to get it in writing.
- It's like getting both team captains to sign a form saying they're okay with you playing on both teams.

Why is this important?

- It prevents conflicts of interest.
- It makes sure both the buyer and seller know exactly what's going on.
- It protects everyone's interests in the deal.

The main point is: If a real estate agent wants to work for both the buyer and the seller in the same deal, they need to get written permission from both sides first. They can't just do it on their own.

16.3. Corrected form. -- If change in a licensee's agency status makes an earlier disclosure inaccurate, incomplete or misleading, the licensee shall prepare a corrected form and immediately present it to all parties to the transaction. The corrected form must be dated and must be acknowledged in writing by all parties.

What if there was an error on the form, you need to change who you represent, or the date was written incorrectly? I mentioned earlier that you couldn't just white out or scratch things out. Here's what you do:

1 **When things change:**

- If the agent's role changes in any way that makes the original form wrong or misleading, they need to fix it.
- It's like realizing your jersey has the wrong number or team name on it.

2 **Make a new form:**

- The agent needs to create a new, corrected form right away.
- Think of it as quickly making a new, accurate jersey.

3 **Tell everyone ASAP:**

- As soon as they make this new form, they need to show it to everyone involved in the deal.
- It's like announcing to both teams that you've switched sides.

4 **Get everyone to sign off:**

- The new form needs to be dated (so everyone knows when the change happened).
- All the people involved need to sign it to show they understand the change.
- It's like getting both team captains to agree that you're now on a different team.

Why is this important?

- It keeps everything honest and up-to-date.
- It makes sure no one is confused about who the agent is working for.
- It protects everyone in the deal from misunderstandings.

The main point is: If anything changes about who the real estate agent is working for, they need to make a new form right away, show it to everyone, and get everyone to agree to the change.

§174-1-17. ADVERTISING.

This area is often overlooked by agents in real life. Let's change that by understanding these things from the law code.

17.1. Advertising of property or specific services. -- Each advertisement shall include the following information: the company name, the name of the responsible broker and the term "Broker," the physical address of a licensed office location, and phone number. The names of associate brokers and salespersons shall not be included in the advertising unless the associate brokers and salespersons are clearly identified as such.

We've all seen the ads around town, on social media, on billboards but have you ever examined the details of what's on there?

1 **The basics that must be on every ad:**

- Company name
- The boss's name: The head broker
- The word "Broker": To show they're legit
- Office address: Where fans can find you
- Phone number: How to contact you

2 **It's all about the boss:**

- The main focus is on the broker (the big boss) and the company.
- This is probably the most confusing, or possibly intentionally ignored part. Us salespeople want recognized and often ignore that we aren't a separate reality from the broker.

3 **Other team members:**

- If you want to include other real estate agents (like associate brokers or salespersons) in the ad, you can.
- But if you do, you need to clearly say what their role is.
- It's like listing your band members on the poster and saying who plays what instrument.

4 **Keep it clear:**

- The point is to make sure people know exactly who they're dealing with.
- No sneaky stuff or confusing info allowed!

Why is this important?

- It helps people know who's really behind the ad.
- It makes sure the main responsible person (the broker) is clearly identified.
- It prevents any confusion about who's offering the service or selling the property.

The main point is: When real estate folks advertise, they need to include specific info about their company and boss. If they mention other team members, they need to be clear about their roles

17.2. Broker supervision. - No salesperson, associate broker or team shall advertise any property under his, her or their own name without the name of the responsible broker. All advertising by an associate broker, salesperson or team must be under the direct supervision of and in the name of the responsible broker. An advertisement for specific property or service by a team is not required to include the name of each team member, or the name of each team member whose photograph may be included in the advertisement, but shall include all of the following information:

17.2.a. The company name, the name of the responsible broker, and the term "Broker" displayed in equal prominence with the team name and with the name of the associate broker or salesperson in the advertisement;

17.2.b. The name of at least one associate broker or salesperson who is a team member, and the term "Associate Broker" or "Salesperson" to identify each associate broker or salesperson whose name is included in the advertisement, as such information appears on his or her license;

Imagine you're in a band, but you're part of a bigger record label. This rule is how you'd advertise your band's gigs.

1. **No solo acts without mentioning the label:**

- Real estate agents (salespersons or associate brokers) can't advertise on their own without mentioning their boss (the responsible broker).
- It's like not being able to promote your band without mentioning your record label.

2. **The boss is always in charge:**

- All ads must be supervised by the main broker and include their name.
- Think of it as your record label approving all your concert posters.

3. **Team ads are special:**

- If you're advertising as a team (like a group of agents working together), you don't have to list every single team member.
- But you do need to include some specific info:

a) The big names:

- Company name (like the record label)
- The boss's name (the main broker)
- The word "Broker"
- These should be as noticeable as the team name and any individual agent names

b) At least one team member:

- Include the name of at least one licensed team member
- Say if they're an "Associate Broker" or "Salesperson"
- It's like mentioning at least one band member and their instrument

17.2.c. The term "Non-Licensed" to identify each team member who does not hold a current valid license and whose name is included in the advertisement; and

17.2.d. Phone number.

c) Non-licensed folks:

- If you mention anyone in the ad who isn't a licensed real estate agent, you have to say they're "Non-Licensed"
- It's like noting which people in your band photo are roadies, not musicians

d) How to reach you:

- Always include a phone number

Why is this important?

- It makes sure people know who's really in charge (the broker).
- It prevents confusion about who's licensed to do what.
- It keeps everything professional and above board.

The main point is: **When real estate agents or teams advertise, they need to make it clear who they work for and who's licensed.** They can't just go off and do their own thing without mentioning their boss.

17.3. Business cards and other promotional items. - Advertising which is not for a specific property or service must include the licensee name, company name and contact information.

When real estate agents are promoting themselves in general (not a specific house), they need to include their name, their company's name, and how to contact them.

This applies to things like:

- Business cards
- Flyers
- Social media profiles

Any other promotional stuff that's about the agent in general, not a specific property

17.4. Internet advertising. -- The information required in section 17.1 and 17.2 of this rule must appear on the home page or the screen that is first seen by the viewer. This information must be accessible with no more than two mouse clicks when advertising on social media.

Imagine you're scrolling through Instagram or TikTok, and you see an ad for a real estate agent. This rule is about making sure you can easily find important info about them. Here's what it means:

1. **Online ads need the basics:**

- Remember all that important stuff we talked about earlier? (Company name, broker's name, etc.)
- When real estate agents advertise online, they need to include this info.

2. **Put it where people can see it:**

- This important info needs to be on the main page or the first screen you see.
- It's like putting the most important details in your Instagram bio or the first few seconds of your TikTok video.

3. **Easy to find on social media:**

- If the ad is on social media (like Facebook, Instagram, or Twitter), you shouldn't have to dig for the info.
- You should be able to find it with no more than two clicks.
- It's like being able to find an influencer's contact info by tapping their bio and then maybe one more link.

Why is this important?

- It makes sure people can quickly see who's behind the ad.
- It prevents agents from hiding important info deep in their websites or profiles.
- It helps potential clients easily find out how to contact the agent or their company.

The main point is: When real estate agents advertise online, they need to put their important info (like who they are and who they work for) front and center. On social media, this info should be easy to find.

17.5. Exemption for property owner. -- A licensee who is the owner of the property has all the rights of an unlicensed person with regard to that property.

No rules, baby! Well, mostly no rules, but the point is if you're selling your own house you have more freedoms about advertising it the way you might want without dealing with all of the rules listed here.

Homeowners who aren't licensed have the right to sell their own home without dealing with rules from the commission. They don't need to worry about this law code 30-40 or Title 174 since these laws apply to people holding a license. The WVREC can't do much with a private citizen, holding no license, since the WVREC is the governing body over licensees.

Look at it this way. If you don't work there how can they fire you? Home owners who are selling their own home don't work under any broker. The commission allows this same rule to apply for a licensee selling their own home even though they have a broker.

§174-1-18. OFFER OF CONSUMER REBATES, INDUCEMENTS AND OTHER DISCOUNTS.

18.1. A licensee may offer, directly or indirectly, to clients or customers rebates, inducements, or other discounts, if such licensee:

18.1.a. Discloses to the client or customer, in a clear and conspicuous manner and in writing, the terms of any rebate, inducement or other discount offered;

This rule is about how you can offer "deals" in real estate:

1 **Can you offer them? Yes, but...**

- Real estate agents can offer special deals to their clients or potential clients.
- These could be things like cash back (rebates), free stuff (inducements), or discounts.
- It's like offering a "buy one, get one free" deal on chips at the grocery store.

2 **But there are some rules:**

a) Spell it out clearly:

- They must explain the deal in writing.
- It needs to be clear and easy to understand.
- No hiding the details in tiny print!

18.1.b. Discloses to the client or customer, in a clear and conspicuous manner, and in writing, the fair market value of any rebate, inducement or other discount offered; and 18.1.c. Offers the rebates, inducements or other discounts only under the direct supervision and in the name of the responsible broker.

b) Show the real value:

- They need to tell you what the deal is actually worth.
- If they're giving you a free home inspection, they need to say how much that usually costs.
- It's like telling you the regular price of the bag of chips before showing you the discounted price.

c) Boss needs to approve:

- The head broker (the big boss) needs to okay these deals.
- The offers should be made under the broker's name, not just the individual agent.
- It's like needing the store managers approval before offering any chip discounts.

Why is this important?

- It keeps things honest and transparent.
- It helps clients understand exactly what they're getting.
- It prevents agents from making wild promises without their boss knowing.

The main point is: Real estate agents can offer special deals to attract clients, but they need to be upfront about what the deals are, what they're worth, and make sure their boss is cool with it.

Remember, in the real estate world, deals and discounts can be tempting, but it's important that everything is clear and above board. This rule helps make sure that when an agent offers you a special deal, you know exactly what you're getting, how much it's worth, and that it's legit and approved by their company. It's all about keeping things fair and transparent for everyone involved!

18.2. No licensee may accept, give or charge any form of undisclosed compensation, consideration, rebate, inducement or other discount to a client or customer.

Here's what it means:

1. **No secret deals:**

- Real estate agents can't give or take any secret perks or payments.
- It's like the car dealer can't secretly knock off $500 from the price just for you, without telling anyone else.

2. **This applies to everything:**

- Money (compensation)
- Favors (consideration)
- Cash back (rebates)
- Free stuff (inducements)
- Discounts

3. **It goes both ways:**

- Agents can't give these secret perks to clients.
- And they can't accept them from clients either.
- It's like the car dealer can't take a secret "tip" from you to give you a better deal.

4. **The key word is "undisclosed":**

- If they want to offer a deal, they have to tell everyone involved about it.
- No under-the-table handshakes or wink-wink agreements.

Pro Tip: This is applicable to innocent gestures you might not think fall into this category. Let's say you offer to mow the lawn to maintain a properties yard that you are to list if they agree to list it with you. This is saying that needs disclosed. It doesn't have to be complicated. Simply type it onto the listing agreement so everyone knows and that suffices for clarity.

18.3. Advertisements of lotteries, contests, prizes, certificates, gifts and lots.

18.3.a. An advertisement by a licensee that employs lotteries or contests or that offers prizes, certificates, gifts or free lots shall be under the direct supervision and in the name of the responsible broker and shall contain:

18.3.a.1. A description of each prize, certificate, gift, lot or other valuable consideration offered;

18.3.a.2. The prerequisites for receiving each prize, certificate, gift, lot or other valuable consideration offered;

18.3.a.3. Limitation on the number of prizes, certificates, gifts, lots or other valuable consideration offered

Imagine you're running a contest on social media to promote your listing. Here's what it means:

1 **The broker is still in charge:**

- Any contests or giveaways need to be run under the main broker's name and supervision.
- It's like needing your school principal's approval for a big school event.

2 **What needs to be in the ad:**

a) Describe the prizes:

- Clearly say what people can win.
- It's like listing "1 pair of designer sneakers" or "Free concert tickets" in your social media contest.

b) How to win:

- Explain what people need to do to get the prize.
- Like "Follow our page and comment to enter" in a social media contest.

c) Limited supply?:

- If there's only a certain number of prizes, say so.
- For example, "Only 5 winners will be chosen!"

18.3.a.4. The fair market value of each prize, certificate, gift or lot offered. If advertised, the statement of fair market value shall be in the same size type as the description of the prize, certificate, gift or lot offered. For purposes of this paragraph, "fair market value" is the price or value that a prospective buyer would expect to pay, or be charged for, if he/she were to acquire a similar item of like quality and quantity in a retail outlet that offers the item for sale to the general public; and

18.3.a.5. The odds of winning or receiving each prize, certificate, gift or lot offered. If advertised, the statement of odds shall be the same size type as the description of the prize, certificate, gift or lot and shall appear immediately adjacent to the description.

d) What's it really worth?:

- Tell people the actual value of the prize.
- The text about the value should be the same size as the text describing the prize.
- "Fair market value" means how much it would cost to buy that thing in a regular store.

e) Chances of winning:

- Say how likely it is that someone will win.
- This info should be right next to the prize description and in the same size text.
- It's like saying "1 in 1000 chance of winning" on your contest post.

Why is this important?

- It prevents misleading ads that make prizes seem better than they are.
- It gives people all the info they need to decide if they want to participate.
- It keeps everything fair and transparent.

The main point is: If real estate agents want to run contests or giveaways, they need to be clear about what people can win, how to win it, how much it's worth, and what the chances of winning are.

18.3.b. A licensee who offers prizes, certificates, gifts or lots shall maintain records on each offering for five (5) years, and the records shall contain:

18.3.b.1. The number and description of each prize, certificate, gift or lot distributed or awarded;

18.3.b.2. The name and address of each person who received a prize, certificate, gift or lot; and

18.3.b.3. The name and address of each person who responded to the advertisement or solicitation but did not receive a prize, certificate, gift or lot.

Imagine you're running a big giveaway on social media for attendance to your open house. Here's what it means:

1 **Keep records for a long time:**

- If a real estate agent runs a contest or giveaway, they need to keep detailed records for 5 years.
- It's like saving all your social media contest info in a special folder for a really long time.

2 **What needs to be in these records:**

a) Prize details:

- Write down exactly what prizes were given out and how many.
- For example: "5 $100 gift cards, 1 free home inspection, 10 moving boxes sets"

b) Winner info:

- Keep a list of everyone who won something.
- Include their names and addresses.
- It's like keeping a spreadsheet of all your TikTok contest winners and how to contact them.

c) Everyone else:

- Also keep a list of everyone who entered but didn't win.
- Again, include their names and addresses.
- This is like saving the info of all your followers who commented on your contest post but didn't win.

Why is this important?

- It helps prove the contest was fair and real.
- It keeps track of who got what, in case there are questions later.
- It shows how many people were interested in the contest.

The main point is: When real estate agents run contests or giveaways, they need to keep super detailed records of everything and everyone involved and hang onto those records for a long time.

18.3.c. The Commission will regard the following as unlawful conduct within the meaning of West Virginia Code §30-40-19(a)(37):

18.3.c.1. Failure to comply with subsection (a) or (b);

18.3.c.2. Failure to disclose the possibility that a particular prize, certificate, gift or lot may not be distributed or awarded;

18.3.c.3. Advertising the availability of a prize, certificate, gift or lot when it is not available for distribution or awarding; and

18.3.c.4. Giving a misleading description of a prize, certificate, gift or lot.

The Real Estate Commission says these things are big no-nos:

1. **Breaking the rules we just talked about:**

- If you don't follow all those rules about describing prizes and keeping records, you're in trouble.
- It's like getting a strike on your YouTube channel for not following contest guidelines.

2. **Not mentioning that prizes might run out:**

- If there's a chance you might not have enough prizes for everyone, you have to say so.
- It's like saying "While supplies last" in your giveaway video.

3. **Advertising prizes you don't have:**

- You can't promise prizes that don't exist or that you can't give away.
- It's like saying you're giving away a PS5 in your video when you don't have one to give.

4. **Describing prizes in a misleading way:**

- You can't make prizes sound better than they really are.
- For example, you can't say "Win a luxury car!" if it's just a toy car model.

Why is this important?

- It keeps contests and giveaways honest and fair.
- It protects people from being tricked by false promises.
- It makes sure real estate agents are being truthful in their promotions.

The main point is: When real estate agents run contests or giveaways, they need to be 100% honest about what they're offering. No tricks, no false promises, and no hiding important information.

18.4. Nothing contained in this section shall be construed to prohibit a licensee from:

18.4.a. Providing a closing gift of nominal value to a party to the transaction, which may be done without the approval of the licensee's responsible broker;

18.4.b. Discussing or negotiating the compensation the licensee agrees to charge for his or her services; or

18.4.c. Disseminating information about special terms, conditions or other offers which are bona fide offers made by a principal to a real estate transaction.

Imagine you're a popular streamer on Twitch. This rule is kind of like explaining what you can and can't do for your viewers. Here's what it means:

1. **Small thank-you gifts are cool:**

- After a deal is done, agents can give a small gift to the people involved.
- It's like giving a subscriber a small merch item as a thank-you.
- They don't need their boss's permission for this.
- Think of it as a "thanks for working with me" gesture.

2. **Talking about their prices is okay:**

- Agents can discuss and negotiate how much they charge for their services.
- It's like being able to talk about your subscription prices or special deals for your Twitch channel.

3. **Sharing real offers is fine:**

- If there's a genuine special offer or deal from someone involved in the real estate transaction, agents can share that info.
- It's like telling your viewers about a real discount code a sponsor gave you to share.

Why is this important?

- It clarifies what agents can do without breaking the rules we talked about earlier.
- It allows for some flexibility in how agents interact with clients.
- It keeps things friendly and professional without crossing ethical lines.

The main point is: While there are strict rules about contests and big promotions, real estate agents are still allowed to do normal, friendly business things like giving small thank-you gifts, discussing their fees, and sharing real offers from the people involved in the deal.

§174-1-19. INVESTIGATIONS AND COMPLAINTS.

19.1. W. Va. Code §30-40-20 and Series 4 of the Commission's rules, as well as other provisions of West Virginia law relating to licensing boards and administrative agencies, set forth various procedures for investigations by the Commission and the filing, processing and resolution of complaints. Complaints may be initiated upon motion by the Commission or filed by licensees or the public.

In the real estate world there is a rule book to lay out how unfair play is handled:

1. **Where is the rulebook:** (Well. It's contained in the code we went over earlier in this textbook)

- There's a specific law (W. Va. Code §30-40-20) and a set of rules (Series 4 IN THIS DOCUMENT) that explain how things work.

2. **What these rules cover:**

- How the Real Estate Commission can investigate issues
- How people can file complaints
- What happens after a complaint is filed
- How problems get solved

3. **Who can start an investigation:**

- The Commission itself can decide to look into something (like game mods checking out suspicious activity)
- Real estate agents can file complaints (like players reporting other players)
- Regular people (like homebuyers or sellers) can also file com plaints (like how non-players might report issues they see in the game community)

4. **It's part of a bigger system:**

- These rules fit into the larger set of laws about how professional licensing boards and government agencies work in West Virginia.
- It's like how gaming rules fit into broader laws about online behavior and consumer protection.

Why is this important?

- It provides a clear process for dealing with problems in the real estate world.
- It allows different people (not just the authorities) to raise concerns.
- It helps keep the real estate industry fair and professional.

The main point is: There's a system in place for investigating and dealing with problems in the real estate world. Whether it's the Real Estate Commission itself, a real estate agent, or a member of the public, there's a way to report issues and have them investigated officially.

19.2. Filing of complaints by licensees or the public. -- Complaints filed by licensees or the public must be submitted in writing on forms prescribed by the Commission and must sufficiently provide the information requested on the form.

Here's what it means:

1. **You've got a problem:**

- Maybe you're a real estate agent who saw another agent doing something shady.
- Or you're a regular person who had a bad experience buying or selling a house.

2. **There's an official way to complain:**

- You can't just send a random email or make a phone call to rant.
- The Real Estate Commission has a specific form you need to use.
- It's like filling out an official "Report a Problem" form on a social media app.

3. **Put it in writing:**

- Your complaint must be written down.
- No verbal complaints allowed - it needs to be on paper (or probably online these days).

4. **Fill it out properly:**

- The form will ask for certain information.
- You need to provide all the details they're asking for.
- It's like when you report a post on social media - you need to pick a reason and sometimes provide extra details.

5. **Be thorough:**

- The more information you provide, the better.
- They want enough details to understand and look into your problem.

Why is this important?

- It keeps things organized for the Commission.
- It makes sure they get all the info they need to investigate.
- It helps prevent vague or unclear complaints.

The main point is: If you want to file a complaint about something in the real estate world, you need to use the official form and fill it out completely. No cutting corners or skipping details!

§174-1-20. LICENSEE'S DUTY TO REPORT OTHER ACTIONS.

20.1 Licensee to inform Commission of disciplinary action by other licensing jurisdiction. -- When any licensee who holds a license in another jurisdiction is found to be in violation of that jurisdiction's license law, it is the duty of the licensee to supply the Commission with a copy of the complaint, any answer(s) filed, and all documents which show the disposition of the matter, including the judgment, findings and sanctions imposed against the licensee. This information must be submitted within thirty (30) days of the disposition.

Here's what it means:

1. **You're licensed in more than one place:**

- You're a real estate agent with a license in West Virginia, but you also have a license in another state.

2. **You get in trouble somewhere else:**

- Let's say you break a rule in that other state where you're licensed.

3. **You have to tell West Virginia:**

- Even though it happened in another state, you need to let the West Virginia Real Estate Commission know about it.

4. **What you need to send them:**

- A copy of the complaint against you
- Any responses you filed
- All documents showing what happened and how it was resolved
- This includes the final decision, what rules they said you broke, and any punishments you got

5. **Do it quickly:**

- You have 30 days from when the issue was resolved to send all this info.

Why is this important?

- It keeps everything transparent across state lines.
- It helps West Virginia know if you're following the rules every where you work.
- It prevents agents from hiding their mistakes in other states.

The main point is: If you're a real estate agent licensed in multiple states and you get in trouble in one of them, you need to tell West Virginia about it ASAP, with all the details.

20.2. Licensee to inform Commission of civil action. -- When any licensee is a party to any civil suit or proceeding arising out of any transaction involving real property other than actions for eviction or for the collection of back rent, it is the duty of the licensee to supply the Commission with a copy of the judgment or final disposition of the case prior to the date of the licensee's next renewal.

Here's what it means:

1. **You're in a legal battle:**

- As a real estate agent, you end up in a lawsuit related to a property deal.
- It's not about kicking someone out (eviction) or chasing unpaid rent.

2. **You have to tell the authorities:**

- You need to let the Real Estate Commission know about this legal stuff.

3. **What you need to send them:**

- A copy of the final decision in your case
- Or any document that shows how the lawsuit ended

4. **When to do it:**

- You don't have to tell them right away
- But you need to send this info before you renew your real estate license
- It's like having to update your streaming platform about legal issues before you can renew your partner status

Why is this important?

- It keeps the Commission informed about your professional conduct
- It helps them decide if you're still fit to hold a real estate license
- It ensures transparency in the real estate industry

The main point is: If you're a real estate agent and you get involved in a lawsuit about a property deal, you need to tell the Real Estate Commission about how it turned out before you renew your license.

20.3. Licensee to inform Commission of criminal action. -- When any licensee is a defendant in any criminal proceeding, it is the duty of the licensee to supply the Commission, within thirty (30) days of the notice of the criminal offense, with a copy of the petition, complaint, warrant, indictment, or information, and the answer filed, if any. The licensee shall also advise the Commission of the disposition of the case and the nature and amount of any judgment, verdict, finding or sentence made, entered or imposed within thirty (30) days of such disposition.

Here's what it means:

1 **You're in hot water:**

- As a real estate agent, you've been accused of a crime.
- It doesn't matter if it's related to your job or not.

2 **You have to spill the beans:**

- You need to tell the Real Estate Commission about this ASAP.

3 **What you need to send them:**

- Any official documents about the criminal case. This could be:
- The official accusation (like a warrant or indictment)
- Your response to the accusation (if you've filed one)

4 **When to do it:**

- You have 30 days from when you first hear about the criminal charges to send this info.
- That's about a month to get your paperwork together and notify them.

5 **Keep them updated:**

- Once the case is over, you need to tell them what happened.
- This includes:
- How the case ended up (guilty, not guilty, charges dropped, etc.)
- Any punishment you received (like a fine or jail time)
- You have 30 days after the case ends to share this info.

Why is this important?

- It keeps the Commission informed about your personal conduct.
- It helps them decide if you should keep your real estate license.
- It ensures that people with serious legal issues aren't selling houses without the authorities knowing.

The main point is: If you're a real estate agent and you get charged with any crime, you need to tell the Real Estate Commission quickly and keep them updated on what happens.

LEGISLATIVE RULE
REAL ESTATE COMMISSION

SERIES 2 LEGISLATIVE RULE REAL ESTATE COMMISSION

SCHEDULE OF FEES

§174-2-1. GENERAL.

1.1. Scope. -- This legislative rule establishes the fees to be charged by the Commission.	
1.2. Authority. -- W. Va. Code § 30-40-8.	There's a law (W. Va. Code § 30-40-8) that gives them the power to set these fees.
1.3. Filing Date. – April 10, 2024.	The rule kicks in on April 10, 2024.
1.4. Effective Date. – April 10, 2024.	That's when these new fees start applying as well.
1.5. Sunset provision. -- This rule shall terminate and have no further force or effect on August 1, 2029.	This rule has an expiration date: August 1, 2029. After that, it's not valid anymore unless they renew it.

§174-2-2. SCHEDULE OF FEES.

This topic area is rather straight forward. We all understand the concept of fees by now, so these are just the current prices for each category. That said, the next few pages are NOT hard to decipher law code. It's a price list. Like scrolling through eBay if people sold real estate licensing fees on there. There is a lot of value to knowing these fees for real life. I have marked with a star fees that are commonly associated with salespeople.

2.1. Salesperson/Broker license application fee: $25.00.

Salesperson/ Broker License App Fee = $25

2.2. Examination fees: Up to $150.00 for each examination taken, which, in the event of a third-party examination provider, shall not exceed the negotiated fee agreed to by the examination provider.

Exam fee = Up to $150

Make note that it's "up to" this amount. Currently the price is not this high.

LICENSING FEES

2.3. Licensure fees:

2.3.1. broker or associate broker license fee: $150.00 for the initial and any subsequent license;

Broker / Associate Broker License Fee = $150

2.3.2. salesperson license fee: $ 75:00 for the initial and any subsequent license; and

Salesperson License Fee = $75

2.3.3. branch office license fee: $150.00.

Branch Office License Fee = $150

RENEWAL FEES

2.4. Annual license renewal fees:

2.4.1. broker / associate broker fee: $150.00;

Broker / Associate Broker Renewal = $150

2.4.2. salesperson fee: $75.00; and

Salesperson Renewal = $75

2.4.3. branch office fee: $150.00.

Branch Office Renewal = $150

2.5. Late renewal fees in addition to the required license renewal fee:

LATE FEES! All of the following fees in 2.5 can be avoided.

2.5.1. For each license renewal paid or postmarked from July 1 through August 31 after the renewal fee was due: $50.00;

July 1 – August 31 is an extra $50 ★

2.5.2. For each license renewal paid or postmarked from September 1 through October 31 after the renewal fee was due: $75.00;

September 1 – October 31 is an extra $75 ★

2.5.3. For each license renewal paid or postmarked from November 1 through December 31 after the renewal fee was due: $100.00.

November 1 – December 31 is an extra $100 ★

2.5.4. Licenses not renewed on or before December 31 after the renewal fee was due cannot be renewed.

Past December 31 and there is no renewal. ★

2.6. Change of employing broker fee: $20.00.	Change broker = $20 ★
2.7. Duplicate license fee: $5.00.	Get another license printed = $5
2.8. Certification of licensure fee: $20.00.	Certification of License fee = $20
2.9. Change of company name fee - $10.00 for each license changed.	Change company name per license = $10
2.10. Change of office address fee: $20.00.	Change office address = $20
2.11. Pre-license education approval fees:	***The fees outlined in this 2.11 are only directed at education providers and NOT salespeople or brokers***
2.11.1. Provider: $75.00 initial approval fee and $50.00 annual renewal fee thereafter.	Education provider = $75 Renewal = $50
2.11.2. Course: $150 initial approval fee and $100.00 annual renewal fee thereafter.	Course = $150 Renewal = $100
2.11.3. Instructor: $75.00 initial approval fee and $50.00 annual renewal fee thereafter.	Instructor of the provider = $75 Renewal = $50

2.12. Continuing education approval fees:

The fees featured in 2.12 are directed at continuing education providers and NOT salespeople or brokers.

2.12.1. Provider: $50.00 initial approval fee and $35.00 annual renewal fee thereafter.	Education Provider = $50 Renewal = $35
2.12.2. Course: $75.00 initial approval fee and $50.00 annual renewal fee thereafter.	Course = $75 Renewal = $50
2.12.3. Instructor: $50.00 initial approval fee and $35.00 annual renewal fee thereafter.	Instructor = $50 Renewal = $35
2.13. Roster of active licensees:	Roster of active licensees- Fees directed at brokers who maintain a roster of this info
All counties - $100.00; $5.00 per county.	Roster = $100 + $5 per county (some brokers have agents in different counties of the state)
2.14. Returned check fee: $25.00 or the actual charge incurred by the Commission, whichever is greater.	Returned check fee = $25 or if the WVREC incurs a fee greater you pay whatever cost more.
2.15. Copies of public records fee: $1.00 per page only if the total charge equals or exceeds $5.00.	Copies of public records = $1 per page if the total equals or exceeds $5

2.16. Transaction fee.

2.16.1. For transactions available on-line via the Commission's website, a transaction fee will be added equal to the amount charged by the transaction processing entity. Paper processing of requests for transactions which are available on-line will be charged a $10.00 processing fee; and

Many times I hear, "You said it cost this so why does it cost this?", when the final bill on let's say, submitting your application to test, isn't what I stated it was from the law code 174-2-2

This is why:

Anyone who has ever managed a business knows credit card processing costs money. The WVREC adds this to the law code so they can add that transaction fee to your total bill. They state here that your bill will reflect the amount the processing company charges them.

It also goes on to say that if you choose to file physical paperwork via mail that you could have otherwise filed online, they will charge you an extra $10 for their hassle of handling it. The WVREC really does not want your paper mail.

2.16.2. Until such time as the Commission notifies its licensees via website or otherwise that licenses are to be renewed online, there will be no processing fee. After the commencement of online renewals, the Commission may continue to accept paper renewals, for which the licensee shall pay a $35.00 processing fee in addition to all other renewal fees.

Currently the WVREC is giving real estate professionals the grace to renew their license either online or via physical paper. They are not going to want to continue to do that as again, the WVREC really doesn't want to handle the paperwork in a physical way any longer.

This is saying that there will come a time that the WVREC will announce, we are not accepting paper renewals anymore and when that time comes you will have to pay a $35 fee associated with submitting it that way, on top of the other fees associated with renewing as explained in 2.4 and 2.5

To keep this simple and modern, just renew and file everything online via the WVREC website.

§174-2-3. INSUFFICIENT FUNDS.

3.1. Funds tendered to the Commission for any fee set forth in this rule which remains unpaid due to insufficient funds or for other reason shall nullify the transaction for which the fee remains unpaid. The Commission will afford the payee a reasonable opportunity to pay the fee. If the non-payment is the result of a returned check, only a certified check, money order or credit card charge will be accepted to cure the non-payment. The Commission may require payment of any actual charges or expenses incurred by the Commission prior to lifting the nullification of the transaction. The Commission may also take appropriate collection action and may require the payee to pay the charges of such action.

Here's what it means:

1 **Your payment bounces:**

- You try to pay a fee to the Real Estate Commission, but it doesn't work.
- Maybe your check bounced, or your card was declined.

2 **What happens next:**

- Whatever you were trying to do (like getting a license) doesn't count until you pay.

3 **Second chance:**

- They'll give you a fair shot to pay the fee correctly.

4 **If it was a bad check:**

- You can't just write another check.
- You'll need to pay with a certified check, money order, or credit card.

5 **Extra costs:**

- If the Commission had to spend money because of your failed payment, you might have to cover those costs too.
- Think of it as paying a small fee for the trouble caused.

6 **They might come after you:**

- If you don't pay, they might take steps to collect the money.
- You could end up paying for the costs of their collection efforts.

Why is this important?

- It ensures the Commission gets paid for its services.
- It discourages people from trying to pay with bad checks or insufficient funds.
- It protects the Commission from losing money on failed transactions.

§174-2-4. FEES NOT REFUNDABLE.

4.1. All fees are non-refundable and will not be pro-rated.

You ain't getting that money back, son.

§174-2-5. EFFECT OF NON-COMPLIANCE.

5.1. Failure to pay any of the fees required under this legislative rule is just cause for refusal to issue or renew a license or the Commission may initiate disciplinary proceedings for violation of this rule.

Here's what it means:

1. **Pay to play:**

- There are certain fees you need to pay to be a real estate agent.

2. **No pay, no play:**

- If you don't pay these fees, you're in trouble.
- The Commission can refuse to give you a license.
- Or they might not let you renew your existing license.

3. **You could get in bigger trouble:**

- The Commission might even start disciplinary proceedings against you.
- This is not just suspending your account but investigating you for breaking the rules.

4. **It's in the rulebook:**

- This is an official rule, not just a suggestion.

Why is this important?

- It makes sure everyone pays their fair share to be part of the real estate profession.
- It gives the Commission a way to enforce payment of fees.
- It helps keep the real estate industry running smoothly.

The main point is: If you want to be a real estate agent (or keep being one), you need to pay your fees on time. If you don't, you could lose your license or face other consequences.

LEGISLATIVE RULE
REAL ESTATE COMMISSION

REQUIREMENTS FOR REAL ESTATE COURSES, COURSE PROVIDERS, AND INSTRUCTORS

99% of you bought this textbook to study for the state portion of the licensing exam. Save yourself some time, being overwhelmed and skip series 3. It's not directed at salespeople. I only included it because I feel totally leaving it out doesn't allow the curious mind to know. However, if your brain is full, there's little reason to know series 3 for the salesperson test.

SERIES 3 INDEX

Index	
Section 1. General	Explaining the general why of this series 3.
Section 2. Definitions	Gonna give you some more definitions to make sense of.
Section 3. Real estate courses, course providers, and instructors.	This is directed at educators, the classes most of you are taking etc. This is really not going to be tested on for the state exam simply because it's not law that is directed at salespeople.
Section 4. Audits of approved providers, courses, and instructors; Report and response required; Investigations.	Like above, this is not directed at salespeople. This is how the WVREC can audit real estate educators. Key word is educators.
Section 5. Disciplinary Actions for Pre-license and Continuing Education Providers and Instructors.	What the WVREC can do to the educators if they are out of line.

Oh,

YES, I DID

JUST STATE YOU COULD SKIP THE NEXT 37 PAGES OF THIS BOOK! AREN'T YOU GLAD YOU HAVE THIS RESOURCE TO SAVE YOU TIME ON YOUR STUDIES!!!

§174-3-1. GENERAL.

STUDY TIP FOR PRE-SALES - For the sake of consistency and providing a breakdown of the full law code, series 3 is included here. However, to the person studying for their pre-sales state portion it is unlikely to be needed info. These are rules aimed at education providers, schools like us, and not the salesperson. I'm not saying to overlook them but if you're looking for an area to not worry about too much to be tested on, these pages of series 3 really should not be a big deal to an aspiring salesperson with their note cards out. The next 31 pages, more or less, are not directed at anything salesperson related. To the salesperson to be, skipping to series 4 on page 273 is most likely fine.

1.1. Scope. -- This legislative rule establishes the minimum requirements and qualifications necessary for approval of real estate courses, course providers and instructors and the regulation of same.

These are the minimum requirements to get a course approved by the WVREC

1.2. Authority. -- W. Va. Code §30-40-8.

The WVREC was given the authority to approve courses and course providers by law code 30-40-8

1.4. Effective Date. – April 10, 2024

This went into effect on April 10, 2024

1.5. Sunset provision. -- This rule shall terminate and have no further force or effect upon the expiration of August 1, 2029.

This rule will go away if the WVREC doesn't renew it by August 1, 2029. You can safely bet they will renew it.

§174-3-2. DEFINITIONS.

2.1. "Applicant" means any person, partnership, association or corporation who is making application to the Commission under this rule	Anyone applying to become a course provider.
2.2. "Approved education provider" means education institution, both accredited post-secondary education institution and proprietary education institution, approved and registered with the Commission to offer Commission approved pre-license and continuing education courses.	You will be called an "approved education provider" if you are approved by the WVREC to do that.
2.3. "ARELLO" means the Association of Real Estate License Law Officials.	ARELLO is a regulator of courses that is independent of the West Virginia Real Estate Commission.
2.4. "Commission" means the West Virginia Real Estate Commission as authorized by W. Va. Code §30-40-6.	When you want to get lazy and use just the word, "commission", it means the full wording, "West Virginia Real Estate Commission
2.5. "Continuing education" means the professional development education as mandated in W. Va. Code §30-40-16 and required to renew a real estate broker or salesperson license on an active status.	When the word "continuing education" is used, they are referring to the education you are required to take each year to maintain licensure in active status as set forth in law code 30-40-16
2.6. "Distance Education" means courses whereby instruction does not take place in a traditional classroom setting but rather where the teacher and student are separated by distance and sometimes by time, or both, and the instruction takes place through media.	When using the word "distance education" it is referencing online learning.

2.7. "Post-Secondary education institution" means any education institution accredited as such by an accrediting agency officially recognized by the United States Department of Education.

When using the word "post-secondary education institution" it means an entity recognized by the US Department of Education.

2.8. "Pre-license education" means courses mandated in W. Va. Code §30-40-14 as prerequisite to obtain a real estate broker or salesperson license.

When using the word "pre-license education" it is the education you are required to take to prepare for your real estate licensing exam. This requirement is outlined in detail in 30-40-14 of this textbook and the law code published by the commission.

2.9. "Primary education provider" means a course developer who has a proprietary interest in the course and may deliver the course and/or market it to secondary providers.

When using the word "primary education provider" it means that that entity created the materials they distribute. They have not handed them by another developer.

2.10. "Secondary course provider" means an approved provider which obtains a distance education course from a primary provider for the purpose of offering it to licensees.

When using the wording "secondary course provider" it means that the provider was handed the materials they distribute by another entity that created the product. The secondary course provider does not create the materials they teach from.

§174-3-3. REAL ESTATE COURSES, COURSE PROVIDERS AND INSTRUCTORS.

3.1. Approval by Commission. -- Unless exempted by statute, all real estate courses, course providers and instructors must be approved by and registered with the Commission prior to advertising or offering prelicense or continuing education courses, although a provider may advertise a course submitted for approval prior to approval by including a plain, visible statement that the course has not yet been approved by the Commission. Applications for approval shall be on forms prescribed by the Commission and through a process prescribed by the Commission. The required approval fees, set forth in Series 2 of these rules, must be submitted with the application. Application fees are non-refundable. Post-secondary education institutions are approved education providers and must go through a modified approval process prescribed by the Commission.

Just like you can't just study for the exam on your own, you also can't just start teaching the content without approval. Here's what the rule means:

1. **Get the green light first:**

- Before you can teach real estate courses or advertise them, you need the Real Estate Commission's approval.
- This goes for the courses themselves, the people or companies teaching them, and the instructors.

2. **One exception:**

- You can advertise a course before it's approved, but you must clearly say it's not approved yet.

3. **How to get approved:**

- You need to fill out specific forms the Commission provides.
- You must follow their process for applying.

4. **Pay to play:**

- There's a fee for getting approved.
- You can find out how much in "Series 2" earlier in this textbook or on the official release from the WVREC without these wonder ful breakdowns.
- Once you pay, you can't get that money back, even if you're not approved.
- Think of it like paying an application fee for a gaming tournament.

5. **Colleges are special:**

- If you're a college or university, you're automatically considered an approved provider.
- But you still need to go through a simpler approval process.
- It's like verified YouTubers getting a faster track for new channel approvals.

Why is this important?

- It ensures that real estate education meets certain standards.
- It prevents just anyone from claiming they can teach real estate courses.
- It gives the Commission control over the quality of real estate education.

The main point is: If you want to teach real estate courses or offer them through your company, you need to get approved by the Real Estate Commission first. There's a process to follow and fees to pay. It might go without saying but yes, Spruce School of Real Estate, who publishes this textbook, is an approved provider.

3.2. Renewal; failure to renew.

3.2.1. To remain active, all course, course provider, and instructor approvals shall be renewed on an annual basis. Such renewal shall be on forms and through a process as prescribed by the Commission. The required, non-refundable, renewal application fee, set forth in Series 2 of these rules, must be submitted with the application.

Here's what it means:

1. **Yearly check-in:**

- If you're approved to teach real estate courses, offer courses, or be an instructor, it's not a one-time deal.
- You need to renew your approval every year.
- It's like having to renew your Netflix subscription annually.

2. **How to renew:**

- The Real Estate Commission has special forms you need to fill out.
- They also have a specific process you need to follow.
- Think of it as going through the steps to renew your streaming service, but with more paperwork.

3. **Pay to stay:**

- You have to pay a fee to renew.
- The cost is listed, where other fees are listed, in "Series 2."
- Once you pay, you can't get that money back, even if your renewal is denied.
- It's like paying for your yearly subscription, but without the option for a refund.

4. **What happens if you don't renew:**

- If you don't go through this process each year, your approval be comes inactive.
- This means you can't keep teaching or offering real estate courses.
- It's like your Netflix account getting suspended if you forget to renew.

Why is this important?

- It helps the Commission keep track of who's actively teaching real estate courses.
- It ensures that course providers and instructors stay up-to-date with any new rules or standards.
- It gives the Commission a chance to review and maintain quality control each year.

The main point is: If you're approved to teach or offer real estate courses, you need to renew that approval every year. There's paperwork to fill out and a fee to pay.

3.2.2. All pre-license course, course provider, and instructor approvals shall be renewed no later than December 31 of each calendar year. Real estate pre-license courses which have not been renewed by this deadline may no longer be offered. Real estate pre-license course providers and instructors, who have not renewed by this deadline, may no longer offer or teach pre-license real estate courses. Any real estate pre-license course, course provider or instructor not renewed by this deadline will need to be approved following the process set out in 3.1 of this rule. Approved and renewed instructors may not teach under a prelicense provider who has not renewed.

Here's what it means:

1. **Yearly deadline:**

- December 31 is the big day.
- It's like your YouTube channel needing to renew its partner status by New Year's Eve.

2. **What needs to be renewed:**

- The courses for new real estate agents
- The people or companies offering these courses
- The instructors teaching these courses

3. **If you miss the deadline:**

- Courses: You can't offer them anymore.
- Course providers: You can't provide any more courses.
- Instructors: You can't teach these beginner courses anymore.
- It's like your YouTube channel losing the ability to post new videos if you don't renew on time.

4. **Starting over:**

- If you miss the deadline, you'll need to go through the whole approval process again from scratch.

5. **A tricky situation:**

- Even if you're an approved instructor who renewed on time, you can't teach for a course provider who didn't renew.
- This is very much like a salesperson must stop working if their brokers license is lost.

Why is this important?

- It keeps everyone on the same schedule.
- It ensures that all courses and instructors are up-to-date each year.
- It prevents outdated courses or unapproved people from teaching new real estate agents.

The main point is: If you're involved in teaching new real estate agents, you need to renew your approval every year by December 31. If you don't, you'll have to stop teaching and go through the whole approval process again.

3.2.3. All continuing education course, course provider, and instructor approvals shall be renewed no later than June 30 of each fiscal year. The Commission, by policy, may add a grace period and late fee for renewal after June 30. Real estate continuing education courses, which have not been renewed by this deadline, may no longer be offered. Real estate continuing education course providers and instructors, who have not renewed by this deadline, may no longer offer or teach continuing education courses. Any real estate continuing education course, course provider or instructor not renewed by this deadline will need to be approved following the process set out in 3.1 of this rule. Approved and renewed instructors may not teach under a continuing education provider who has not renewed.

This is much like the above rule but it is directed at continuing education providers rather than pre sales license providers. Here's what it means:

1. **Yearly deadline for CE providers:**

- June 30 is the big day.
- It's like your YouTube channel needing to renew its special "advanced tutorials" status by the end of June.

2. **What needs to be renewed:**

- The courses for existing real estate agents
- The people or companies offering these courses
- The instructors teaching these courses

3. **If you miss the deadline:**

- Courses: You can't offer them anymore.
- Course providers: You can't provide any more courses.
- Instructors: You can't teach these ongoing education courses any more.
- It's like your YouTube channel losing the ability to post new advanced tutorials if you don't renew on time.

4. **Possible grace period:**

- The Commission might give you a little extra time after June 30.
- But you might have to pay a late fee.
- It's like YouTube giving you a few extra days to renew, but charging you extra for being late.

5. **Starting over:**

- If you miss the deadline (and any grace period), you'll need to go through the whole approval process again from scratch.
- It's like having to reapply for your special "advanced tutorials" status if you let it lapse.

6. **A tricky situation:**

- Even if you're an approved instructor who renewed on time, you can't teach for a course provider who didn't renew. It's like the rule above this one.
- It's like being a verified advanced tutor but not being able to post on a channel that lost its advanced status.

3.2.4. To be eligible to renew, all pre-license and continuing education instructors shall complete annual instructor development workshops when offered by the Commission, unless the attendance is waived by the Commission.

Here's what it means:

1. **Who this is for:**

- Anyone who teaches real estate courses
- This includes courses for beginners (pre-license) and courses for existing agents (continuing education)

2. **What you need to do:**

- The Real Estate Commission offers special workshops for instructors
- You need to attend these workshops every year
- It's like attending a yearly YouTube creator conference to learn new skills

3. **Why you need to do this:**

- It's required if you want to keep teaching
- Think of it as updating your skills to stay current, just like a gamer learning new strategies

4. **When it happens:**

- The Commission will offer these workshops annually
- You need to go whenever they're offered

5. **One exception:**

- Sometimes, the Commission might say you don't have to go
- But don't count on this – assume you need to attend unless told otherwise

6. **What happens if you don't go:**

- You might not be allowed to renew your instructor approval
- It's like losing your verified status on YouTube if you don't keep up with their latest guidelines

Why is this important?

- It keeps instructors up-to-date with the latest teaching methods and real estate information
- It ensures all instructors are on the same page and learning the same new stuff
- It helps maintain the quality of real estate education

The main point is: If you teach real estate courses, you need to attend special workshops each year to keep your teaching approval. It's all about staying current and improving your teaching skills.

3.3. Out-of-state providers.
-- Out-of-state education providers must
register with the West Virginia Secretary of State prior to offering any
education services in the State and take all other necessary steps to
legally conduct business in West Virginia prior to their application with
the Commission.

This is directed at people who want to teach real estate courses in West Virginia that are outside of WV. Here's what it means:

1. **Who this is for:**

- Education providers (people or companies that offer real estate courses) from outside of West Virginia

2. **First step:**

- Before you can teach in West Virginia, you need to register with the West Virginia Secretary of State.
- It's like setting up an American bank account for your Twitch earnings before you start streaming to a U.S. audience.

3. **Do your homework:**

- You need to figure out all the legal stuff required to do business in West Virginia
- This might include things like getting certain permits or paying specific taxes

4. **Timing is important:**

- You need to do all of this BEFORE you apply to the Real Estate Commission.
- It's like making sure your streaming setup is fully legal and compliant before you hit that "Go Live" button.

5. **Then you can apply:**

- Once you've done all the legal stuff, you can apply to the Real Estate Commission to offer your courses.
- This is like finally being able to apply for Twitch partner status after getting all your paperwork in order.

Why is this important?

- It makes sure out-of-state educators are following West Virginia's laws
- It puts local and out-of-state educators on a level playing field
- It helps protect West Virginia students by ensuring all educators are properly registered

The main point is: If you're from outside West Virginia and want to teach real estate courses there, you need to register with the state and make sure you're legally allowed to do business there before you even apply to the Real Estate Commission.

3.4. Pre-License education.

This is the breakdown of what is mandated by the WVREC for a **pre license course** to consist of hourly. This is why our course is laid out like it is. To everyone asking and throwing their fists in the air and asking, why? This is why.

3.4.1. The ninety hours (six college credit hours) course prescribed for applicants for a salesperson's license shall consist of:

3.4.1.a. 30 clock hours -- Real Estate Principles and Practice

3.4.1.b. 20 clock hours -- Real Estate Law

3.4.1.c. 20 clock hours -- Real Estate Finance

3.4.1.d. 20 clock hours -- Real Estate Appraisal

90 hours total

30 clock hours of Real Estate Principles and Practice
20 clock hours of Real Estate Law
20 clock hours of Real Estate Finance
20 clock hours of Real Estate Appraisal

3.4.2. The additional ninety hours (six college credit hours) course prescribed for applicants for a broker's license shall consist of:

3.4.2.a. 30 clock hours -- Brokerage Operation and Management

3.4.2.b. 25 clock hours -- Human Resources Management and Interpersonal Skills

3.4.2.c. 35 clock hours -- West Virginia-Specific Real Estate for Brokers

These are the required content hours of what must be in the **brokers course** as mandated by the WVREC.

It is noteworthy that the brokers course is a total of 180 hours but is made up of the 90 hours from the presales curriculum above, with an addition 90 hours of what is laid out below:

90 hours total + 90 hours from the presales curriculum = **180 hours**

30 clock hours of Brokerage Operation and Management
25 clock hours of Human Resource Management & Interpersonal Skills
35 clock hours of WV Specific Real Estate for Brokers

3.4.3. In order to sit for the real estate examination, the applicant must score 70% or higher in each subject area.

This is why the grading structure exists as it does within the course. "Passing is defined as above 70%".

3.4.4. After a student has successfully completed an approved pre-license education course, the approved provider shall supply the student with a certificate of course completion which certifies the student's name and address, 90% attendance but for absences excused in accordance with Commission policy, the course completion date, the number of hours in each subject area, and the score of 70% or higher.

Here's what it means:

1. **You've finished the course:**

- You've taken all the classes needed to start your real estate career.

2. **You get a special certificate:**

- The school (or "provider") gives you an official document.

3. **What's on this certificate:**

a) Your name and address

- So everyone knows it's really you who completed the course.

b) Attendance record

- You need to have shown up for at least 90% of the classes.
- If you missed some classes for good reasons (that the Commission accepts), that's okay.

c) When you finished

- The date you completed the course.

d) What you learned

- A breakdown of how many hours you spent on each topic.
- It's like listing all the different game skills you mastered.

e) Your score

- You need to have scored at least 70% on your tests.
- Think of it as proving you've really learned the material.

Why is this important?

- It proves you've completed the necessary education to become a real estate agent.
- It shows you've put in the time and effort to learn the basics.
- It gives you an official document to show when you apply for your license.

The main point is: When you finish your pre-license real estate course, you get an official certificate that shows you attended regularly, passed your tests, and learned what you needed to learn.

3.4.5. All approved providers shall maintain records indicating the students who have registered for each course, the completion date of the course and the final results of their attendance. These records must be maintained for a minimum period of five (5) years and are subject to inspection by the Commission or its authorized representative. On December 31 of each year, every approved education provider shall compile a list of the students completing each class during the previous calendar year and submit the information to the Real Estate Commission's digital education tracking system or on a form prescribed by the Commission prior to January 31 of the succeeding year.

For people who teach real estate courses. Here's what it means:

1. **Keep good records:**

- You need to write down who signed up for each course.
- Note when each student finished the course.
- Keep track of how often they showed up.

2. **Hold onto these records:**

- You can't just delete this info after the course is over.
- You need to keep it for at least 5 years.

3. **Be ready for inspections:**

- The Real Estate Commission might want to check these records anytime.

4. **Year-end report:**

- At the end of each year (December 31), make a list of all students who finished your courses that year.
- It's like creating an annual "Hall of Fame" for your gaming school.

5. **Submit your report:**

- You need to send this list to the Commission by January 31 of the next year.

You can either:

a) Upload it to their online system, or
b) Use a special form they provide.

Why is this important?

- It helps keep track of who's completed the necessary education.
- It allows the Commission to verify course completions if needed.
- It ensures schools are keeping accurate, long-term records.

The main point is: If you're teaching real estate courses, you need to keep detailed records of your students for a long time, and report your graduates to the Commission each year.

3.4.6. The Commission will accept pre-license education courses approved by the real estate regulatory agency of any other licensing jurisdiction in meeting West Virginia pre-license education requirements if the jurisdiction offers the same privilege to West Virginia. The Commission will not give credit for classroom hours earned in excess of the number of hours awarded by the other jurisdiction.

This is a very often question from out of state people looking to come here and test for licensure. I wish there was a formal list of states, but the answer is vague and along the lines of "if they do this then we will do this." Making it ever changing since their states commission could always change the way they handle their end and thus affect the way our commission in WV handles our end. Clear as mud, right? Here's a break down of what it means:

1. **Education from other states can count:**

- If you've taken real estate classes in another state, they might count in West Virginia.
- It's like being able to use your game character's skills on a different server.

2. **But there's a catch:**

- This only works if that other state would do the same for West Virginia's courses.
- It's like a "you scratch my back, I'll scratch yours" deal between states.

3. **No extra credit:**

- You can't get more credit in West Virginia than you got in the other state.
- For example, if your course was 60 hours in another state, West Virginia won't give you credit for more than 60 hours.

4. **Who decides:**

- The West Virginia Real Estate Commission makes the final call on accepting these courses.

Why is this important?

- It makes it easier for people to move between states and become real estate agents.
- It recognizes that good real estate education in one state is probably good in another.
- It encourages states to work together and respect each other's education standards.

The main point is: If you've taken real estate classes in another state, they might count towards your West Virginia requirements, but only if that state would do the same for West Virginia's courses.

3.4.7. The Commission will prepare and supply a suggested course outline of the material to be taught in the pre-license courses, and will supply supplemental material when the Commission deems it necessary. In addition, the Commission may recommend suggested textbooks to be used in the courses.

For people learning to become real estate agents. Here's what it means:

1. **The Commission makes a study guide:**

- The Real Estate Commission creates an outline of what should be taught in beginner real estate courses.
- It's like getting a list of all the skills you need to learn.

2. **They'll give you this outline:**

- The Commission will share this outline with schools and teachers.

3. **Extra help when needed:**

- If the Commission thinks something important is missing, they'll provide extra material.
- It's like getting bonus tips and tricks for specific games or streaming techniques.

4. **Book recommendations:**

- The Commission might suggest certain textbooks to use.
- This is like recommending the best guides or tutorials for aspiring streamers to read.

Why is this important?

- It ensures everyone learning real estate basics is getting the same important information.
- It helps teachers know what they should be covering in their courses.
- It makes sure the education meets the Commission's standards.

The main point is: The Real Estate Commission provides a roadmap for what should be taught in beginner real estate courses, and they might suggest books or provide extra info to make sure everything important is covered.

3.5. Continuing education.

3.5.1. Guidelines.

3.5.1.a. All continuing education courses shall cover real estate subjects which the Commission finds relevant to fulfilling the statutory duty or best practices of licensees, and contribute directly to the professional competence of the individual.

3.5.1.b Course content and all course materials should be developed by qualified individuals for use with specified teaching methods.

3.5.1.c. Program content must be current.

Rules regarding continuing education courses:

1. **What these courses are about:**

- Continuing education courses are like level-up classes for real estate agents who are already working.
- They need to cover stuff that's actually useful for real estate work.
- It's like learning new game strategies that will actually help you win more matches.

2. **Making agents better at their job:**

- These courses should directly improve how good agents are at their work.
- Think of it as training that makes you a noticeably better player.

3. **Who creates the courses:**

- The people making these courses should really know their stuff.
- It's like having pro gamers or game developers design your training sessions.

4. **How the courses are taught:**

- The creators need to think about the best ways to teach the material.
- It's not just about what you learn, but how you learn it.
- Like choosing between hands-on practice, watching tutorials, or team exercises in gaming.

5. **Keep it fresh:**

- The information in these courses needs to be up-to-date.
- No teaching old, outdated stuff that doesn't apply anymore.
- It's like making sure you're learning the latest game patches and meta strategies, not last year's outdated tactics.

Why is this important?

- It helps real estate agents stay sharp and knowledgeable.
- It ensures the courses are useful, not just time-fillers.
- It keeps the real estate industry up-to-date with current practices.

The main point is: Continuing education for real estate agents should be relevant, practical, well-designed, and current. It's all about helping agents get better at their jobs.

3.5.2. Approved providers shall make application to the Commission for approval of every continuing education course. The application shall be accompanied by a copy of all course materials proposed to be used in the course, a copy of any proposed advertisements, and any other information that may be required by the Commission

The main point is: If you want to offer a continuing education course for real estate agents, you need to get it approved by the Real Estate Commission first, and you need to show them everything about the course when you ask for approval.

3.5.3. The minimum length of a continuing education course will be three (3) hours with each hour equaling fifty (50) minutes of instruction. The Commission shall determine the amount of credit to be awarded for each course.

Continuing education courses for real estate agents need to be at least 3 hours long, but remember, each "hour" is really 50 minutes of learning time. The Commission decides how much each course is worth.

3.5.4. The Commission may approve courses that deal with real estate related subjects, including but not limited to real estate law, agency, ethics, civil rights, equal opportunity, appraisal, contract law, finance, and principal/agent relationships

The Real Estate Commission approves courses on topics that are directly related to real estate work. They've got a list of common topics, but they can approve other stuff too, as long as it's relevant.

3.5.5. When approved instructional elements (videos, interactive exercises, external links, assessments, etc.) are used, the instructor must be present at all times while class is in session.

Real estate teachers can use cool tech and tools to teach, but they can't use these to replace themselves. They need to be present and active throughout the entire class.

3.5.6. Instructors of continuing education courses who are also licensees may obtain credit toward the continuing education requirement in the same amount as the number of hours awarded to the students but only for the first time the course is taught. No continuing education credit shall be given for subsequent teaching of the same course.

If you're a licensed real estate agent and you teach a continuing education course, you can get credit for it, but only the first time you teach that specific course.

3.5.7. Each approved education provider approved to offer continuing education courses shall maintain records indicating the student's name and address, the completion date of the course, the course title, and the number of hours awarded. These records must be maintained for a minimum period of five (5) years and shall be open to inspection by the Commission or its authorized representative. Each approved provider shall annually report to the Commission's digital continuing education tracking system or on a form prescribed by the Commission a comprehensive list of all students who have completed a course in continuing education at their institution during the fiscal year July 1 through June 30 no later than July 15 of the succeeding fiscal year.

If you're teaching continuing education courses for real estate agents, you need to keep detailed records of your students for a long time, and report your graduates to the Commission each year.

3.6. Distance education.

3.6.1. Real estate pre-license and continuing education may be offered through distance education formats. Real estate courses offered through distance education must be well-structured and allow monitoring.

You can learn about real estate online, but these online courses need to be well-organized and have ways to check that you're learning.

3.6.2. All distance education courses of both the primary and the secondary provider shall be approved by the Commission in accordance with such policy as shall be adopted by the Commission.

If anyone wants to offer an online real estate course, they need to get it approved by the Real Estate Commission first. This applies to everyone, no exceptions.

3.6.3. The design and delivery of each distance learning course shall be certified by the Association of Real Estate License Law Officials or by another institution whose certification standards are deemed equivalent by the Commission. The credit hours for a certified distance learning course shall be based upon the same number of hours that would be credited for an equivalent live course and must include a commission approved comprehensive assessment.

Online real estate courses need to be officially approved, be the same length as classroom courses, and include a big test at the end to make sure you learned the material.

It's official approval:

1. **Online courses need a seal of approval:**

- Each online real estate course needs to be certified.

2. **Who gives this approval:**

- There's a group called ARELLO (Association of Real Estate License Law Officials) that can certify courses.

- Or, it could be another organization that the Real Estate Commission thinks is just as good.

3. **How long should the course be:**

- The online course should take about the same time as if you were in a classroom.
- If a classroom course is 3 hours, the online version should also count as 3 hours.
- It's like saying a gaming tutorial should take the same time whether you're watching it live or pre-recorded.

3.6.4. Each distance education course must contain a comprehensive final exam that includes a sufficient number of questions to assure the student has a thorough knowledge of the course material.	When you finish an online real estate course, you'll face a big, thorough test that covers everything you should have learned. It's designed to make sure you really understand the material.
3.6.5. The minimum passing score on the final comprehensive examination shall be 70%.	You have to pass the final exam with a minimum score of 70%
3.7. Instructors of Pre-license and Continuing Education Courses.	These are the requirements of an instructor for these courses.
3.7.1. The approval requirement set forth in 3.1. of this rule shall not apply to any guest speaker or to any professor of a post-secondary educational institution teaching real estate or related college courses.	While most real estate instructors need official approval, guest speakers and college professors teaching real estate don't need to go through that process. They can just come in and share their knowledge.

3.7.2. An instructor will be approved by the Commission only if he or she:

3.7.2.a. Is an attorney at law with a minimum of five (5) years of active practice in the area of study he or she proposes to teach;

3.7.2.b. Holds a degree in real estate from an accredited college or university;

3.7.2.c. Is a licensed real estate broker, associate broker, or salesperson with a minimum of five (5) years experience in the area of study he or she proposes to teach;

3.7.2.d. Holds a degree from an accredited college or university and has at least (2) years of teaching experience and possesses a minimum of two hundred (200) classroom hours in the area of study he or she proposes to teach; or

3.7.2.e. Has a minimum of five (5) years of professional or teaching experience in the area of study he or she proposes to teach.

The Real Estate Commission will only approve you as an instructor if you fit into one of these categories:

1. **The Legal Eagle:**

- You're a lawyer who's been practicing for at least 5 years.
- But not just any kind of law - it has to be in the area you want to teach.

2. **The Academic:**

- You have a college degree specifically in real estate.

3. **The Experienced Pro:**

- You're a licensed real estate agent (broker, associate broker, or salesperson).
- You've been doing it for at least 5 years in the area you want to teach.

4. **The Educated Teacher:**

- You have any college degree.
- Plus, you've been teaching for at least 2 years.
- And you've spent at least 200 hours in classrooms learning about what you want to teach.
- Imagine having a degree, teaching gaming for 2 years, and spending 200 hours in gaming workshops.

5. **The Seasoned Expert:**

- You've been either working in or teaching your subject for at least 5 years.
- It doesn't matter if it's professional experience or teaching experience.
- Like being either a pro gamer or a gaming coach for 5 years in your specific game.

Why is this important?

- It ensures instructors really know their stuff.
- It makes sure teachers have either lots of real-world experience or solid academic backgrounds.
- It helps maintain high-quality education in the real estate field.

The main point is: To teach real estate courses, you need to be seriously qualified in one way or another. Whether it's through long-term experience, specific education, or a mix of both, you need to prove you're an expert before you can teach others.

3.8. Instructors of distance education courses shall obtain Distance Education Instructor Certification from IDECC (International Distance Education Certification Center) prior to their application for approval by the Commission and must submit verification of the certification.

If you want to teach real estate courses online, you need to get a special certification for online teaching first, before you can even apply to be approved as an instructor.

Here's what it means:

1. **Special certification for online teachers:**

- If you want to teach real estate courses online, you need an extra badge.
- This badge is called "Distance Education Instructor Certification." And yes, the author of this book is a Certified Distance Education Instructor.

2. **Who gives out this badge:**

- There's an organization called IDECC (International Distance Education Certification Center).
- Think of them as the YouTube of online education - they're the experts in teaching stuff over the internet.

3. **Do this first:**

- You need to get this certification BEFORE you even ask the Real Estate Commission to approve you as an instructor.

4. **Prove you've got it:**

- When you apply to the Real Estate Commission, you need to show them your IDECC certification.

Why is this important?

- It ensures online instructors know how to teach effectively in a virtual environment.
- It maintains the quality of online real estate education.
- It shows that the instructor understands the unique challenges of teaching without being face-to-face.

3.9. All approved pre-license and continuing education instructors shall complete annual instructor development workshops when offered by the Commission, unless the attendance is waived by the Commission or the individual is an out-of-state instructor who a) is approved by the National Association of Realtors (NAR) or b) holds a Distinguished Real Estate Instructor (DREI) designation.

Here's what it means:

1. **Yearly skill-up sessions:**

- If you're approved to teach real estate courses (both for beginners and pros), you need to attend special workshops each year.

2. **Who runs these workshops:**

- The Real Estate Commission organizes these sessions.
- Think of them as the Twitch HQ for real estate education.

3. **You gotta go, unless:**

- The Commission says you don't have to.

4. **Special rules for out-of-state teachers:**

- If you're not from the state, you might get a pass if:

a) You're approved by NAR (National Association of Realtors)

b) You have a special title called DREI (Distinguished Real Estate Instructor)

Why is this important?

- It keeps instructors up-to-date with the latest teaching methods and real estate info.
- It ensures all instructors are on the same page and learning new stuff regularly.
- It recognizes that some instructors might already be at a super high level.

The main point is: If you teach real estate courses, you usually need to attend special workshops each year to keep your teaching skills sharp. But if you're from out of state and have certain high-level qualifications, you might not have to.

3.10. No product or service may be promoted or sold during a real estate pre-license or continuing education offering.

When you're taking a real estate course, it should be all about learning. The instructor isn't allowed to try and sell you stuff or promote their side business during class time.

§174-3-4. AUDITS OF APPROVED PROVIDERS, COURSES AND INSTRUCTORS; REPORT AND RESPONSE REQUIRED; INVESTIGATIONS.

4.1. All approved providers, courses and instructors shall be subject to audit by the Commission or its authorized representative(s) to ensure compliance with the West Virginia Real Estate License Act and the Commission's rules.

Here's what it means:

1. **Everyone can be checked:**

- The people who offer courses (providers)
- The courses themselves
- The instructors teaching the courses

2. **Who's doing the checking:**

- The Real Estate Commission itself
- Or people they've given permission to do it for them

3. **What they're looking for:**

- They want to make sure everyone's following the rules
- There are two main sets of rules:

a) The West Virginia Real Estate License Act (like the main rulebook for real estate in WV)

b) The Commission's rules (like the specific guidelines for how to play the game)

4. **It's like a surprise inspection:**

- They can do this anytime
- You don't get to say "no" or "come back later"

Why is this important?

- It keeps everyone honest and following the rules
- It helps maintain the quality of real estate education
- It protects students by ensuring they're getting proper training

The main point is: If you're involved in real estate education in West Virginia - whether you're teaching, offering courses, or creating course content - you need to be ready for the Commission to check up on you at any time to make sure you're doing things right.

4.2 In the event of such an audit, all documentation and information requested and deemed necessary to complete the audit, shall be made available to the Commission or its representative(s). This may include, but is not limited to:

4.2.1. Registrations;

4.2.2. Attendance records;

4.2.3. Course completion records and certificates of course completion;

4.2.4. Advertisements, including information published on social media;

4.2.5. Course materials used in conducting the course; and 4.2.6. Any additional documentation reasonably requested by the Commission.

Here's what it means:

1. **Show them everything:**

- If the Real Estate Commission comes to check on you, you've got to be ready to show them whatever they ask for.

2. **What they might want to see:**

a) **Who signed up:**

- Lists of people who registered for your courses

b) **Who actually showed up:**

- Records of who attended your classes

c) **Who finished the course:**

- Proof that people completed your classes
- Including any certificates you gave out

d) **How you advertised:**

- Any ads you made for your courses
- Even stuff you posted on social media

e) **What you taught:**

- All the materials you used in your courses

f) **Anything else they want:**

- The Commission can ask for other stuff if they think it's important

Why is this important?

- It helps the Commission make sure you're teaching what you're supposed to
- It checks that you're being honest about who's taking and completing your courses
- It ensures you're advertising your courses correctly

The main point is: If you're involved in real estate education and the Commission decides to check up on you, you need to be ready to show them pretty much everything about how you run your courses.

4.3. The Commission representative(s) may make photocopies of any documentation the approved education provider or instructor has submitted relative to the audit and required to maintain by the Commission.

When the Real Estate Commission checks up on your real estate education business or your teaching, they can make copies of pretty much any paperwork you show them or are supposed to have.

4.4. The Commission representative(s) conducting the audit shall make report that is provided to the approved provider within sixty (60) days of the audit.

Here's what it means:

1. **They'll write up what they found:**

- After checking everything out, the people from the Real Estate Commission will create a report.

2. **You'll get to see the results:**

- They have to share this report with you (the course provider).

3. **There's a time limit:**

- They can't take forever to get this report to you.
- They have 60 days (that's about 2 months) to give you the report.

4. **What might be in the report:**

- What they looked at
- What they found (good and bad)
- Any areas where you might need to improve

Why is this important?

- It keeps the process transparent - you get to know what they found.
- It gives you a clear idea of how you're doing and if you need to make any changes.
- It puts a time limit on the process so you're not left waiting forever.

The main point is: After the Real Estate Commission checks up on your real estate education business, they must give you a report of what they found within 60 days.

4.5. The Commission will review and approve the written audit report prior to being delivered by certified mail, to the audited real estate course provider or instructor.

Here's what it means:

1. **The big bosses check it first:**

- Before you get to see the report about your real estate course or teaching, the Real Estate Commission itself looks it over.

2. **They give it the thumbs up:**

- The Commission has to approve the report.

3. **Special delivery:**

- Once approved, they don't just email it to you or drop it in regular mail.
- They send it by certified mail.

4. **Who gets this special mail:**

- If you're a course provider (like a real estate school), you'll get the report.
- If you're an instructor who was audited, you'll get the report.

Why is this important?

- It ensures the report is accurate and fair before you see it.
- It makes the process more official and serious.
- It creates a record that you definitely received the report.

The main point is: After the Real Estate Commission checks your real estate course or teaching, they carefully review the report, approve it, and then send it to you in a way that proves you got it.

4.6. The real estate course provider or instructor will receive a written warning and be given a specified amount of time to correct the issues, if there is an audit violation of any of the following:

If the Real Estate Commission finds any of these problems, they'll give you a warning and some time to fix things:

4.6.1. Does an inadequate job of teaching the curriculum required by the Commission as evidenced by the use of inaccurate, inappropriate or outdated teaching materials and strategies, students' poor performance on the licensing examination, student evaluations, and/or Commission audits. This shall include failing to teach the content contained in the detailed content outline(s) approved by the Commission;

1. **Teaching the wrong stuff or badly:**

- Using outdated or wrong information
- Not covering all the topics you're supposed to
- Your students doing poorly on their real estate exams
- It's like teaching outdated game strategies or skipping important game mechanics

4.6.2. Engages in unprofessional behavior and/or inappropriate conduct in the classroom including but not limited to regular tardiness or excessive disorganization; the use of profanity or ridicule; making inappropriate or offensive remarks; or engaging in conduct prohibited by local, state or federal law relating to human rights, anti-discrimination and similar laws;

2. **Being unprofessional:**

- Showing up late all the time
- Being super disorganized
- Using bad language or making fun of students
- Saying offensive things or breaking discrimination laws

4.6.3. Fails to display adequate knowledge of the subject matter in the presentation of information or in answering questions related to the subject matter;

3. **Not knowing your stuff:**

- Can't answer questions about the topic you're teaching
- It's like a gaming tutor who can't explain game mechanics properly

4.6.4. Fails to utilize a variety of teaching methods to accommodate visual, auditory and tactile learning styles;

4. **Boring teaching style:**

- Not using different ways to teach (like visuals, discussions, hands-on practice)
- It's like only lecturing and never showing gameplay or letting viewers practice

4.6.5. Makes inaccurate comments to students regarding course content or West Virginia real estate law to students which are in conflict with the West Virginia Real Estate License Act, the Commission's rules, or any material contained in a Commission approved course.

5. **Giving wrong info:**

- Telling students things that don't match up with real estate laws or official course content
- It's like giving advice that goes against the official rules

What happens if you mess up:

- You'll get a written warning (like a yellow card in soccer)
- They'll give you a specific amount of time to fix the problems

Why is this important?

- It helps maintain the quality of real estate education
- It gives instructors a chance to improve before facing serious con sequences
- It ensures students are getting accurate and useful information

The main point is: If you're teaching real estate courses and you're not doing a good job in these specific ways, you'll get a warning and a chance to fix things before any serious trouble happens.

4.7. The audited real estate course provider and/or instructor shall submit a written response to the Commission, at the end of the time specified in the written warning, outlining the actions taken to resolve the issues.

Here's what it means:

1. **You got a warning:**

- Remember, if the Real Estate Commission found problems with your teaching or course, they gave you a warning.
- It's like YouTube sending you a notification about issues with your content.

2. **They gave you time to fix things:**

- In that warning, they told you how long you have to sort out the problems.
- Think of it as YouTube saying, "You have X days to fix these is sues."

3. **Now it's your turn to respond:**

- When that time is up, you need to write back to the Commission.

4. **What to include in your response:**

- You need to explain what you did to fix the problems they pointed out.
- Be specific about the actions you took.
- It's like telling YouTube, "Here's how I've improved my content based on your feedback."

5. **Put it in writing:**

- This isn't a phone call or a casual chat. You need to write it down.

6. **Who needs to do this:**

- If you're the course provider (like a real estate school), you need to respond.
- If you're an individual instructor who got warned, you need to respond.
- It's like both a YouTube channel owner and an individual creator being responsible for addressing issues.

Why is this important?

- It shows you're taking the warning seriously.
- It gives you a chance to prove you've made improvements.
- It helps the Commission decide if further action is needed or if the issues are resolved.

4.8. Failure to respond or take the necessary corrective measures may result in non-renewal and/or disciplinary action set forth in this rule.

Here's what it means:

1. **You've got to act:**

- Remember that warning you got? You can't just ignore it.
- It's like Twitch telling you to fix something on your channel, and you can't just pretend you didn't see it.

2. **Two things you need to do:**

a) Respond: Write back explaining what you did to fix the problems.

b) Actually fix the problems: Make the changes they asked for.

3. **What happens if you don't:**

- If you ignore the warning or don't make the necessary changes, you're in trouble.
- It's like not addressing issues Twitch pointed out on your channel.

4. **Possible consequences:**

a) Non-renewal: They might not let you keep teaching or offering courses.

b) Disciplinary action: You could face other punishments laid out in their rules.

5. **It's in the rulebook:**

- These consequences aren't just made up on the spot. They're part of the official rules.
- It's like Twitch having a clear policy on what happens if you break rules and don't fix things.

Why is this important?

- It shows that warnings are serious and need to be addressed.
- It gives real consequences for not improving or responding.
- It helps maintain the quality and integrity of real estate education.

The main point is: If you get a warning about problems with your real estate teaching or course, you need to respond and fix those problems. If you don't, you could lose your ability to teach or face other serious consequences.

4.9. The Commission may investigate any approved course provider and/or instructor, regarding matters of concern in the areas set forth in this section.

Here's what it means:

1. **The Commission has detective powers:**

- The Real Estate Commission can decide to investigate any course provider or instructor.

2. **Who can they investigate:**

- Course providers: Think of these as the "channels" or schools offering real estate courses.
- Instructors: These are like the individual "creators" or teachers.

3. **What they're looking into:**

- Any of the issues mentioned in the previous rules we talked about.
- This could include things like teaching quality, professionalism, accuracy of information, etc.
- It's like YouTube investigating concerns about video content, community guidelines, or creator behavior.

4. **They don't need a formal complaint:**

- The Commission can start an investigation on their own if they have concerns.
- They don't have to wait for someone to report a problem.
- It's like YouTube deciding to review a channel even if no viewers have complained.

5. **It's not just about audits:**

- This is different from the regular checks (audits) we talked about earlier.
- It's more like a special investigation when something seems off.

Why is this important?

- It allows the Commission to be proactive in maintaining quality.
- It means problems can be addressed even if no one has officially complained.
- It helps keep everyone on their toes, knowing they could be investigated at any time.

The main point is: The Real Estate Commission has the power to investigate any real estate course provider or instructor if they're concerned about something, without needing a formal complaint or waiting for a scheduled audit.

§174-3-5. DISCIPLINARY ACTIONS FOR APPROVED PRE-LICENSE AND CONTINUING EDUCATION PROVIDERS AND INSTRUCTORS.

5.1. The Commission may take disciplinary action(s) against an approved provider or instructor in accordance with the procedural rules of the Commission and other applicable law if found in violation of any of the following:

The Real Estate Commission can punish course providers or instructors if they:

5.1.1. Is a party to any falsification of any document or other information provided to the Commission;

1. **Lie on paperwork:**

- Like faking your streaming stats

5.1.2. Publishes or causes to be published any advertisement which is not in compliance with the provisions of the West Virginia Real Estate Licensing Act and the Commission's rules;

2. **Post misleading ads:**

- Similar to promoting your stream with false information

5.1.3. Does not comply with any provision of the West Virginia Real Estate Licensing Act or the Commission's rules;

3. **Break any real estate education rules:**

- It's like violating a streaming platforms terms of service

5.1.4. Engages in conduct which constitutes or demonstrates dishonest dealings, bad faith or untrustworthiness;

4. **Act shady or untrustworthy:**

- Think of it as scamming your viewers or being dishonest

5.1.5. Awards credit to any student who fails to comply with the attendance requirements as set forth in Commission's rules;

5. **Give credit to students who didn't show up enough:**

- Falsifying attendance

5.1.6. Fails to file with the Commission accurate and complete records as required by these rules or fails to furnish any documents requested by the Commission by the stated deadline;

6. **Don't keep good records or ignore the Commission's requests:**

- Similar to not providing them with required info when they ask

5.1.7. Does not correct problems identified in a Commission audit report; or

7. **Ignore problems the Commission pointed out:**

- Not fixing issues they found during a review

5.1.8. Conducts any course of education without active approval by the Commission;

8. **Teach courses without approval:**

- It's like streaming without being an approved partner

If you do any of these things:

- The Commission can take disciplinary action
- They'll follow their official procedures and laws when deciding what to do
- It's like Twitch having a process for punishing rule-breaking streamers

Why is this important?

- It keeps real estate education honest and high-quality
- It gives the Commission power to deal with bad actors
- It protects students from subpar or dishonest education

5.2. Sanctions.

5.2.1. The Commission may impose sanctions against any provider or instructor found to be in violation of any provision of subsection 5.1 of this section in accordance with the general powers and duties of W. Va. Code §30-40-7(l) and any other applicable provisions of the West Virginia Real Estate License Act and the Commission's rules.

5.2.2. A revocation of provider and/or instructor approval shall be for a period of two years. Any provider or instructor whose approval has been revoked shall need to be approved following the process set out in 3.1. of this rule.

Here's what it means:

1. **The Commission can dish out punishments:**

- If you break any of those rules we just talked about, you can get in trouble.
- It's like YouTube having the power to punish channels that violate their policies.

2. **They've got official power to do this:**

- There's a law (W. Va. Code §30-40-7(l)) that gives them this authority.
- Think of it as YouTube's terms of service that allow them to take action against rule-breakers.

3. **Different types of punishments:**

- They can choose from various sanctions (punishments).
- It's not just one-size-fits-all; they can decide what's appropriate.
- Like how YouTube might give warnings, demonetize, or ban channels depending on the offense.

4. **The big punishment - Revocation:**

- If they revoke your approval, it's serious business.
- You're banned from teaching or providing courses for two whole years.
- It's like YouTube banning your channel for two years - a really big deal!

5. **Starting over after a ban:**

- After those two years, you can't just jump back in.
- You have to go through the whole approval process again from scratch.
- It's like having to reapply as a brand new YouTuber after a long ban, even if you were famous before.

Why is this important?

- It shows there are real consequences for breaking the rules.
- It gives the Commission tools to maintain quality in real estate education.
- It creates a deterrent for bad behavior.

The main point is: If you break the rules as a real estate course provider or instructor, the Commission can punish you. The worst punishment is a two-year ban, and even after that, you have to start all over to get approved again.

PROCEDURAL RULE
WEST VIRGINIA REAL ESTATE COMMISSION

PROCEDURE FOR THE INVESTIGATION AND RESOLUTION OF COMPLAINTS AND CONTESTED CASE HEARINGS.

SERIES 4 INDEX.

Index

Section 1. General.	Explains the general purpose of what Series 4 is about.
Section 2. Definitions.	Gives you definitions so we know the slang these legal folk use.
Section 3. Causes for Denial of Licenses or Discipline of Licensees.	Gives you reasons why you can be denied licensure and how you can be disciplined for things done badly.
Section 4. Disposition of Complaints.	Handling Complaints: How complaints are dealt with and resolved.
Section 5. Contested Case Hearings.	Formal Dispute Hearings: Meetings to settle disagreements officially.
Section 6. Subpoena Powers.	Power to Demand Information: Authority to require people to provide evidence or testify.
Section 7. Conduct of Hearing.	Running the Hearing: How the formal meeting or trial is managed.
Section 8. Disposition.	Deciding the Outcome: How the final decision is made.
Section 9. Final Decision.	Last Word: The ultimate ruling on the matter.
Section 10. Judicial Review.	Court Review: When a higher court looks over the decision.
Section 11. Application for Reinstatement.	Asking to Rejoin: How someone can request to be allowed back in after being removed.
Section 12. Publication of Decisions.	Making Decisions Public: Sharing the rulings with everyone.

§174-4-1. GENERAL.

1.1. Scope. -- This rule specifies a procedure for the investigation and resolution of complaints against real estate brokers, associate brokers and salespersons and the conduct of contested case hearings.	If you are a salesperson, associate broker, or broker, these are the rules for how the WVREC can investigate and resolve matters of complaints against you.
1.2. Authority. -- W. Va. Code '30-40-8.	The authority the WVREC has to implement these rules are laid out earlier in 30-40-8
1.3. Filing Date. -- March 21, 2007.	Series 4 was filed on March 21st, 2007.
1.4. Effective Date. -- April 20, 2007.	Series 4 went into effect on April 20th, 2007.

§174-4-2. DEFINITIONS.

The following words and phrases as used in this rule have the following meanings, unless the context otherwise requires:

Like elsewhere in this law code, they spend a brief amount of time explaining what certain words mean in the context of their documents. This is the same process.

2.1. "Commission" means the West Virginia real estate commission.

When you text message your friends, "Commission" you mean the West Virginia Real Estate Commission and not the television drama from 1990

2.2. "Executive Director" means the executive director of the West Virginia real estate commission.

"Executive Director implies the executive director of the West Virginia Real Estate Commission and not some random executive director of your choice.

2.3. "License" means a license to act as a broker, associate broker or salesperson.

"License" is in reference to you holing a real estate license as a salesperson, broker, or associate broker, and not any other type of license (Hair dresser, drivers, so on)

2.4. "Licensee" means a person holding a license.

"Licensee" is what you are referred to as a salesperson, broker, anyone holding a license.

§174-4-3. CAUSES FOR DENIAL OF LICENSES OR DISCIPLINE OF LICENSEES.

3.1. The Commission may deny an application for license, place a licensee on probation, limit or restrict a license, suspend or revoke any license, or otherwise discipline any licensee in accordance with these rules and W. Va. Code '30-40-1, et seq., upon satisfactory proof that a licensee has been convicted of a felony or is engaged in conduct, or committed other acts, practices or acts constituting professional negligence or a willful departure from accepted standards of professional conduct in violation of W. Va. Code '30-40-1, et seq., or the rules of the Commission.

The Real Estate Commission has the power to take action against real estate agents who break the rules or laws. This is what they can do:

1. Deny a license application
2. Put an agent on probation
3. Limit what an agent can do
4. Take away an agent's license temporarily (suspend)
5. Take away an agent's license permanently (revoke)
6. Give other punishments

The Commission can do these things if they have good proof that:

1. An agent has been found guilty of a serious crime (felony)
2. An agent is doing something unprofessional or against the rules
3. An agent has made big mistakes in their work
4. An agent is deliberately not following the accepted ways of doing their job

All of this is based on West Virginia laws and the Commission's own rules. The goal is to make sure real estate agents are doing their jobs properly and ethically.

§174-4-4. DISPOSITION OF COMPLAINTS.

4.1. The Commission may upon its own motion and shall upon the filing of a complaint by any person setting forth a cause of action under W. Va. Code '30-40-1, et seq., or the rules promulgated thereunder, ascertain the facts and if warranted hold a hearing to determine whether disciplinary action should be imposed against a licensee.

The West Virginia Real Estate Commission has the power to investigate and take action against real estate agents who might have done something wrong. This can happen in two ways:

1. **The Commission decides on its own to look into something.**
2. **Someone files a complaint against a real estate agent.**

When either of these things happen, the Commission will try to find out what really occurred. If they think there might be a problem, they'll hold a meeting (called a hearing) to decide if the real estate agent should be punished.

This whole process is based on West Virginia laws about real estate agents and the rules that go along with those laws. The goal is to make sure real estate agents are following the rules and doing their jobs properly.

4.2. The Commission will consider complaints of alleged violations of W. Va. Code '30-40-1, et seq., and the rules promulgated thereunder, only when they are submitted in writing on forms supplied by the Commission and set forth all details of the transaction, giving full names of all persons having knowledge of such transactions, together with specific addresses, dates, monetary amounts involved, copies of contracts, closing statements, correspondence and other pertinent documents and information. Only in this way can the Commission handle such matters expediently and satisfactorily.

When someone wants to complain about a real estate agent in West Virginia, they need to follow a specific process:

1. **Use the right form:** The complaint must be written on special forms provided by the Real Estate Commission.

2. **Include all the details:** The person complaining needs to give a complete picture of what happened. This means:

- Full names of everyone involved
- Specific addresses
- Exact dates
- How much money was involved
- Copies of important papers like contracts and closing statements
- Any relevant letters or emails
- Any other important information or documents

3. **Be thorough:** The more complete and detailed the information, the better.

The Commission asks for all this information for a good reason. When they have all the facts and documents, they can:

- Handle the complaint more quickly
- Make a fair decision based on solid evidence

By requiring this level of detail, the Commission is trying to be efficient and fair in dealing with complaints about real estate agents.

4.3. Upon initiation or receipt of the complaint, the Commission shall provide a copy of the complaint to the licensee for his or her response to the allegations contained in the complaint. The accused party shall file an answer within twenty days of the date of service. Failure of the licensee to file a timely response may be considered an admission of the allegations in the complaint: Provided, That nothing contained herein shall prohibit the accused party from obtaining an extension of time to file a response, if the Commission, its Executive Director or other authorized representative permits the extension.

When someone files a complaint against a real estate agent in West Virginia, this is what happens next:

1. **Sharing the complaint:** The Real Estate Commission sends a copy of the complaint to the real estate agent who's being accused. This lets the agent know what they're being accused of.

2. **Time to respond:** The real estate agent has 20 days to write back and explain their side of the story. This response is called an "answer."

3. **Importance of responding:** If the agent doesn't respond within those 20 days, it could be seen as admitting that the complaint is true. So it's really important for them to reply on time.

4. **Getting more time:** If the agent needs more than 20 days to respond, they can ask for extra time. They need to get permission from:

- The Commission itself
- The Executive Director of the Commission, or
- Someone else authorized by the Commission

The main idea here is to give the real estate agent a fair chance to defend themselves, while also making sure the process moves along in a timely manner. It's all about balancing fairness with efficiency.

20 days to respond

4.4. Requests for a response to the allegations contained in a complaint, or requests for additional information will be considered properly served when sent to the licensees last known address. It is the responsibility of the licensee or applicant to keep the Commission informed of his or her current address.

This rule is about making sure real estate agents can be contacted when there's a complaint against them. Here's what it means:

1. **Sending notices:** When the Commission needs to ask a real estate agent to respond to a complaint or provide more information, they'll send it to the agent's last known address.

2. **Proper delivery:** If the Commission sends something to this address, it counts as "properly served." This means the agent can't claim they didn't get the notice just because they moved and didn't tell anyone.

3. **Agent's responsibility:** It's up to the real estate agent to make sure the Commission always has their current address. This applies to:

- Licensed real estate agents
- People applying for a real estate license

4. **Why it matters:** If an agent doesn't keep their address up to date, they might miss important notices. This could lead to problems, like not responding to a complaint in time.

The main point here is that real estate agents need to be responsible about keeping their contact information current with the Commission. If they don't, they could miss out on their chance to defend themselves in a complaint situation. It's a simple way to protect themselves and stay in good standing with the Commission.

4.5. After receiving the licensee's response to the complaint and reviewing any information obtained through investigation, the Commission shall determine if probable cause exists that the licensee has violated any provision of W. Va. Code '30-40-1, et seq., the rules promulgated thereunder, or any order or final decision issued by the Commission.

After a complaint is filed against a real estate agent, there's a process to decide if it's worth moving forward with. Here's how it works:

1. **Getting the agent's side:** First, the Commission waits to receive the real estate agent's response to the complaint.
2. **Investigating:** The Commission might also look into the situation on their own to gather more information.
3. **Reviewing everything:** They then look at all the information they have:
    - The original complaint
    - The agent's response
    - Any extra info from their investigation
4. **Making a decision:** Based on all this, the Commission decides if there's "probable cause." This means they're trying to figure out if there's a good reason to believe the agent might have broken the rules.
5. **What they're looking for:** They're checking if the agent might have violated:
    - West Virginia real estate laws
    - Rules that go along with those laws
    - Any orders or decisions the Commission has made before
6. **What "probable cause" means:** It doesn't mean they're sure the agent did something wrong. It just means there's enough evidence to look into it further.

If they do find probable cause, it usually means the case will move forward, possibly to a hearing. If they don't, the complaint might be dismissed.

The main point is that the Commission tries to be fair by looking at both sides and gathering information before deciding to take any serious action against a real estate agent.

4.6. Investigation of complaints

4.6.a. The Commission may, upon receipt of a complaint or upon its own motion, review and investigate alleged acts or omissions which the Commission reasonably believes constitute cause for disciplinary action. In order to determine if probable cause exists for a hearing on a complaint, the Executive Director, investigator(s) designated by Commission staff, or the chairperson of the Commission shall cause an investigation to be made into the allegations of the complaint. If the Commission determines that the complaint does not present facts which constitute a basis for disciplinary action, the Commission shall take no further action.

4.6.b. In connection with the investigation of a complaint, the Commission is authorized to subpoena witnesses, books, papers, records and any other evidence to help it determine whether a contested case proceeding should be instituted.

4.6.c. Every licensee has an affirmative duty to assist the Commission, or its authorized representative, in investigations performed by the Commission.

When the West Virginia Real Estate Commission receives a complaint or suspects something's wrong, they follow these steps:

1 **Initial Review:**

- They look into the complaint or the situation they're concerned about.
- The Executive Director, investigators, or the Commission chair person leads this process.
- If they don't find anything that seems like a real problem, they'll stop here.

2 **Gathering Evidence:**

- If needed, the Commission can require people to testify or pro vide documents and other evidence.
- This helps them decide if they need to take the case further.

3 **Real Estate Agents' Duty:**

- All licensed real estate agents must help with these investigations when asked.

4.6.d. Upon completion of the investigation, the Commission may:

4.6.d.1. Order the matter to be further investigated;

4.6.d.2. Allow the licensee, who is the subject of the complaint, an opportunity to appear before the Commission for an informal discussion regarding the facts and circumstances of the alleged violations;

4.6.d.3. Determine there is no probable cause to believe a disciplinary violation has occurred and close the case; or

4.6.d.4. Determine there is probable cause to believe that a disciplinary violation has occurred and proceed with a contested case hearing or dispose of the matter through a consent agreement or otherwise.

4 After the Investigation:

The Commission has four options:

1. Investigate more if they need more information.

2. Ask the real estate agent to come in for an informal chat about what happened.

3. Decide there's no real problem and close the case.

4. Decide there probably is a problem and either:

    - Hold a formal hearing, or
    - Try to resolve it through an agreement with the agent.

The main goals here are:

- To be thorough in checking out complaints
- To be fair to the real estate agents
- To protect the public from any bad practices in real estate

This process helps the Commission decide which complaints are serious and need more attention, and which ones can be resolved quickly or dismissed

§174-4-5. CONTESTED CASE HEARING.

5.1. Hearings shall be conducted in accordance with the provisions of article five, chapter twenty-nine-a of this code and the Commission's rules.

When the West Virginia Real Estate Commission decides to hold a hearing about a complaint against a real estate agent, they have to follow specific rules. These rules are designed to make sure the process is fair for everyone involved.

The main points about these hearings are:

1 **Legal Basis:**

- The hearings follow rules set out in West Virginia law, specifically in Article 5, Chapter 29A of the state code.
- This law is about how government agencies should conduct hearings.

2 **Commission Rules:**

- In addition to the state law, the Real Estate Commission has its own set of rules for hearings.
- These rules work alongside the state law to provide more specific guidance.

3 **Fair Process:**

- The goal of having these rules is to ensure that everyone gets a fair chance to present their case.
- It helps make sure that decisions aren't made arbitrarily but follow a consistent process.

4 **What to Expect:**

- While the specific details can be complex, generally these rules cover things like:

- How evidence is presented
- Who can speak at the hearing
- How decisions are made
- What rights the real estate agent has during the process

5 **Importance:**

- Following these rules is crucial because it protects both the public and the real estate agents.
- It helps ensure that any action taken against a real estate agent is done properly and legally.

5.2. Hearings shall be held at a time and place determined by the Commission, but in no event less than thirty days after the notice of hearing is given.

When and where it happens:

1. **Scheduling:**

- The Commission gets to choose when and where the hearing will take place.
- They have the flexibility to pick a time and place that works for everyone involved.

2. **Advance Notice:**

- The most important rule here is about giving people enough time to prepare.
- The Commission must give at least 30 days' notice before the hearing.
- This means if they decide to have a hearing on December 1st, they need to tell everyone involved by November 1st at the latest.

3. **Why 30 Days?**

- This 30-day rule is important because it gives people time to:

- Gather evidence
- Prepare their arguments
- Find witnesses if needed
- Possibly get legal advice or representation

4. **Fairness:**

- This rule helps make sure the process is fair.
- It prevents the Commission from surprising anyone with a sudden hearing.
- It gives the real estate agent enough time to prepare their defense.

5. **Flexibility with Location:**

- While the time has a specific rule, the place doesn't.
- This allows the Commission to choose a location that's convenient and appropriate for the hearing

5.3. Any member of the Commission has the authority to administer oaths and to examine any person under oath.

Let's break it down:

1. **Administering Oaths:**

- Any member of the Commission can ask people to swear an oath.
- An oath is a formal promise to tell the truth.
- It's like when you see in movies or TV shows where someone puts their hand on a Bible and swears to "tell the truth, the whole truth, and nothing but the truth."

2. **Examining Under Oath:**

- After someone takes the oath, Commission members can ask them questions.
- Being "under oath" means the person has to answer honestly or face legal consequences for lying.

3. **Why This Matters:**

- It makes the hearing more official and serious.
- It helps ensure that people tell the truth during the hearing.
- Lying under oath is a crime called perjury, which can have serious consequences.

4. **Any Member Can Do This:**

- It's not just the head of the Commission who has this power.
- Any member of the Commission can administer oaths and ask questions.
- This makes the process more flexible and efficient.

5. **Purpose:**

- This power helps the Commission get to the truth of what happened in a complaint against a real estate agent.
- It adds a level of seriousness to the proceedings, encouraging honesty.

The main point is that this rule gives Commission members a tool to help ensure they're getting honest, truthful information during hearings. It's part of making sure the process is fair and that decisions are based on accurate information.

5.4. If, after hearing, the Commission determines the licensee has violated any provision of W. Va. Code '30-40-1, et seq., the Commissions rules or any order or final decision issued by the Commission, a formal decision shall be prepared which contains findings of fact, conclusions of law and specifically lists the disciplinary actions imposed.

This rule is about a special power that members of the West Virginia Real Estate Commission have during hearings. Let's break it down:

1 **Administering Oaths:**

- Any member of the Commission can ask people to swear an oath.
- An oath is a formal promise to tell the truth.
- It's like when you see in movies or TV shows where someone puts their hand on a Bible and swears to "tell the truth, the whole truth, and nothing but the truth."

2 **Examining Under Oath:**

- After someone takes the oath, Commission members can ask them questions.
- Being "under oath" means the person has to answer honestly or face legal consequences for lying.

3 **Why This Matters:**

- It makes the hearing more official and serious.
- It helps ensure that people tell the truth during the hearing.
- Lying under oath is a crime called perjury, which can have serious consequences.

4 **Any Member Can Do This:**

- It's not just the head of the Commission who has this power.
- Any member of the Commission can administer oaths and ask questions.
- This makes the process more flexible and efficient.

5 **Purpose:**

- This power helps the Commission get to the truth of what happened in a complaint against a real estate agent.
- It adds a level of seriousness to the proceedings, encouraging honesty.

The main point is that this rule gives Commission members a tool to help ensure they're getting honest, truthful information during hearings. It's part of making sure the process is fair and that decisions are based on accurate information.

5.5. The Commission may elect to have an administrative law judge or hearing examiner conduct the hearing.

This rule is about how the West Virginia Real Estate Commission can handle hearings in a different way. Let's break it down:

5.5.a. In such cases where the Commission elects to utilize an administrative law judge or hearing examiner, the administrative law judge or hearing examiner shall:

1 **Bringing in an Outside Expert:**

- Instead of conducting the hearing themselves, the Commission can choose to have an administrative law judge or hearing examiner run it.
- These are legal experts who are trained to handle these kinds of proceedings.

2 **Powers of the Administrative Law Judge or Hearing Examiner:**

5.5.a.1. Be in control of the proceedings as presiding officer,

5.5.a.2. Have the authority to administer oaths,

5.5.a.3. Have the authority to admit or exclude testimony or other evidence, and

5.5.a.4. Have the authority to rule on all motions and objections.

They get to:

- Be in charge of the whole hearing
- Ask people to swear to tell the truth (administer oaths)
- Decide what evidence or testimony is allowed
- Make decisions on any arguments or objections during the hearing

5.5.b. At the conclusion of a hearing, the administrative law judge or hearing examiner shall prepare a proposed order which shall contain findings of fact and conclusions of law. The Commission may request that the administrative law judge or hearing examiner additionally prepare and submit proposed disciplinary action, if any and where warranted, to be taken against the licensee in the proposed order. The Commission may accept, reject or modify the proposed decision of the administrative law judge or hearing examiner.

3 After the Hearing:

- The judge or examiner writes up a proposed decision
- This includes:

- Findings of fact (what they think happened)
- Conclusions of law (how they think it relates to the rules)

- They might also suggest what should happen to the real estate agent if they broke the rules

4 The Commission's Role:

- The Commission doesn't have to just accept what the judge or examiner says

They can:

- Accept the proposed decision as is
- Reject it completely
- Change parts of it

Why This Matters:

- It can make the process more impartial, as the person running the hearing isn't part of the Commission
- It brings in someone with specific expertise in conducting these kinds of hearings
- It still allows the Commission to have the final say

The main point is that this rule gives the Commission an option to have an outside expert run the hearing, but the Commission still gets to make the final decision based on the expert's recommendations. This approach can help balance fairness, expertise, and the Commission's authority in these important decisions about real estate agents' conduct.

5.6. Contested case hearings shall be recorded either by mechanical or electrical means or by certified shorthand reporters. Contested case hearings or any part thereof shall be transcribed at the request of any party, with the expense of the transcription to be charged to the requesting party. The recording, stenographic notes or transcription of oral proceedings shall be filed with and maintained by the Commission for at least five years.

This rule is about how hearings for real estate agents are recorded and what happens to those recordings. Let's break it down:

1. **Recording the Hearing:**

- Every hearing must be recorded.
- This can be done in two ways:

  a) Using audio or video recording equipment
  b) Having a certified shorthand reporter write everything down

2. **Getting a Written Copy:**

- If anyone involved in the case wants a written transcript of the hearing, they can ask for one.
- However, whoever asks for it has to pay for it. It's not free.

3. **Keeping the Records:**

- Whether it's an audio recording, a video, or written notes, the Commission has to keep these records.
- They must keep them for at least five years.

4. **Why This Matters:**

- Having a record helps ensure accuracy. If there's ever a question about what was said, they can go back and check.
- It's useful if someone wants to appeal the decision later.
- It helps maintain transparency in the process.

5. **Fairness in Costs:**

- By making the person who wants a transcript pay for it, it keeps costs down for the Commission.
- But it also ensures that anyone who really needs a transcript can get one.

6. **Long-Term Record Keeping:**

- Keeping records for five years allows for any follow-up or review that might be needed, even years after the hearing.

The main point of this rule is to make sure there's always a reliable record of what happens in these hearings. This protects everyone involved - the real estate agent, the Commission, and anyone else who's part of the case. It's all about maintaining a fair, transparent, and accountable process when dealing with complaints against real estate agents.

§174-4-6. SUBPOENA POWERS.

6.1. Commission subpoenas for books, papers, records, and other evidence will be issued to a party upon request. Subpoenas for witnesses may also be obtained. The Executive Director of the Commission, or other representative designated by the Commission, shall issue all subpoenas for both parties upon reasonable cause shown. The request must specify the documents sought to be obtained and the full names and addresses of the witnesses whose testimony is sought.

This rule is about how people can get important information and witnesses for a hearing about a real estate agent. Let's break it down:

1 **What's a Subpoena?**
- A subpoena is an official order that requires someone to provide information or appear at a hearing.

2 **Types of Subpoenas:**
- For Documents: You can ask for books, papers, records, or other evidence.
- For People: You can ask for specific people to come and testify at the hearing.

3 **Who Can Ask for Subpoenas?**
- Both sides in the case can ask for subpoenas.
- This means the person complaining and the real estate agent being complained about both have this right.

4 **How to Get a Subpoena:**
- You have to ask the Commission for it.
- The Executive Director or another designated person from the Commission will issue the subpoena.

5 **What You Need to Provide:**
- For Documents: You need to specify exactly what documents you want.
- For Witnesses: You need to give the full names and addresses of the people you want to testify.

6 **"Reasonable Cause":**
- The Commission won't just give out subpoenas for anything. You need to show a good reason why you need this information.

7 **Why This Matters:**
- It helps both sides gather the evidence they need to present their case.
- It ensures that important witnesses can be required to testify.
- It helps make the hearing fair by giving both sides access to important information.

The main point of this rule is to give both sides in a hearing a way to get the information and witnesses they need to make their case. It's about making sure the process is fair and thorough. But it also includes some checks to make sure people aren't asking for unnecessary things or wasting time. This balance helps keep the hearings focused and effective.

6.2. Discovery procedures shall consist of those procedures authorized under the State Administrative Procedure Act found in W. Va. Code '29A-5-1, et seq.

This rule is about how people involved in a hearing about a real estate agent can gather information before the actual hearing. Let's break it down:

1 **What is Discovery?**

- Discovery is the process of collecting information before a hearing or trial.
- It helps both sides understand what evidence and arguments the other side has.

2 **Following State Law:**

- The rule says that discovery procedures must follow the West Virginia State Administrative Procedure Act.
- This is a set of laws that govern how state agencies conduct their business, including hearings.

3 **What's Allowed:**

- The specific procedures allowed are listed in that state law.
- These might include things like:

- Requesting documents
- Asking written questions (called interrogatories)
- Taking sworn statements from witnesses (called depositions)

4 **Why It Matters:**

- It ensures that both sides have access to the same information.
- It helps prevent surprises during the hearing.
- It can make the hearing process more efficient by clarifying issues beforehand.

5 **Fairness:**

- By following state law, it ensures that the discovery process is fair and consistent for all cases.

6 **Limitations:**

- The state law also sets limits on what can be requested, protecting against unreasonable or invasive requests.

The main point of this rule is that when preparing for a hearing about a real estate agent's conduct, both sides can gather information, but they have to do it according to specific state laws. This helps keep the process fair, organized, and consistent with how other state agencies handle similar situations. It's all about making sure everyone has a fair chance to prepare their case before the actual hearing.

6.3. In the event of a refusal to obey a subpoena, either party or the Commission may petition the circuit court for its enforcement. If a proper showing is made, the circuit court shall order the person to obey the subpoena; if the person fails to obey the order of the court, the person may be found guilty of contempt of court.

This rule is about what happens if someone doesn't follow a subpoena during a real estate agent hearing process. Let's break it down:

1. **What if Someone Ignores a Subpoena?**
   - Sometimes, people might refuse to provide documents or show up to testify when they're ordered to by a subpoena.

2. **Who Can Take Action?**
   - If this happens, either side in the case or the Real Estate Commission itself can ask for help.

3. **Where Do They Go for Help?**
   - They go to the circuit court, which is a higher-level court.

4. **What Does the Court Do?**
   - The court will look at the situation.
   - If they agree that the subpoena is valid and important, they'll order the person to obey it.

5. **What if the Person Still Refuses?**
   - If the person still doesn't follow the subpoena after the court order, they can be found in "contempt of court."
   - This is a serious situation where someone is disobeying a court order.

6. **Consequences of Contempt of Court:**
   - This can lead to penalties like fines or even jail time in extreme cases.

7. **Why This Matters:**
   - It gives the subpoena "teeth" - real consequences for not following it.
   - It helps ensure that important information or testimony is provided for the hearing.
   - It shows that the hearing process is serious and backed by the legal system.

The main point of this rule is to make sure that when subpoenas are issued for real estate agent hearings, they're taken seriously. It provides a way to enforce these subpoenas if someone tries to ignore them. This helps make sure that all the necessary information and witnesses are available for a fair and thorough hearing. It's about maintaining the integrity and effectiveness of the hearing process.

§174-4-7. CONDUCT OF HEARING.

7.1. If a licensee, upon who a proper notice of hearing has been served, fails to appear in person at the hearing, the Commission or presiding officer may proceed to conduct the hearing (or may enter such other order or judgement deemed appropriate) and the licensee shall be bound by the results of such hearing to the same extent as if the licensee were present.

This rule is about what happens if a real estate agent doesn't show up for their hearing. Let's break it down:

1. **The Set-Up:**

- A real estate agent (licensee) is given proper notice about a hearing.
- This means they've been officially told when and where the hearing will be.

2. **What if They Don't Show Up?**

- If the agent doesn't come to the hearing in person, the hearing doesn't automatically stop.

3. **What the Commission Can Do:**

- They have two main options:

  a) Go ahead with the hearing without the agent there
  b) Make another decision or judgment about the case

4. **The Consequences:**

- Whatever the Commission decides will apply to the agent.
- It doesn't matter that they weren't there - they're still bound by the results.

5. **Why This Matters:**

- It prevents agents from avoiding consequences by simply not showing up.
- It allows the process to move forward even if an agent tries to delay things.
- It emphasizes the importance of taking these hearings seriously.

6. **Fairness Consideration:**

- The rule specifies that the notice must be "proper," ensuring the agent had a fair chance to know about the hearing.

7 **The Message:**

- This rule basically says, "If you're told about a hearing, you should show up. If you don't, decisions can still be made about your case, and you'll have to live with the results."

The main point of this rule is to ensure that the hearing process can't be derailed just because an agent decides not to show up. It keeps the system efficient and prevents agents from avoiding potential consequences by simply not attending. It's a way of saying that these hearings are serious business, and not participating doesn't make the issue go away.

7.2. Before testimony is presented, the record shall show the identity of any Commission members present, of the presiding officer, and of the primary parties and their representatives, and shall reflect that all testimony is being recorded. The licensee may challenge any member of the Commission for cause prior to the commencement of the hearing; the members of the Commission (with the challenged member abstaining) shall decide by the majority vote whether cause exists and whether the challenged member shall participate in the hearing. The Commission or presiding officer shall set dates, times and rules for hearings and shall rule on all issues. Hearings shall generally be conducted in the following order, subject to modification at the discretion of the Commission or presiding officer:

This rule describes how a hearing for a real estate agent is set up and run. Let's break it down:

1 **Before the Hearing Starts:**

- They record who's there: Commission members, the person in charge (presiding officer), the main people involved, and their representatives.
- They note that everything will be recorded.

2 **Challenging Commission Members:**

- The real estate agent can challenge any Commission member if they think they might be unfair.
- The other Commission members vote on whether that person should stay or go.

3 **Setting the Rules:**

- The Commission or presiding officer decides on dates, times, and rules for the hearing.

4 The Order of the Hearing:

7.2.a. The Presiding Officer may read a summary of the charges and answers thereto, and other responsible pleadings filed by the licensee prior to the hearing.

a) The charges against the agent might be read out.

7.2.b. The Assistant Attorney General representing the State's interest before the Commission may make a brief opening statement, which may include a summary of charges and the witnesses and documents to support such.

b) The state's lawyer (Assistant Attorney General) can make an opening statement.

7.2.c. The licensee shall be offered the opportunity to make an opening statement.

c) The agent gets a chance to make an opening statement.

7.2.d. The presentation of evidence on behalf of the State, including a summary at the close of the evidence on behalf of the State.

d) The state presents its evidence and witnesses.

7.2.e. The presentation of evidence on behalf of the licensee.

e) The agent presents their evidence and witnesses.

7.2.f. Rebuttal evidence on behalf of the State, if any.

f) The state can present more evidence to counter what the agent said.

7.2.g. Rebuttal evidence on behalf of the licensee, if any.

g) The agent can present more evidence to counter what the state said.

7.2.h. Closing arguments, if any, by all interested parties on behalf of the Commission and on behalf of the licensee

h) Both sides can make closing arguments.

5 **Flexibility:**

- This order can be changed if needed.

6 **Why This Matters:**

- It ensures the hearing is fair and organized.
- Both sides get a chance to present their case.
- It's similar to how a court trial works, but less formal.

The main point of this rule is to lay out a clear, fair process for these hearings. It makes sure everyone knows what to expect and gets a chance to present their side

7.3. The Commission may grant immunity from disciplinary action to a witness, but only upon a majority vote of the Commission members present. If the hearing is being presided over by an administrative law judge or hearing examiner, the administrative law judge or hearing examiner, shall have authority to grant immunity from disciplinary action before the Commission to a witness. The official record of the hearing shall include the reasons for granting the immunity.

This rule is about a special protection that can be given to witnesses in a hearing about a real estate agent. Let's break it down:

1. **What is Immunity?**

- Immunity means protection from punishment or consequences.
- In this case, it's protection from disciplinary action by the Real Estate Commission.

2. **Who Can Get Immunity?**

- Witnesses in the hearing can be granted immunity.
- These might be people who have important information but are worried about getting in trouble themselves.

3. **Who Can Grant Immunity?**

- The Commission can grant immunity if most of the members present agree.
- If there's an administrative law judge or hearing examiner running the hearing, they can also grant immunity.

4. **Why Grant Immunity?**

- It encourages witnesses to tell the truth without fear of consequences.
- It can help the Commission get important information they might not otherwise hear

5. **Recording the Decision:**

- If immunity is granted, they have to write down the reasons why.
- This becomes part of the official record of the hearing.

6. **Why Record the Reasons?**

- It ensures transparency in the decision-making process.
- It provides a justification if anyone questions the decision later.

7. **Why This Matters:**

- It can help the Commission get to the truth in complicated cases.
- It protects witnesses who might have valuable information but are afraid to speak up.
- It shows that the main goal is finding out what really happened, even if it means not punishing everyone involved.

7.4. Admissibility of evidence at the hearing shall be governed by the terms of the West Virginia Administrative Procedure Act. Copies of documents offered as evidence at the hearing shall be provided to opposing parties. Copies must also be furnished to members of the Commission. Notwithstanding the foregoing, to the extent the licensee believes he or she is being asked to reply to accusations, charges, innuendoes, or facts for the first time in the hearing, the licensee shall be afforded the opportunity to respond to any such evidence to the Commission either in writing or at a subsequent scheduled meeting of the Commission; the Assistant Attorney General assigned to prosecute the case before the Commission shall, however, be allowed to continue to present evidence during the hearing.

This rule is about how evidence is handled during a hearing for a real estate agent. Let's break it down:

1 **Rules for Evidence:**

- They follow the West Virginia Administrative Procedure Act to decide what evidence is allowed.
- This is a set of state laws that guide how these kinds of hearings work.

2 **Sharing Evidence:**

- If someone wants to use a document as evidence, they have to give copies to the other side.
- They also need to give copies to the Commission members.

3 **Surprise Evidence:**

- Sometimes, new information might come up during the hearing that the real estate agent hasn't heard before.
- If this happens, the agent has rights:

a) They can ask to respond in writing later.
b) They can ask to respond at another Commission meeting.

4 **Continuing the Hearing:**

- Even if the agent asks for time to respond to new information, the hearing doesn't stop.
- The state's lawyer (Assistant Attorney General) can keep presenting evidence.

5 **Why This Matters:**

- It ensures fairness by making sure everyone has access to the same information.
- It protects the agent from being blindsided by new accusations.
- It keeps the process moving forward while still allowing for fair responses.

6 Balance:

- This rule tries to balance efficiency (keeping the hearing going) with fairness (giving the agent a chance to respond to new information).

The main point of this rule is to make sure the hearing process is fair, especially when it comes to evidence. It makes sure that:

- Everyone knows what evidence is being used
- The real estate agent has a chance to defend themselves against any new accusations
- The hearing can keep moving forward efficiently

7.5. When a majority of the Commission presides over the reception of evidence at the hearing, the decision is a final decision.

This rule is about how decisions are made in hearings about real estate agents. Let's break it down:

1. **What's a "Majority of the Commission"?**

- This means more than half of the Commission members are present at the hearing.

2. **"Presides Over the Reception of Evidence":**

- This fancy phrase just means they're there listening to all the evidence presented during the hearing.

3. **Final Decision:**

- If a majority of the Commission is present for the whole hearing, their decision is final.
- This means it's the last word on the matter, unless someone appeals to a higher authority like a court.

4. **Why This Matters:**

- It gives weight to the Commission's decision.
- It shows that when most of the Commission is there to hear ev erything, they can make a definitive ruling.

5. **Efficiency:**

- This rule helps make the process more efficient by avoiding the need for additional reviews or discussions after the hearing.

6. **Authority:**

- It emphasizes the Commission's authority to make important decisions about real estate agents' licenses and conduct.

7. **Responsibility:**

- It also puts a big responsibility on the Commission members to be present and attentive during hearings.

The main point of this rule is to establish when a decision made by the Real Estate Commission is considered final. When most of the Commission members are there to hear all the evidence, their decision carries more weight and is considered the final say on the matter. This helps create a clear and authoritative process for dealing with issues involving real estate agents. It's a way of saying, "If most of us are here and we've heard everything, we can make a decision that sticks."

7.6. Upon the motion of the Commission or any party assigning error or omission in any part of any transcript, the Commission or its appointed administrative law judge or hearing examiner shall settle all differences arising as to whether such transcript truly discloses what occurred at the hearing and shall direct that the transcript be corrected and/or revised as appropriate so as to make it conform to the truth.

This rule is about making sure the written record of a hearing is accurate. Let's break it down:

1 1. **What's a Transcript?**

- A transcript is a written record of everything that was said during the hearing.

2 2. **Spotting Mistakes:**

- Sometimes, there might be errors or missing parts in the tran script.
- Either the Commission or any person involved in the case can point out these mistakes.

3 3. **Who Fixes It?**

- The Commission, or the administrative law judge or hearing examiner they appointed, is in charge of fixing these issues.

4 4. **What They Do:**

- They listen to both sides if there's a disagreement about what was actually said.
- They decide what really happened during the hearing.

5 5. **Making Corrections:**

- They can order changes to the transcript to make it accurate.
- This might involve adding missing information or correcting errors.

6 6. **The Goal:**

- The aim is to make sure the transcript truly reflects what happened at the hearing.

7 7. **Why This Matters:**

- An accurate transcript is crucial for:
- Reviewing the case later
- Potential appeals
- Understanding the reasons for decisions

8 Fairness:

- This process ensures that no one is disadvantaged by mistakes in the record.
- It gives everyone a chance to make sure their words are correctly recorded.

The main point of this rule is to ensure that the official written record of a hearing about a real estate agent is as accurate as possible. It recognizes that mistakes can happen when recording or transcribing a hearing and provides a way to fix those mistakes. This is important because these transcripts can be used in future decision-making or appeals, so they need to be correct.

§174-4-8. DISPOSITION.

8.1. At the conclusion of any contested case hearing the Commission or presiding officer shall make Findings of Fact and Conclusions of Law and may:

8.1.a. Dismiss the charges. In the event the charges are dismissed, and before a decision by the Commission is reported, the file shall be confidential;

8.1.b. Impose one or more sanctions as considered appropriate in the circumstances for the discipline of a licensee. Available sanctions include, but are not limited to, denial of a license or renewal thereof, administrative fine not to exceed one thousand dollars per day per violation, probation, revocation, suspension, reexamination, restitution, require additional education, censure, denial of future license, downgrade of license, reprimand, impose all costs associated with the investigation and prosecution of the licensee upon the licensee, order the return of compensation collected from an injured consumer, or any other sanction pursuant to W. Va. Code '30-40-1, et seq.

This rule is about what happens after a hearing about a real estate agent's conduct. Let's break it down:

1. **Making a Decision:**

- After the hearing, the Commission or the person in charge has to do two things:

  a) Make "Findings of Fact" (decide what actually happened)

  b) Make "Conclusions of Law" (decide if what happened broke any rules)

2. **Two Main Outcomes:**

   A. Dismiss the Charges:

   - ▸ If they decide the agent didn't do anything wrong, they can dismiss the case.
   - ▸ If this happens, the case file stays private.

   B. Impose Sanctions:

   - ▸ If they decide the agent did something wrong, they can choose from a range of punishments.

3. **Types of Sanctions:**

- There are many options, including:

- Denying or not renewing a license
- Fining the agent (up to $1,000 per day per violation)
- Putting the agent on probation
- Revoking or suspending the license
- Requiring the agent to retake exams
- Making the agent pay back money to consumers they hurt
- Requiring more education
- Officially criticizing the agent (censure or reprimand)
- Downgrading the license
- Making the agent pay for the costs of the investigation and hearing
- Any other punishment allowed by West Virginia law

4. **Flexibility:**

- The Commission can choose one or more of these sanctions based on how serious the situation is.

§174-4-9. FINAL DECISION.

9.1. The final decision of the Commission shall be filed with the Executive Director. A copy of the decision and order shall immediately be sent by certified mail, return receipt requested, to the licensee's last known address or may be served in the manner of original notices upon the licensee.

This rule is about what happens after the Commission makes its final decision about a real estate agent's case.

1 **Filing the Decision:**

- Once the Commission decides what to do, they file their decision with the Executive Director.
- This is like officially recording the decision.

2 **Notifying the Real Estate Agent:**

- The Commission has to let the agent know about their decision right away.
- They do this by sending a copy of the decision and order to the agent.

3 **How They Send It:**

- They use certified mail with a return receipt requested.
- This means:

    a) The letter is tracked
    b) Someone has to sign for it when it's delivered
    c) The Commission gets proof that it was received

4 **Where They Send It:**

- They send it to the last address they have for the agent.
- This is why it's important for agents to keep their contact info up to date.

5 **Alternative Method:**

- If they can't use mail for some reason, they can serve the decision "in the manner of original notices."
- This usually means having someone personally deliver the decision to the agent.

6 **Why This Matters:**

- It ensures the agent definitely gets the decision.
- It provides proof that the agent was informed.
- It starts any time limits for appeals or for following the order.

7 **Fairness:**

- This process makes sure the agent knows exactly what was decided and can take any necessary next steps

§174-4-10. JUDICIAL REVIEW.

10.1. Any person adversely affected by any decision or final order made by the Commission, after a hearing, is entitled to judicial review by the circuit court of the county where the hearing was held.

This rule is about what a real estate agent (or anyone else affected) can do if they don't agree with the Commission's final decision.

1. **Right to Appeal:**
   - If someone doesn't like the Commission's decision, they have the right to ask a higher authority to look at it.
   - This process is called "judicial review."

2. **Who Can Appeal:**
   - Anyone who is "adversely affected" by the decision can appeal.
   - This usually means the person who got in trouble or faced negative consequences from the decision.

3. **Where to Appeal:**
   - The appeal goes to the circuit court.
   - Specifically, it's the circuit court in the county where the original hearing took place.

What This Means:
- The circuit court is a higher-level court that can review what the Commission did.
- They can check if the Commission followed all the rules and made a fair decision.

Why This Matters:
- It provides a safeguard against unfair decisions.
- It gives people a chance to have their case looked at by a different authority.
- It helps ensure that the Commission's power is balanced by over sight from the court system.

Important Points:
- This only applies to decisions made after a hearing.
- The person has to actually be affected by the decision to appeal it.

The Process:
- The person would need to file paperwork with the circuit court explaining why they think the Commission's decision was wrong.
- The court would then review the case and make its own decision.

The main point of this rule is to provide a way for people to challenge the Commission's decisions if they think they're unfair. It's like a safety net in the legal system. If someone feels the Commission made a mistake or was unfair, they have the option to take their case to a higher authority. This helps ensure that the process of regulating real estate agents is fair and open to scrutiny, protecting both the agents and the public.

§174-4-11. APPLICATION FOR REINSTATEMENT.

11.1. Any person whose license or certification has been revoked or suspended by the Commission may apply to the Commission for reinstatement in accordance with the terms of the order of revocation or suspension. If an order of revocation does not establish terms upon which reinstatement might occur, an initial application for reinstatement may not be made until two (2) years has elapsed from the date the order becomes effective, and successive applications shall be made no more often than once every two (2) years.

This rule is about how a real estate agent can try to get their license back after it's been taken away or suspended.

1 **Applying for Reinstatement:**

- If an agent's license has been revoked (taken away) or suspended, they can ask the Commission to give it back.

2 **Following the Order:**

- They have to follow the rules set out in the original order that took away or suspended their license.

Two Types of Situations:

A) When the Order Has Specific Terms:

- Some orders might say exactly when and how an agent can apply to get their license back.
- In this case, the agent needs to follow those specific instructions.

B) When the Order Doesn't Have Specific Terms:

- If the order doesn't say anything about getting the license back, there are default rules:
- The agent has to wait at least 2 years before they can first apply.
- After that, if they're rejected, they can only apply again every 2 years.

Why the Wait Period:

- This gives time for the agent to learn from their mistakes and make changes.
- It also shows the seriousness of having a license revoked or suspended.

Commission's Decision:

- Just because an agent applies for reinstatement doesn't mean they'll get their license back.
- The Commission will review the application and decide if the agent should get their license again.

Why This Matters:

- It gives agents a chance to redeem themselves and get back into the profession.
- It also protects the public by making sure agents who've had serious problems can't immediately come back without proving they've changed.

The main point of this rule is to provide a path for real estate agents to potentially get their licenses back after serious disciplinary action. It balances the opportunity for second chances with the need to protect the public and maintain high standards in the real estate profession. The rule shows that losing a license isn't always permanent, but getting it back isn't automatic or easy either. It requires time, effort, and likely proof that the agent has addressed whatever issues led to the loss of their license in the first place.

§174-4-12. PUBLICATION OF DECISIONS.

12.1. Final decisions of the Commission relating to disciplinary actions, including consent agreements and consent orders, may be transmitted to the appropriate professional association(s), other licensing jurisdictions, news media and other interested persons or organizations.

This rule is about what happens with the information after the Commission makes a final decision about disciplining a real estate agent. Let's break it down:

1. **What Information Can Be Shared:**
   - The final decisions about disciplinary actions
   - This includes agreements where the agent accepts the punishment (consent agreements)
   - It also includes orders that the agent has agreed to follow (consent orders)

2. **Who Can They Share It With:**
   - Professional Associations: Groups that real estate agents might belong to
   - Other Licensing Jurisdictions: Other states or areas that give out real estate licenses
   - News Media: Newspapers, TV stations, websites that report news
   - Other Interested Persons or Organizations: This could be almost anyone who has a valid reason to know

3. **Why This Matters:**
   - Transparency: It keeps the process open and honest
   - Public Protection: It lets people know if an agent has had problems
   - Professional Standards: It helps maintain high standards in the real estate industry

4. **What It Means for Agents:**
   - Their disciplinary actions might become public knowledge
   - This could affect their reputation and future job prospects

5. **What It Means for the Public:**
   - People can find out about an agent's disciplinary history
   - This helps them make informed decisions about who to work with

6. **Professional Consequences:**
   - Other states might use this information when deciding whether to give an agent a license
   - Professional associations might take their own actions based on this information

7. **Media Involvement:**
   - Sometimes, these decisions might end up in the news, especially if it's a big case

The main point of this rule is that when the Commission makes a final decision about disciplining a real estate agent, they can tell a lot of different people and organizations about it. This is part of keeping the real estate profession accountable and protecting the public. It means that disciplinary actions aren't kept secret – they can be shared widely to make sure everyone who needs to know about them does know. This can have big consequences for the agent involved, but it's seen as necessary for maintaining trust and standards in the real estate industry.

LEGISLATIVE RULE
WEST VIRGINIA REAL ESTATE COMMISSION

SERIES 5 LEGISLATIVE RULE REAL ESTATE COMMISSION

COMPLIANCE WITH REQUIREMENTS THAT BROKERS' TRUST FUND ACCOUNTS BE INSURED AGAINST LOSS.

REPEALED

This page is left to document that there WAS a series 5 in these law rules. It was REPEALED on July 1, 2018

LEGISLATIVE RULE
WEST VIRGINIA REAL ESTATE COMMISSION

SERIES 6
LEGISLATIVE RULE REAL ESTATE COMMISSION

APPLICATION FOR WAIVER OF INITIAL LICENSING FEES FOR CERTAIN INDIVIDUALS.

SERIES 6 INDEX.

Section 1. General.	Overall, what series 6 is about.
Section 2. Definitions.	Terms to know so you can understand the law code.
Section 3. Request for Waiver of Initial Licensure Fee.	How you request for not having to pay the fee.
Section 4. Required Documentation for Waiver of Initial License Fee.	What you need to provide to qualify to not have to pay the fee.

§174-6-1. GENERAL.

1.1. Scope. -- This rule establishes procedures for waiving the initial licensing fee for low income individuals and military personnel and their spouses.	This rule is to help certain groups of people become real estate agents by removing the financial hurdle of the initial licensing fee. It's a way of opening doors for people who might otherwise find it difficult to enter the profession, either because of financial constraints or because of their service to the country. This can lead to more diversity in the real estate industry and provide new career opportunities for these groups.
1.2. Authority. -- WV Code §30-40-8	The authority to do this was given to the WVREC in 30-40-8
1.3. Filing Date. – April 1, 2020	Was placed into the grand old filing cabinet on April fools day, 2020
1.4. Effective Date. – July 1. 2020	Went into effect on July 1, 2020
1.5. Sunset Provision. -- This rule shall terminate and have no further force or effect upon July 1, 2025.	Expires on July 1, 2025 if they don't renew it.

§174-6-2. DEFINITIONS.

2.1. "Commission" means the West Virginia Real Estate Commission.

Here we go again. When you're throwing around the word, "**commission**" you are talking about the West Virginia Real Estate Commission.

2.2. "REC-LIW" means the Real Estate Commission Low Income Waiver form used to request a waiver of the initial licensing fee for low income individuals, as authorized in W.Va. Code §30-1-23;

When you text into the chat "**RECLIW**" you are referencing the form that requests a waiver of fees for low income individuals as authorized in 30-1-23

2.3. "Initial license" means an individual applying for a license in West Virginia sought for the first time;

The wording "**initial license**" means that's the persons FIRST application to gain a license.

2.4 "Local labor market" means every county in West Virginia, and any county outside of West Virginia if any portion of that county is within fifty miles of the border of West Virginia, pursuant to W.Va. Code §21-1C-2;

The main point of the term "**local labor market**" is to establish a clear idea of what counts as the local job market for West Virginia. It's not just limited to the state itself but includes nearby areas in other states. This broader view helps in understanding the full picture of job opportunities and workforce issues for West Virginians, recognizing that people often work across state lines, especially in border areas. It's a practical approach that reflects the reality of how people look for and find work in the region.

2.5. "Low-income individuals" means individuals in the local labor market as defined in West Virginia Code §21-1C-2, whose household adjusted gross income is below 130 percent of the federal poverty line. This term also includes any person enrolled in a state or federal public assistance program including, but not limited to, the Temporary Assistance for Needy Families Program, Medicaid, or the Supplemental Nutrition Assistance Program;

The main point of this definition is to clearly spell out who can be considered "low-income" for the purpose of getting the initial real estate licensing fee waived. It casts a fairly wide net, including both people with low incomes and those receiving various forms of public assistance. This approach aims to make the real estate profession more accessible to people who might otherwise find the initial costs too high. It's a way of removing financial barriers for people who want to start a career in real estate but are facing economic challenges.

Let's look at some details on this one:

1 **Two Ways to Qualify as Low-Income:**

A. Based on Income:

- Your household's adjusted gross income is below 130% of the federal poverty line.
- This means you make less than a certain amount, which changes based on family size and is updated yearly.

B. Based on Participation in Assistance Programs:

- You're enrolled in certain state or federal public assistance programs.

2 **Examples of Qualifying Programs:**

- Temporary Assistance for Needy Families (TANF)
- Medicaid
- Supplemental Nutrition Assistance Program (SNAP, formerly known as food stamps)
- The list isn't limited to just these; other similar programs might qualify too.

3 **Local Labor Market:**

- This refers to every county in West Virginia, plus nearby counties in other states (within 50 miles of WV's border).

4 **Why This Matters:**

- It helps determine who can get their initial real estate licensing fee waived.
- It recognizes that people in these situations might need financial help to start a new career.

5 Broader Impact:

- This definition makes it easier for people facing financial challenges to enter the real estate profession.
- It could help increase diversity in the field and provide new opportunities for people.

6 Important Notes:

- The 130% of poverty line is higher than the standard poverty line, allowing more people to qualify.
- Being on public assistance automatically qualifies you, regardless of your exact income.

2.6. "Military families" means any person who serves as an active member of the armed forces of the United States, the National Guard, or a reserve component as described in 38 U. S. C. §101, honorably discharged veterans of those forces, and their spouses. This term also includes surviving spouses of deceased service members who have not remarried; and

The main point of this definition is to clearly outline who qualifies as "military families" when it comes to getting the initial real estate licensing fee waived. It's quite inclusive, covering not just active service members but also veterans, spouses, and even some surviving spouses. This broad definition reflects an effort to support and provide opportunities to those who have served in the military and their families, recognizing the unique challenges they face, including frequent moves and the need for portable career options like real estate.

This definition explains who counts as "military families" for the purpose of waiving the initial real estate licensing fee.

1 **Who's Included:**

A. Active Service Members:

- People currently serving in the U.S. armed forces
- Members of the National Guard
- Members of reserve components

B. Veterans:

- People who used to serve in these forces and were honorably dis charged

C. Spouses:

- Husbands or wives of current service members
- Husbands or wives of veterans

D. Surviving Spouses:

- Husbands or wives of service members who died
- But only if they haven't remarried

2 **Specific Military Branches:**

- This includes all branches of the U.S. military (Army, Navy, Air Force, Marines, Coast Guard)

3 **Legal Reference:**

- The definition refers to 38 U.S.C. §101, which is a federal law that provides more detailed definitions of these terms

4 **Why This Matters:**

- It determines who can get their initial real estate licensing fee waived under the "military families" category
- It recognizes the service and sacrifices of military personnel and their families

5 **Broader Impact:**

- This definition makes it easier for people connected to the military to enter the real estate profession
- It can help military families find new career opportunities, which is especially important given how often they might move

6 **Important Notes:**

- The inclusion of surviving spouses who haven't remarried shows consideration for those who've lost a partner in service
- The honorable discharge requirement for veterans ensures the benefit goes to those who served well

2.7 "REC-MFW" means the Real Estate Commission Military Family Waiver form used to request a waiver of the initial licensing fee for military service members and their spouses as described in §30-1-22.

This definition is to introduce a specific form (REC-MFW) that military families can use to request a waiver of the initial real estate licensing fee. It's a practical tool that puts the policy of helping military families into action. By having a standardized form, it makes the process clearer and potentially easier for military service members and their spouses who are interested in becoming real estate agents. This form represents a concrete step in making the real estate profession more accessible to those who have served in the military and their families.

This definition is about a specific form used in the process of waiving the initial real estate licensing fee for military families.

1 **What REC-MFW Stands For:**

- REC = Real Estate Commission
- MFW = Military Family Waiver

2 **What It Is:**

- It's a form you fill out to ask for the initial licensing fee to be waived (not charged)

3 **Who It's For:**

- Military service members
- Spouses of military service members

4 **What It Does:**

- It's used to request that you don't have to pay the fee normally charged when first getting a real estate license

5 **Legal Basis:**

- This form is mentioned in West Virginia state law, specifically in §30-1-22
- This law likely provides the details on who qualifies and how the waiver process works

6 Why It Matters:

- It's a specific tool to help military families enter the real estate profession
- It shows there's an official process for requesting this fee waiver

7 How It Helps:

- Makes it easier for military families to understand and access the fee waiver
- Standardizes the process of requesting the waiver

8 What It Doesn't Do:

- Just having this form doesn't automatically waive the fee
- You still need to qualify based on the military family definition we discussed earlier

§174-6-3. REQUEST FOR WAIVER OF INITIAL LICENSURE FEES.

3.1. An applicant seeking a low-income individual or military family waiver of the initial licensing fee shall apply for licensure to the Commission and provide the required documentation of eligibility for waiver.

This rule is about how to apply for a waiver of the initial real estate licensing fee if you're a low-income individual or part of a military family.

1. **Who This Is For:**

- Low-income individuals
- Military families (including service members, veterans, and their spouses)

2. **What You Need to Do:**

a) Apply for the License:

- You still need to go through the regular process of applying for a real estate license.

b) Request the Waiver:

- At the same time, you ask for the initial fee to be waived.

3. **Providing Documentation:**

- You can't just say you qualify; you need to prove it.
- You'll need to provide official documents that show you're eligible for the waiver.

4. **Types of Documentation:**

- For low-income individuals: This might include proof of income or enrollment in assistance programs.
- For military families: This could be military ID, discharge papers, or marriage certificates.

5. **Why Documentation is Important:**

- It ensures that only those who truly qualify get the fee waived.
- It keeps the process fair for everyone.

6 **Applying to the Commission:**

- All of this goes directly to the Real Estate Commission.
- They're the ones who will review your application and documentation.

7 **What This Doesn't Cover:**

- This is just for the initial licensing fee.
- Other fees or costs associated with becoming a real estate agent might still apply.

8 **The Process:**

- Apply for the license
- Submit the waiver request
- Provide the required documentation
- Wait for the Commission's decision

3.2. The Commission shall provide the application form and instructions on what documentation is necessary to submit with the license application requesting the low-income individual or military family initial licensing fee waiver

This rule is about how the Real Estate Commission helps people apply for the initial licensing fee waiver. Let's break it down:

1 **What the Commission Provides:**

a) Application Form:

- They give you the specific form you need to fill out.

b) Instructions:

- They tell you exactly what you need to do to apply.

2 **Documentation Guide:**

- The Commission explains what papers or proof you need to show you qualify for the waiver.

3 **For Both Groups:**

- This applies to both low-income individuals and military families.

4 **Part of the License Application:**

- The waiver request is included with your regular license application.
- It's not a separate process; it's all done together.

5 **Why This Matters:**

- It makes the process clearer and easier to understand.
- You don't have to guess what documents you need; they tell you.

6 **Reducing Mistakes:**

- By giving clear instructions, it helps people submit complete and correct applications.
- This can speed up the process and reduce the chance of your application being rejected.

7 **Accessibility:**

- Having the Commission provide everything makes the process more accessible to everyone.

8 **Standardization:**

- By using a specific form, it ensures everyone provides the same type of information.

The main point of this rule is that the Real Estate Commission takes an active role in helping people apply for the fee waiver. They don't just say "apply for a waiver" and leave you to figure it out. Instead, they give you the exact form you need and tell you precisely what documents to include.

3.3. An applicant shall submit all required documentation to the Commission and upon the submission of a complete application, the Commission shall review the application and issue a decision within 30 days of receipt of the completed application.

This rule is about what happens after you submit your application for a real estate license with a fee waiver request.

1. **Submitting Your Application:**

- You need to send in all the required paperwork to the Real Estate Commission.
- This includes both your license application and the documents for the fee waiver.

2. **Complete Application:**

- Your application is only considered "complete" when you've sent in everything they asked for.
- If you're missing any documents, it might not be processed yet.

3. **Commission's Review:**

- Once they have your complete application, the Commission will look it over.

4. **Time Frame:**

- They have 30 days to make a decision.
- This 30-day countdown starts from the day they receive your completed application.

5. **What They're Deciding:**

- Whether to approve your license application
- Whether to grant you the fee waiver

6 **Why 30 Days Matters:**

- It gives you a clear idea of how long you'll have to wait for an answer.
- It ensures the Commission processes applications in a timely manner.

7 **What This Means for You:**

- Once you submit everything, you should hear back within a month.
- If 30 days pass and you haven't heard anything, it might be worth following up.

8 **Importance of Completeness:**

- The 30-day clock doesn't start until your application is complete.
- It's in your best interest to make sure you submit everything at once.

The main point of this rule is to set clear expectations for how long the application process should take. It tells you that once you've submitted a complete application, you should get an answer within 30 days. This helps make the process more transparent and efficient. It also puts some pressure on the Commission to process applications quickly, which is good for applicants. Remember, the key is submitting a complete application - if you miss anything, it could delay the whole process.

3.4. The Commission may issue a license to an applicant who meets the requirements for licensure, under the West Virginia Real Estate License Act and the rules promulgated by the Commission, and the Commission shall waive the initial licensing fee for an applicant that meets the requirement of "low income individuals" or "military families" as defined in W.Va. Code §30-1-23.

This rule is about how the Real Estate Commission makes decisions on license applications and fee waivers.

1 **Issuing a License:**

- The Commission can give you a real estate license if you meet all the requirements.

2 **What Requirements?**

- You need to satisfy the rules in the West Virginia Real Estate License Act.
- You also need to meet any additional rules the Commission has made.

3 **Fee Waiver:**

- If you qualify as a "low income individual" or part of "military families," they will waive your initial licensing fee.
- This means you don't have to pay the fee that's usually charged when you first get your license.

4 **Who Qualifies for the Waiver?**

- The definitions of "low income individuals" and "military families" are found in West Virginia state law (W.Va. Code §30-1-23).
- We've discussed these definitions in earlier parts.

5 **Two Separate Decisions:**

- The Commission decides if you can get a license.
- They also decide if you can get the fee waived.

6 **Important to Note:**

- Meeting the requirements for a license doesn't automatically mean you get the fee waived.
- Meeting the requirements for a fee waiver doesn't automatically mean you get a license.

7 **Why This Matters:**

- It makes the process of becoming a real estate agent more accessible for certain groups.
- It maintains professional standards while also providing financial help to those who need it.

8 **The Commission's Role:**

- They have the authority to both issue licenses and waive fees.
- They're responsible for checking that you meet all the necessary criteria.

The main point of this rule is that the Real Estate Commission has the power to give you a license if you meet all the regular requirements, AND they will waive your initial fee if you fall into specific categories (low in come or military families). This shows an effort to maintain professional standards in real estate while also making the profession more accessible to certain groups who might find the initial costs challenging. It's a balance between upholding the quality of the profession and opening doors for people who might otherwise struggle to enter the field.

§174-6-4. REQUIRED DOCUMENTATION FOR WAIVER OF INITIAL LICENSURE FEES.

4.1. Individuals requesting a waiver of initial licensure fees for low income or military service personnel and their spouses, shall submit with the application for licensure the initial licensure waiver REC-LIW or REC-MFW form and the appropriate documentation as specified in this section.

This rule is about the specific steps you need to take to get your initial real estate licensing fee waived if you're a low-income individual or part of a military family.

1. **Who This Is For:**

- Low-income individuals
- Military service personnel
- Spouses of military service personnel

2. **What You Need to Submit:**

a) Your regular application for a real estate license
b) A special waiver form
c) Specific documents to prove you qualify

3. **The Waiver Forms:**

- For low-income individuals: Use the REC-LIW form
- For military families: Use the REC-MFW form
- REC likely stands for Real Estate Commission

4. **Submitting Everything Together:**

- You don't apply for the license first and then ask for the waiver later
- Everything needs to be submitted at the same time

5. **Appropriate Documentation:**

- The rule mentions you need to include "appropriate documentation"
- This means official papers that prove you qualify for the waiver
- The specific documents needed are explained in other parts of the rules

6 **Why This Matters:**

- It ensures you follow the correct process to get your fee waived
- Using the right form helps the Commission process your request efficiently

7 **Being Prepared:**

- Before you apply, make sure you have all the necessary forms and documents
- This can help avoid delays in processing your application

8 **Following Instructions:**

- It's crucial to follow these instructions exactly
- Missing a form or document could result in your waiver request being denied

The main point of this rule is to clearly spell out what you need to do if you want your initial real estate licensing fee waived. It's not just about saying you qualify; you need to use the right form (either REC-LIW or REC-MFW) and provide proper documentation. By submitting everything together with your license application, you're making it easier for the Commission to review your case and potentially approve your waiver.

4.2. To establish low income eligibility for the initial licensing fee waiver, an applicant shall submit to the Commission evidence that the adjusted gross income of the household of the applicant is below 130% of the federal poverty level by submitting documentation of eligibility for:

4.2.1. Temporary Assistance for Needy Families Program;

4.2.2. Medicaid;

4.2.3. Supplemental Nutrition Assistance Program; or

4.2.4. A Federal Tax Return.

This rule explains how to prove you qualify for the low-income waiver of the initial real estate licensing fee.

1 **The Goal:**

- You need to show that your household's adjusted gross income is below 130% of the federal poverty level.

2 **What to Submit:**

- You don't just tell them you're low-income; you need to provide proof.

3 **Four Ways to Prove Eligibility:**

You can submit documentation showing you're eligible for one of these programs:

a) Temporary Assistance for Needy Families (TANF):

- This is a program that helps families with children when parents are unemployed or underemployed.

b) Medicaid:

- This is a health coverage program for people with low income.

c) Supplemental Nutrition Assistance Program (SNAP):

- Often known as food stamps, this helps low-in come people buy food.

d) Federal Tax Return:

- If you're not in any of these programs, you can submit your tax return to show your income level.

4 **Why These Programs?**

- Being eligible for these programs usually means your income is already at or below the required level.

5 **Choosing Your Proof:**

- You only need to submit proof for one of these options, not all of them.

6 **Tax Return Option:**

- This is useful if you're not in any of the assistance programs but still have low income.

7 **Submitting to the Commission:**

- Whatever proof you choose, you need to send it directly to the Real Estate Commission.

8 **Privacy Considerations:**

- Remember, you're sharing personal financial information, so make sure you're comfortable with that.

The main point of this rule is to give you clear options for proving you qualify as low-income for the fee waiver. By accepting proof of participation in these specific programs or a tax return, the Commission is trying to make it as straightforward as possible for truly low-income individuals. This approach recognizes that if you're eligible for these assistance programs, you're likely to meet the income requirements for the fee waiver. And if you're not in these programs, you can still prove your income level with your tax return. It's all about making sure the fee waiver goes to those who genuinely need it while providing multiple ways to demonstrate that need.

4.3. To establish military family eligibility for the initial licensing fee waiver, an applicant shall submit to the Commission proof of qualifying military service and proof of eligibility as a qualifying spouse , as follows:

4.3.1. A service member's DD-214 form;

4.3.2. A service member's NGB-22 form;

4.3.3. A service member's DD-1300 form; or

This rule explains how to prove you qualify for the military family waiver of the initial real estate licensing fee.

1 **The Goal:**

- You need to show that you're part of a military family.

2 **Two Things to Prove:**

a) Qualifying military service
b) Being a qualifying spouse (if applicable)

3 **Documents for Proving Military Service:**

You can submit one of these forms:

a) DD-214 form:

- This is a document given to service members when they leave the military.
- It's often called a "discharge paper" or "separation document."

b) NGB-22 form:

- This is similar to the DD-214, but it's for National Guard members.

c) DD-1300 form:

- This is a "Report of Casualty" form.
- It's used when a service member has died.

4 **What These Forms Show:**

- They prove that you or your family member served in the military.
- They include details about the type and length of service.

5 **Choosing the Right Form:**

- Which form you use depends on your specific situation (active duty, veteran, National Guard, etc.).

6 **For Spouses:**

- The rule mentions proving eligibility as a qualifying spouse, but doesn't specify how in this section.
- This might involve additional documents like a marriage certificate.

7 **Submitting to the Commission:**

- You need to send these documents directly to the Real Estate Commission.

8 **Privacy Considerations:**

- These forms contain personal information, so handle them carefully.

4.3.4. A copy of the service member's current military orders; or

4.3.5. Other official military documentation, determined to be appropriate by the Commission, demonstrating the service member's qualifying past or current military service; and

4.3.6. A copy of the marriage certificate with the qualifying service member and, where applicable, the death certificate of the qualifying service member if the spouse is applying for the military family waiver.

This continues the list of ways to prove you qualify for the military family waiver of the initial real estate licensing fee. Let's break down these additional options:

1 **More Documents for Proving Military Service:**

d) Current Military Orders:
- This is for active duty service members.
- It shows they're currently serving in the military.

e) Other Official Military Documentation:
- This is a flexible option.
- The Commission can accept other military documents if they think it's appropriate.
- This allows for situations that might not fit the standard forms.

2 **Proving You're a Qualifying Spouse:**

a) Marriage Certificate:
- You need to show you're married to the service member.
- Submit a copy of your marriage certificate.

b) Death Certificate (if applicable):
- If you're a surviving spouse, you might need to submit the service member's death certificate.
- This is to show you were married to a service member who has passed away.

3 **Why These Additional Options Matter:**

- They cover more situations, like current active duty or unique service circumstances.
- They provide a way for spouses to prove their connection to the service member.

4 **Flexibility in Documentation:**

- The "other official military documentation" option shows the Commission is willing to consider various proofs of service.

5 **For Surviving Spouses:**

- The inclusion of death certificates recognizes that surviving spouses of service members are also eligible for this waiver.

4.4. Honorably discharged service members applying for waiver of the initial licensing fee shall submit a completed application, and a DD-214 form, a NGB-22 form, or other official military documentation determined to be appropriate by the Commission, showing the applicant has been honorably discharged from military service.

This rule is specifically about how veterans (honorably discharged service members) can apply for the waiver of the initial real estate licensing fee. Let's break it down:

1 **Who This Is For:**

- Veterans who have been honorably discharged from military service

2 **What You Need to Submit:**

a) A completed application for a real estate license
b) Proof of honorable discharge

3 **Options for Proving Honorable Discharge:**

- DD-214 form: This is the standard discharge paper for most military branches
- NGB-22 form: This is for National Guard members
- Other official military documentation: The Commission can accept other forms if they think it's appropriate

4 **What These Forms Show:**

- They prove you served in the military
- They show that you were honorably discharged

5 **Why "Honorable Discharge" Matters:**

- Only those who were honorably discharged qualify for this waiver
- It's a way of ensuring the benefit goes to those who served well

6 **Flexibility in Documentation:**

- By allowing "other official military documentation," the Commission recognizes that some veterans might have different paper work

7 **Submitting to the Commission:**

- You need to send both your license application and your proof of honorable discharge together

8 **Importance of "Completed Application":**

- Make sure your application is fully filled out
- An incomplete application might delay the process

LEGISLATIVE RULE
WEST VIRGINIA REAL ESTATE COMMISSION

SERIES 7
LEGISLATIVE RULE REAL ESTATE COMMISSION

CONSIDERATION OF PRIOR CRIMINAL CONVICTIONS IN INITIAL LICENSE ELIGIBILITY DETERMINATION.

SERIES 7 INDEX.

Index

§174-7-1. GENERAL.

1.1. Scope. -- This rule establishes procedures for consideration of prior criminal convictions in initial licensure eligibility determination.

This rule is about how the Real Estate Commission deals with people who have criminal records when they apply for a real estate license.

1 **Purpose of the Rule:**
- It sets up a process for deciding if someone with a criminal record can get a real estate license.

2 **Initial Licensure:**
- This is about people applying for their first real estate license, not renewals.

3 **Consideration of Criminal History:**
- The Commission will look at an applicant's past criminal convictions.
- **But having a criminal record doesn't automatically disqualify you.**

4 **Establishing Procedures:**
- The rule creates a standard way to evaluate these cases.
- This helps ensure fairness and consistency in decisions.

5 **Why This Matters:**
- It gives people with criminal records a chance to enter the real estate profession.
- It also protects the public by ensuring proper screening of applicants.

6 **Balancing Act:**
- The Commission has to balance giving second chances with protecting public safety.

7 **Not Just a Yes/No Decision:**
- The rule suggests **there's a process for looking at each case individually.**

8 **Transparency:**
- By having a set procedure, it makes the process clearer for applicants with criminal records.

This rule is to create a fair and standardized way of evaluating real estate license applications from people who have criminal convictions in their past. It recognizes that people with criminal records might want to start careers in real estate, and it provides a framework for deciding if that's appropriate. This approach aims to be both fair to applicants who have turned their lives around and responsible in terms of public safety.

1.2. Authority. -- WV Code §30-40-8	The authority to do this was given to the WVREC in law code 30-40-8
1.3. Filing Date. – April 1, 2020	These rules entered the big ol filing cabinet on April 1, 2020
1.4. Effective Date. – July 1, 2020	These rules went into effect on July 1, 2020
1.5. Sunset Provision. -- This rule shall terminate and have no further force or effect upon July 1, 2025.	If the WVREC does not renew this it will expire on July 1, 2025. Like all of the other rules that are set to expire, my hunch is they renew them.

§174-7-2. DEFINITIONS.

2.1. "Commission" means the West Virginia Real Estate Commission established pursuant to W. Va. Code §30-40-4 et seq.

Here we go again. When the word "commission" is used it refers to the WV Real Estate Commission.

2.2. "Initial license" means obtaining a license in West Virginia for the practice of real estate brokerage services for the first time.

When using the wording "initial license" it refers to someone trying to gain their license for the first time.

2.3. "License" or "licensure" means the official authorization by the Commission to engage in the practice of real estate.

The word "real estate **license**" is an official permission given by the state's Real Estate Commission that allows someone to work legally in the real estate field. It's not just a formality; it's a crucial authorization that separates professional real estate agents from those who aren't qualified or approved to practice. This definition sets the foundation for understanding the importance of **licensure** in the real estate profession and why the Commission takes the licensing process, including considerations about criminal history, so seriously.

2.4. "Unreversed", as that term refers to a criminal conviction, means that a conviction has not been set aside, vacated, pardoned, or expunged.

What counts as an "unreversed" conviction when the Real Estate Commission is considering someone's criminal history. It's saying that unless a conviction has been officially changed through specific legal processes (set aside, vacated, pardoned, or expunged), it's still considered valid and will be taken into account. This is important for license applicants to understand because it affects how their criminal history might be viewed in the application process. It also highlights that there are legal ways to address past convictions, which could be relevant for some applicants.

1. **Four Ways a Conviction Could be Reversed:**

   a) Set Aside: A court has canceled or nullified the conviction.

   b) Vacated: The conviction has been voided or withdrawn.

   c) Pardoned: An official (like a governor or president) has forgiven the crime.

   d) Expunged: The conviction has been erased from official records.

2. **If None of These Have Happened:**

- Then the conviction is considered "unreversed."

3. **Why This Matters for Licensing:**

- The Real Estate Commission likely looks at unreversed convictions when deciding on license applications.

4. **It's About Current Status:**

- This definition focuses on the current legal status of a conviction, not the original guilty verdict.

5. **Importance for Applicant**

- If you have a criminal record, knowing if your convictions are "unreversed" is crucial when applying for a license.

6. **Legal Processes:**

- This definition indirectly points out that there are legal ways to change the status of a conviction

§174-7-3. RATIONAL NEXUS TO THE PRACTICE OF REAL ESTATE BROKERAGE.

3.1. The commission may not disqualify an applicant from initial licensure because of a prior criminal conviction (s) that remains unreversed unless that conviction is for a crime(s) that bears a rational nexus to the practice of real estate. In determining whether a criminal conviction bears a rational nexus to a real estate, the commission shall consider at a minimum:

This rule is about how the Real Estate Commission handles license applications from people with criminal records.

1 **The Basic Rule:**

- Having a criminal record doesn't automatically disqualify you from getting a real estate license.

2 **When They Might Disqualify You:**

- **If your conviction is for a crime that's related to working in real estate.**
- The term they use is "bears a rational nexus" - which means there's a logical connection.

3 **What They Look At:**

- The Commission has to consider certain things before they can disqualify you.

4 **"Unreversed" Convictions:**

- They only look at convictions that haven't been set aside, vacated, pardoned, or expunged.

5 **Considering the Connection:**

- They have to think about how your specific crime might relate to working in real estate.

6 **Minimum Considerations:**

- The rule says "at a minimum," which means there's a list of things they must consider, but they might look at other factors too.

7 **Fair Chance:**

- This rule is about giving people with criminal records a fair chance at getting licensed.

8 **Case-by-Case Basis:**

- It means they look at each application individually, not with a one-size-fits-all approach.

3.1.a. The nature and seriousness of the crime for which the individual was convicted;

The Real Estate Commission must consider when looking at an applicant's criminal record.

1. **Nature and Seriousness of the Crime:**

- They look at what kind of crime it was and how serious it was.
- For example, a minor theft might be viewed differently than a major fraud.

3.1.b. The passage of time since the commission of the crimes;

2. **Time Since the Crime:**

- They consider how long ago the crime happened.
- This recognizes that people can change over time.

3.1.c. The relationship of the crime(s) to the ability, capacity, and fitness required to perform the duties and discharge the responsibilities of a licensed salesperson, associate broker or broker; and

3. **Relationship to Real Estate Work:**

- They think about how the crime relates to working in real estate.
- They look at:

a) Ability: Can you do the job?
b) Capacity: Are you mentally and physically able to handle the work?
c) Fitness: Are you suitable for the responsibilities of the job?

- They consider this for different levels: salesperson, associate broker, or broker.

3.1.d. Any evidence of rehabilitation or treatment undertaken by the individual.

4. **Evidence of Rehabilitation:**

- They look for proof that you've turned your life around.
- This could include:
- Treatment programs you've completed
- Positive changes in your life since the conviction

5. **Why These Factors Matter:**

- Nature of Crime: Shows if it's relevant to real estate work.
- Time Passed: Gives context to your current character.
- Relationship to Work: Helps determine if the crime affects your ability to do the job.
- Rehabilitation: Shows your efforts to change and improve.

6. **Comprehensive Look:**

- By considering all these factors, they get a fuller picture of you as an applicant.

§174-7-4. APPLICATION AFTER DENIAL.

4.1. Notwithstanding any other provision of the W. Va. Code to the contrary, if an applicant has been denied licensure because of a prior criminal conviction, the commission shall permit the applicant to apply for initial licensure if:

4.1.a. A period of five years has elapsed from the date of conviction of the disqualifying event or the date of release from incarceration, whichever is later;

4.1.b. The individual has not been convicted of any other crime (s) during the period of time following the disqualifying offense (s); and

This rule is about giving people a second chance at getting a real estate license after being denied due to a criminal conviction. Let's break it down:

1 **The Basic Idea:**

- Even if you were denied a license before because of a criminal record, you might get another chance.

2 **When You Can Reapply:**

- You have to wait for a certain period before you can try again.

3 **The Waiting Period:**

- It's 5 years from either:

  a) The date you were convicted, or
  b) The date you got out of jail (if you were incarcerated)

- Whichever of these happened most recently is the one that counts.

4 **Staying Clean:**

- During those 5 years, you can't have been convicted of any other crimes.

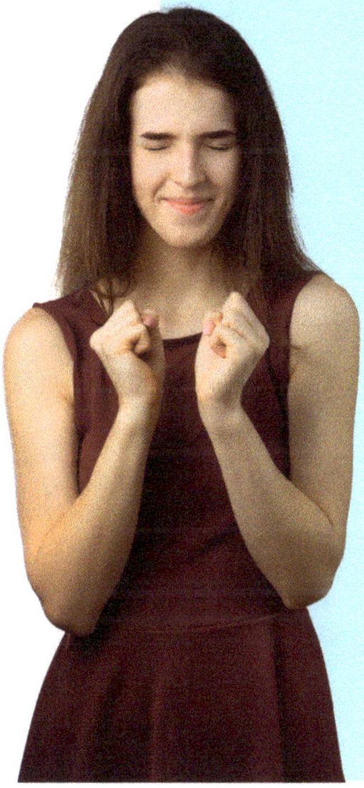

4.1.c. The conviction(s) was not for an offense of a violent or sexual nature: Provided, that a conviction for an offense of a violent or sexual nature may subject an individual to a longer period of disqualification from licensure, to be determined by the commission on a case by case basis.

5 **Types of Crimes:**

- This rule doesn't apply to violent or sexual crimes.
- If your conviction was for a violent or sexual crime, you might have to wait even longer.
- For these types of crimes, the Commission decides on a case-by-case basis.

6 **Why This Matters:**

- It gives people a path to redemption and a second chance at a career.
- It recognizes that people can change and reform over time.

7 **Commission's Discretion:**

- For violent or sexual crimes, the Commission has more flexibility in deciding how long you have to wait.

8 **Not Automatic:**

- Meeting these criteria doesn't guarantee you'll get a license; it just means you can apply again.

The main point of this rule is to provide a structured way for people with criminal records to have another shot at getting a real estate license. It sets clear timelines and conditions, recognizing that people can change over time and deserve a chance to prove themselves. However, it also maintains safeguards, especially for more serious crimes, to ensure public safety and the integrity of the real estate profession

§174-7-5 PETITION FOR LICENSURE ELIGIBILITY DETERMINATION.

5.1. An individual with a criminal record who has not previously applied for licensure may petition the commission at any time for a determination of whether the individual's criminal record will disqualify the individual from obtaining a license.

This rule is about giving people with criminal records a chance to check if they can get a real estate license before they actually apply.

1. **Who This Is For:**

- People with criminal records
- Who have never applied for a real estate license before

2. **What You Can Do:**

- You can ask the Commission to review your criminal record
- They'll tell you if your record would stop you from getting a license

3. **When You Can Do This:**

- "At any time" - you don't have to wait for a specific period

4. **Why This Matters:**

- It helps you know where you stand before you go through the whole application process
- You can find out if it's worth applying or if you need to wait

5. **It's Called a Petition:**

- This means you're formally asking the Commission to make a decision

6. **Not an Application:**

- This isn't the same as applying for a license
- It's just asking for information about your eligibility

7. **Saves Time and Effort:**

- If your record would disqualify you, you know in advance
- If it wouldn't, you can feel more confident about applying

8. **No Guarantee:**

- Even if they say your record won't disqualify you, you still need to meet all other licensing requirements

5.2. The petition shall be submitted on an application form prescribed by the commission and shall include sufficient details about the individual's criminal record to enable the commission to identify the jurisdiction where the conviction occurred, penalties imposed, the date of the conviction, and the specific nature of the conviction.

This rule explains how to ask the Real Estate Commission about your chances of getting a license if you have a criminal record.

1 **Using a Special Form:**

- You can't just write a letter; you need to use the Commission's official form.

2 **What You Need to Include:**

- Details about your criminal record

3 **Specific Information Required:**

a) Where the Conviction Happened:

- Which city, state, or country you were convicted in

b) Penalties You Received:

- What punishment you got (like fines, probation, jail time)

c) Date of Conviction:

- When you were found guilty or pleaded guilty

d) Nature of the Conviction:

- What specific crime you were convicted of

4 **Why All This Detail:**

- It helps the Commission understand exactly what happened
- They need this info to make an accurate decision about your eligibility

5 **Being Thorough:**

- The more complete your information, the better they can assess your situation

6 **Honesty is Important:**

- You need to provide accurate information
- Lying or hiding information could hurt your chances later

7 **Not Just for One Conviction:**

- If you have multiple convictions, you should include details for all of them

8 **It's Not an Application:**

- Remember, this is just to get information, not to actually apply for a license

5.3. The applicant may submit with the petition for licensure eligibility determination, evidence of rehabilitation, letters of reference, and any other information the applicant deems relevant to show fitness and the ability to practice real estate sales.

This rule is about what extra information you can provide when asking the Real Estate Commission about your eligibility for a license if you have a criminal record. Let's break it down:

1. **Additional Information:**

- You're allowed to submit more than just the details of your conviction.

2. **Evidence of Rehabilitation:**

This could include:

- Certificates from programs you've completed
- Proof of counseling or therapy
- Records showing positive changes in your life

3. **Letters of Reference:**

- You can ask people to write letters about your character
- These could be from employers, teachers, or community leaders

4. **Other Relevant Information:**

- Anything else you think shows you're fit to work in real estate
- This might include:
- Job history
- Volunteer work
- Educational achievements

5. **Showing Fitness:**

- The goal is to demonstrate that you're capable and trustworthy enough to work in real estate

6. **Ability to Practice:**

- You want to show that your past doesn't prevent you from being a good real estate professional

7. **It's Optional:**

- The rule says "may submit," which means it's your choice to provide this extra information

8. **Making Your Case:**

- This is your chance to present a full picture of who you are now, not just who you were when you got in trouble

5.4. The commission shall provide the determination within 60 days of receiving the petition and the applicable fee from the applicant. The fee shall be equal to the Application fee required in WV CSR §174-2-2.

This rule is about what happens after you submit your petition asking if your criminal record will affect your chance of getting a real estate license. Let's break it down:

1 **Time Frame:**

- The Commission has 60 days to give you an answer.
- That's about two months from when they receive your petition.

2 **What You'll Get:**

- A "determination" - which means their decision or answer about your eligibility.

3 **Fee Required:**

- You have to pay a fee when you submit your petition.
- It's not free to ask for this information.

4 **How Much is the Fee:**

- It's the same amount as the regular application fee for a real estate license.
- You can find the exact amount in a document called "WV CSR §174-2-2".

5 **When the Clock Starts:**

- The 60-day countdown begins when the Commission has both:

  a) Your completed petition
  b) Your payment of the fee

6 **Why There's a Fee:**

- It covers the cost of reviewing your petition and criminal record.
- It shows you're serious about your inquiry.

7 **No Guarantee:**

- Paying the fee doesn't guarantee a favorable answer.
- It just ensures they'll review your case and give you an answer.

8 **Planning Ahead:**

- This process lets you know where you stand before you invest time in training or a full application.

The main point of this rule is to set clear expectations about how long it will take to get an answer about your eligibility and what it will cost you. By giving a specific timeframe (60 days) and a set fee (equal to the regular application fee), it helps you plan and know what to expect.

Index

ABOUT THE AUTHOR

BILLY ZWIENER

Billy Zwiener has taught with Spruce School of Real Estate for 20 years. As an early founder of online education, long before the post-COVID shift into "online everything", Billy developed an online platform for educating in the early 2000s, making Spruce School of Real Estate the first school in WV to offer such a thing. He is a graduate of WVU, a proud human parent, and a pet one as well. In Billy's free time, he usually attempts to make his ADHD a superpower rather than a disability, and you can find him obsessing over a project like authoring a textbook, playing with tech, being creative with music, gardening, failing at skateboarding well beyond his years of trying, and woodworking, Praise and thanks to God, my mother, Vickie, and Wade Caskey, for allowing me to be a part of the Spruce legacy. I'm sure they would have loved to see this go to print.

www.ingramcontent.com/pod-product-compliance
Lightning Source LLC
LaVergne TN
LVHW070848210926
848482LV00016B/890
9798992500202